READY

FOR HIM

TODAY

PREPARING WISELY FOR THE FUTURE
LIVING FULLY IN THE PRESENT

By Yaasha Moriah

To my First Love and Best Friend. If life with You is this exciting already, I can't wait for eternity.

To my second love and second best friend. When I meet you, I'll recognize my First Love in you.

READY FOR HIM TODAY
PREPARING WISELY FOR THE FUTURE
LIVING FULLY IN THE PRESENT

SHIRES PRESS
4869 Main Street
P.O. Box 2200
Manchester Center, VT 05255
www.northshire.com/printondemand

NORTHSHIRE BOOKSTORE

Building Community, One Book at a Time
This book was printed at the Northshire Bookstore, a family-owned, independent bookstore in Manchester Ctr., Vermont, since 1976. We are committed to excellence in bookselling. The Northshire Bookstore's mission is to serve as a resource for information, ideas, and entertainment while honoring the needs of customers, staff, and community.

Printed in the United States of America
using an Espresso Book Machine
from On Demand Books

Acknowledgments

God: Your plan for my life and my writing are still mysteries, but I'm grateful for the gift of Your Word, in both flesh and written form. Give me the ability to represent it excellently in both my writing and my life.

Dad: Thank you for never letting me get away with mediocre work. You always challenge me to do justice to God's message and to my own potential. Your guidance focuses me and your vision empowers me.

Mom: Thank you for refusing to let me give up on my writing or on this project. Your faith has inspired my own faith and your words of encouragement mean far more than you know.

My siblings: Thank you for letting me bounce ideas off of you and for your honest opinions. I have learned more from you about God, myself, and my writing than I ever thought possible. You are my biggest fans, harshest critics, and best friends.

Jonny and Keren: Thanks for being willing to share your unique love story. Your future together is baptized with many prayers.

Lisa Manchester (and family): Thank you all for being so generous with your time, your skill, and especially your friendship. Lisa, the cover is truly representative of both my vision and your talent.

CM: Thank you for your attention to detail and your willingness to proofread. More importantly, your constancy in friendship and your clarity on God's Word have encouraged me innumerable times and have motivated much of this project. You are truly a wonderful friend.

AB: Thank you for your willingness to share with me the ups and downs of newly-married life, for faithfully praying for this project, and for posing as my model. You are beautiful—inside and out!

RT: Thank you for the resources you sent to encourage me over the years and for our stimulating discussions on many of this book's topics. I greatly value your godly encouragement and our friendship.

Debbi Wraga and the others at Shires Press: Our first talk on the phone convinced me that Shires Press was the best publisher for me. Your honesty, flexibility, and service have been extremely encouraging.

Gilbert Newbury: Since you have only sons, I'm sure a "ladies' book" isn't of much use to you or them, but your publishing advice and your family's friendship will always recall fond memories. Thank you!

MG: Your mirror is now famous. Congratulations.

NH: Thanks for the use of your wedding bouquet!

Friends and family: For years, you kept asking when I would publish this book. When I doubted my book's value, your interest encouraged me to keep going. I am in your debt and I hope you will find that the finished product is worth your long wait.

Table of Contents

Introduction

For as long as I can remember, I have wanted to be a wife and a mother. It's a dream that has never faded. It is a dream that I share with many Christian young women I know.

As I headed into my twenties, I found that the desire became an increasing weight. I wanted to be married, but I saw no chance of such a thing ever happening. All around me, my friends and relatives were forming relationships, getting engaged, and getting married, but I stood in the middle of the whirlwind, untouched by the swirling winds of promise.

As I wrestled with feelings of being "overlooked," I found myself facing questions I thought I would never ask myself, questions about the worth of singleness, about the worth of marriage, even about the worth of living Christ-like. I never thought I would face these doubts and frustrations. Not me. I was raised in a Christian family, I loved the Lord with all my heart, I studied the Bible constantly, I had connections with strong Christian family and friends, and my parents had been teaching me about marriage and relationships since I was a child. If anyone was spiritually and mentally prepared for marriage, it was I.

Or so I thought.

As I struggled to understand God's way, I thought my doubts and frustration showed that I was somehow weaker than everyone else. But when I looked around me, I realized that other young women faced the same doubts. I began to wonder: How many of us are out there? How many, like me, need to know that they aren't alone in their struggles regarding marriage and singleness? How can we prepare in practical ways for marriage? How can we learn contentment in singleness?

When I perused material to answer these questions, I found that the resources just made me ask more questions. I wondered: "Why are most of the books on singleness written by married people? When authors claim to be content in singleness, does this mean that they daily live in this mindset, or that they know that's what they should say to struggling young women like me? If they actually do feel content, how do I get to that place? Isn't that something only 'super-Christians' can do?"

That's when I decided to write the book that I had been planning since my early teens. The process took an effort of over four years. Like the authors of the books I read, I may not answer all your questions. You may not agree with everything I say. That's okay. I intend only to open up the dialogue, so that we can explore God's expectations for our lives. I have not tried to be spiritual or to be "religiously correct." I have only tried to be honest. My main concern is truth—the truth about God, about ourselves, and about normal daily life.

Writing this book was in itself an answer to many of my questions, and I learned two main things from the journey. First, I learned that God really is enough. I know how glib this may sound to a young woman who wants to get married. God is all that we need, but He is not always all that we want. I admit I don't always feel that God is sufficient, but I know it is true. If we know that something is true, we should act on that truth, regardless of our feelings. This book discusses the daily reality—and the immense rewards—of stumbling along, following truths that we cannot feel but that we *know*.

Furthermore, as I wrote this book, I recognized the danger of the "someday" mentality.

"Someday, I will learn how to have a fantastic relationship."

"Someday, I will break these patterns of sin in my life."

"Someday, I will learn important life skills and fill my time with meaningful activities."

"Someday, I will start my real life, but until then, I'll try to be as productive as possible."

We often say "someday" when we mean "when I get married." We allow relationships in our lives today to grow lukewarm or cold, expecting that our future marriage relationship will be different. We continue patterns of sexual sin, expecting that our marriage relationship will fulfill all of those sexual needs. We delay learning important life skills, expecting that we'll somehow learn them easily once we reach marriage. We delay pursuing productivity in a career or a ministry, expecting that those activities are just to keep us meaningfully occupied while we're single. We expect that marriage will be the beginning of our "real lives," the birth of our fully mature and productive selves.

With this book, I intend to obliterate the "someday" mentality. Everything we do or don't do today influences everything that will happen tomorrow. We should not be ready "someday" for the life God has given to us. We should be ready today, now, at this moment. Our lives have already started. Opportunities have already arrived—and maybe passed by. We don't need husbands in order to begin living as God expects us to live. We only need God Himself.

Whether or not you meet the man of your dreams, you will have to meet the Lord. This book is less about preparing you for your future husband than about preparing you for our God. Our lives have a single purpose and that purpose is very clear from the Bible: We are called to love, serve, fear, and obey our God.[1] That purpose is the same whether we are single or married.

If you read this book and think, "Wow! I'm better prepared for marriage than ever!" then I've failed and I hope you'll forgive me for being unclear. But if you read this book and think, "Wow! I love the Lord more than ever!" then I've succeeded and I pray your relationship with Him will continue to be the most important relationship in your life.

I can't lie; even when we know the truth, it isn't always easy to practice on a daily basis. Sometimes I didn't like writing this book, even though I felt compelled to write it. There were times when a subject emotionally drained me, and most of the time I didn't know how to say what I felt I had to say. It was especially difficult to write about the benefits of singleness during times when the benefits of marriage looked so much better. I have spent many years learning to say, "Thy will be done" one more time. I have wrestled to understand singleness, marriage, and love as God sees them, and not as my culture sees them. I have never received complete answers to my questions, even though I search for them. Perhaps that is God's way of making me pursue Him; why would I need Him if I had all the answers?

If I have ever sounded confident about what I have written here, it is only because I am confident that God's way is best, even

[1] Micah 6:8

though I am not confident in my ability to recognize or act upon that truth consistently. If you are tempted to believe that I have arrived at some wonderful place of spiritual maturity, remember that I am always striving and I never arrive. If you are at that place of striving and seeking, please believe that I walk through this with you. Every day, I have to choose to enjoy my singleness and to use it for God's glory. Some days, that choice is difficult; some days, it is not difficult at all. I am no more or less than you are. I am simply a woman, with all the faults and desires of any other woman.

Yet even when I am most discouraged, one thought spurs me onward: My God loves me and, even if all other relationships fail me, He will never fail me.[2] He is worthy of my praise and obedience. I pray that this thought will become foremost in your mind as well, whether you remain single or whether you marry. This is a truth that marriage will never change.

No matter how you feel, don't waste the life that God has given you. You get *one* chance to live. Don't spend it wishing that you had something different or waiting for the perfect moment to go into action; use what you've been given—today—and see what God will do with it. Only then will you truly be ready today.

Yaasha Moriah

---

[2] Psalm 27:10

Authority
&
Relationships

℘ 1 ℭ

The True Definition of Love

You may be thinking to yourself, "Okay, I can skip this chapter because I learned about love in youth group." Or "I already heard this in a sermon." Or "I read a whole book on love!"

Although my parents have been teaching me about God's definition of love ever since I could understand words, I'm *still* learning about love. The way we define love determines the way we live our lives. It influences how we approach all of our relationships, particularly marriage. That is why it is important to start out any discussion about relationships with a good, detailed, honest discussion of love. What is true love? How can we tell it apart from false love? What does true love look like in a relationship, and what is the result of putting it into practice? Fortunately, 1 Corinthians chapter 13, commonly called "The Love Chapter," spells out God's definition of true love.

The Love Chapter
(verse 4) Charity suffereth long...

Love behaves itself with patience and keeps giving chances. Often when a person repeatedly fails, injures, or disappoints us, we mentally give him only so much more time, only so many more chances. But true love has no expiration date. Love does not just tolerate annoyances; it suffers real pain (hence *"suffereth long"*), and it suffers that pain indefinitely, for the sake of the other person.

...and is kind;

Love shows genuine thoughtfulness and other-centeredness, and directly fulfills the command: "You shall love your neighbor as yourself." [3] When we love ourselves, we show kindness to ourselves, we are mindful of our needs and wants, we are concerned about our well-being, we desire respect, and we do

---

[3] Mark 12:31

whatever is necessary to secure what seems good for us. Love takes that definition of kindness and transfers it to another person. Now, instead of treating ourselves with special care, we concern ourselves with the special care of others.

Charity envieth not;

Envy desires something that belongs to another person, and is blind to both joy and pain. When we envy, we cannot share the other person's joy because we feel frustrated that we cannot call that joy our own. We also cannot minister to another person's pain because they seem to have more things or better things than we do; we view *them* as the "lucky" ones and feel that *we* deserve more than they do. On the other hand, love rejoices with others, even when we wish we had what others have, and shows compassion for others' suffering, even if that suffering does not seem as great as our own. Love allows no envy to cloud a relationship or to interfere with a Christ-like response to the situations of others. Love is other-centered.

Charity vaunteth not itself...

To "vaunt" means to display yourself, to push yourself forward, to be the center of attention. Loudness is a form of vaunting; we try to draw attention to ourselves through noise. Immodesty is a form of vaunting; we try to draw attention to our bodies. Showing off our talents, intelligence, and skill can be a way of vaunting; we may do it subtly and quietly, but the intention is to show off. Vaunting is all about making ourselves look and feel better than others. Love, in contrast, esteems others as better than ourselves.[4] Love is not concerned with getting attention, but with giving attention. Love is humble and makes itself a servant to others.[5] The Bible says that we should not seek glory for ourselves, but should rather take the lowest place and give the higher place to others.[6] Let others give us glory[7]—not ourselves—and let God honor us when He sees our

---

[4] Philippians 2:3
[5] Mark 10:43-45
[6] Luke 14:8-10
[7] Proverbs 27:2

humility.[8] That honor will be worth far more than the temporary admiration of those who respond to our vaunting of ourselves.

...is not puffed up,

"Puffed up" implies being made bigger and more important in appearance than one's actual substance would allow. A balloon, for example, is a small thing in actuality, but when it is inflated, it looks bigger than it really is—even though it is 99% air! The problem with inflated things is that they eventually deflate and shock others with their lack of substance. Love does not try to make itself look bigger or better than others. It is the "real deal" and gives us growth only when we can support that growth. Love never deflates, as vanity does, and is therefore constant. It is steady, firm, and strong. Once again, love makes itself other-centered, and reaps the rewards of lasting maturity.

(verse 5) Doth not behave itself unseemly...

Many things can fall into the category of unseemliness— loudness, immodesty, unkindness, rashness, crudeness, arrogance, selfishness, impatience... In contrast, love is the model of good behavior. "Seemliness" would cover behaviors like good manners and graciousness. Seemliness is the tact and social grace of an experienced diplomat or an accomplished hostess. I suppose it is a sense of kingliness (or queenliness) in manner, behavior that puts others at their ease and inspires their trust and confidence. Love never flies off the handle or invites insecurity; love is constant, stable, and trustworthy.

Seeketh not her own,

Every attribute of love can be summed up in the phrase "other-centered." This phrase "seeketh not her own" just underscores the obvious theme. Love does not look for what it can get, but for what it can give. Love revolves around serving others, placing their needs above our own, and sacrificing our desires for the sake of securing another person's well-being and happiness.

---

[8] James 4:10

Is not easily provoked,

The Bible warns against anger and constantly advises us to be slow to wrath[9] and to rule our spirits and our tongues.[10] The fruits of the Spirit include patience and self-control,[11] both of which are strong shields against the danger of being easily provoked. We can be provoked in so many ways, and whether we snap or simmer, neither is a loving response. The Bible does not condemn *all* anger—some is justifiable and right[12]—but I believe that much anger is inspired by a sense of entitlement, entitlement to be treated a certain way, entitlement to pursue our own happiness, entitlement to have a certain type of relationship, entitlement not to have to deal with certain faults in the other person. The list is endless, but the bottom line is that we expect more than we get and we are provoked when we feel like the other person is not holding up their end.

Love covers a multitude of sins.[13] It doesn't look the other way when sin is committed, but it does respond to sin with truth, forgiveness, and an attitude that encourages the other person in righteousness. An attitude that easily ignites into anger is self-centered and untrusting; an attitude that overlooks provocation is other-centered, constant, and ready to give the benefit of the doubt. This is the attitude of love.

Thinketh no evil;

Another way of interpreting "thinketh no evil" is "not ready to suspect evil." A suspicious mind is one of the greatest barriers to the healing or building of a relationship. Few things are as destructive as obvious mistrust, the tendency to assume the worst in other people, and the poison of accusing words. Assuming that the other person's motivations and intentions are evil often causes problems where there are none. Sometimes, acting as if the other person does not intend harm—even when it is quite possible that they do—spurs the other person to behave in an honorable and

---

[9] Proverbs 14:29
[10] Proverbs 16:32
[11] Galatians 5:22-23
[12] Ephesians 4:26, John 2:13-17
[13] 1 Peter 4:8

4

trustworthy way. Love does not have to be blind or naïve in order to be gracious and to give the benefit of the doubt. Love also does not expect the other person to fail. Love recognizes that the other person may fail, but to expect and predict weakness or sin does nothing to encourage others to pursue righteousness. Rather, it discourages them from trying.

An attitude that thinks evil is more ready to accuse than to forgive. This attitude holds grudges and keeps a record of all real or imagined wrongs committed by the other person, to be retrieved and used as missiles at opportune moments. Such an attitude is also sensitive and suspicious even when little or no evidence supports the suspicion. Nothing the other person does is good enough; even improvements seem inadequate or go unnoticed by the accuser's eye. Love, on the other hand, strains to facilitate, encourage, inspire, and notice improvement. Love forgives rather than accuses, gives the benefit of the doubt rather than suspecting evil, responds to real or imagined provocations with patience rather than anger, and releases resentment rather than treasuring it. Love does everything it can to build mutual trust.

(verse 6) Rejoiceth not in iniquity, but rejoiceth in the truth...

Some people get a kick out of making sarcastic rejoinders or witty put-downs; love gets a kick out of speaking the truth graciously and kindly, respecting the other person's dignity and feelings. Some people enjoy seeing other people fail or sin; they hate to see a goody-two-shoes and they feel better about themselves when they can expose the hypocrisy of others. Love enjoys seeing other people overcome weakness and sin and works to cultivate genuine righteousness and pure truth. Love celebrates progress, recognizes the danger and deception of sin, and combats it with the truth of God. Love rejoices not to see the enemy fall, but to see the enemy repent.

(verse 7) Beareth all things...

Love is willing to bear pain and suffering for the sake of another. Jesus Christ was willing to bear the ultimate pain—God's wrath and punishment for sin—because of His overwhelming love for us. The humiliation, pain, and unkindness that we bear from each other is *nothing* compared to what He bore for us and still bears from us. Our longsuffering Christ shows us the meaning of true love by extending love and forgiveness even when we are unworthy and ungrateful. If we are the receivers of such incredible love, how can we not also be givers of it?

Believeth all things...

Love is fueled by trust and results in righteousness. The Bible says that Abraham believed God and it was accounted to him as righteousness.[14] Trust in the Lord is never misplaced.[15] We believe all things He tells us and we believe in His Son; this is an expression of our trust and love for Him. When we doubt, we are showing distrust, which is the enemy of love.

When we love others, we cultivate trust, and we encourage each other to develop Christ-like trustworthiness. Eventually, this leads the relationship into a level of trust in which we can believe anything the other person says, because we know their love for us would never allow them to lie to us. In this way, trust and belief in our Lord translates into belief, love, and trust for others.

Hopeth all things...

Hope is more than a wishful feeling; it is the conviction that God will work all things together for good, for those who are called according to His purpose.[16] When we do not yet see the evidence or the fulfillment of a promise with our own eyes, we trust the eyes of another person. Part of loving God, therefore, is believing in the hope He has promised us, the hope of eternal life.[17] Love extends a hopeful attitude to others by looking to the fulfillment of God's work in their lives and by not expecting failure. It desires the best and hopes that the effort will be rewarded and will see fulfillment. Love never gives up hope in another person, no matter how many times that person fails. We may give up on love, but love will never give up on us.

---

[14] Romans 4:3
[15] Psalm 18:30, Proverbs 3:5-6
[16] Romans 8:28
[17] 1 John 2:25

Endureth all things...

We can only endure if we have hope. If there is nothing for which to endure—no prize at the end—then enduring is just a futile exercise in longevity. Scripture says that for the joy set before Him, Christ endured the cross.[18] Our hope and joy is this: Glory and eternal life with the Father. We endure suffering now because we hope in the promise of God.[19] Similarly, when we love others, we are given the strength to endure much hardship, disappointment, discouragement, ill-treatment, sacrifice and service.

(verse 8) Charity never faileth.

Many people in our lives fail us and disappoint us—we even fail and disappoint ourselves—but Love Himself never fails us. He will never leave us or forsake us, even if all others leave us behind. Love Himself always comes through on His promises, and always remains completely trustworthy. Love Himself is a safe place for our hearts.

Because of our contact with Love Himself, we are able to extend the same unfailing love to others. Our love has no conditions, no expiration date, and no record of wrongs. Imagine what such a love could do to our relationships, our communities, and our whole world! When Love Himself died on a cross, the whole universe turned upside down and Love ripped apart Death itself. If Love can conquer something as powerful as Death, what might it accomplish in the hearts and hands of ordinary women?

Love God

Someone once asked Jesus Christ, "What is the greatest commandment?" His answer: "You shall love the Lord your God with all your heart, with all your soul, with all your mind, and with all your strength."[20] When I first considered that commandment, I realized I had no hope of living up to it. Make God my one consuming passion? How could I love Him like that?

---

[18] Hebrews 12:2
[19] 2 Corinthians 1:7
[20] Mark 12:30

We love Him because He first loved us.[21]

In this was manifested the love of God toward us, because that God sent his only begotten Son into the world, that we might live through him. Herein is love, not that we loved God, but that he loved us, and sent his Son to be the propitiation for our sins.[22]

Our relationship with the Lord is the litmus test for all our other relationships. A young woman once explained to me that, as much as she valued her relationship with the Lord, it was just not the type of relationship she wanted to have right then. She wanted a husband. Now I know *exactly* what this young woman was talking about, because I've felt the same way myself. I knew that I should love Jesus more than anything else, but Jesus didn't seem like enough. His love seemed so distant and dim in comparison with the love of a human being that I could see and touch and hear. How could I love Jesus when I had never seen Him?

Funny thing. I have never seen my future husband either—I still don't know who he might be—yet I already "loved" him so much that I was putting my love for him above my love for Jesus Christ!

Consider this: Jesus loves us unconditionally. He is perfect, He never changes, and He *always* does good to us. Compare that to a husband. Husbands are imperfect. They may intend to do everything for our good, but their good intentions will sometimes fail. Husbands will also change. Essentially, we're comparing a perfect, complete, and secure love with an imperfect, incomplete, and insecure love. If our love for the perfect Lover is lukewarm, how can we truly love an imperfect lover?

Our relationship with the Lord is the doorway to all other relationships. This relationship must become the basis for relationships with others, so that our relationships will be strong and long-lasting.

Of course, we will always struggle to love the Lord as He ought to be loved. We will not always feel a spiritual sense of closeness to Him. But loving God is not about feeling lovingly toward Him; it is about acting in a way that demonstrates our love for Him. I once confessed to my father, "I feel like I don't love the Lord anymore. I

---

[21] 1 John 4:19
[22] 1 John 4:9-10

feel like I'm just doing what He wants me to do out of habit and not because I love Him."

My father asked, "What's wrong with that?"

At the time, it seemed barbaric that I could obey God out of habit rather than out of love, but as time went on, I began to see what my father had meant.

My mother helped me to fill in the blanks when I shared my guilt that I was not completely passionate about the Lord.

"Yaasha," Mom said. "Love isn't all about having those wonderful, loving feelings. Love is doing your duty. For example, sometimes I don't feel affection for my husband, but I still love him and I do my duty by him. I behave like a good wife should. When I show my love for him, even when I don't feel it, eventually I feel loving toward him again. The love was there in what I was doing."

The Christian life is not about dredging up feelings of love toward God, but rather about acting out love at those times when we do not feel it. Most times when we are told to love God, this command is immediately followed up with the command to keep His commandments—in other words, to *do* something.

Therefore thou shalt love the LORD thy God, and keep his charge, and his statutes, and his judgments, and his commandments, alway.[23]

Once I grasped this concept of loving God even when I didn't feel like it, I began to see a change in my life. I no longer felt depressed about my spiritual life. Instead, I began to view it all as a journey. I knew there would be highs and lows, but so long as I kept my focus on Christ, it would all turn out right. Consequently, I was able to love others even when I didn't feel like it, and *that* is the key to building a lasting and growing relationship.

We must love God with all our hearts, all our souls, all our minds, and all our strength. We must grasp for Him like we've grasped for nothing else. We must desire Him like we've desired no one else. We must love Him like we've loved no one else. He is worth it. Even if all other relationships grow cold, we will find that *He is enough.*

---

[23] Deuteronomy 11:1

Love Others

Imagine getting a birthday present with this message on the package, "As soon as you get this, give it away to someone else!" It's a strange thing, but when God gives us His love, He expects us to give it away at once. Almost every time there is a commandment in the Bible to love the Lord, it is followed by a commandment to love others.

For example, when Jesus revealed that the greatest commandment is to love God with all your heart, soul, mind, and strength,[24] He added, "And the second is like it: You shall love your neighbor as yourself. There is no other commandment greater than these."[25] We are encouraged over and over in the Scriptures to love each other, as proof of our love for the Lord. If we do not show love for our brothers and sisters in Christ, our faith is under suspicion, because those who truly love God would have God's love inside of them, and God's love behaves in a certain way.

Beloved, let us love one another: for love is of God; and every one that loveth is born of God, and knoweth God. He that loveth not knoweth not God; for God is love. In this was manifested the love of God toward us, because that God sent his only begotten Son into the world, that we might live through him. Herein is love, not that we loved God, but that he loved us, and sent his Son to be the propitiation for our sins. Beloved, if God so loved us, we ought also to love one another. No man hath seen God at any time. If we love one another, God dwelleth in us, and his love is perfected in us... If a man say, I love God, and hateth his brother, he is a liar: for he that loveth not his brother whom he hath seen, how can he love God whom he hath not seen? And this commandment have we from him, That he who loveth God love his brother also.[26]

Love Your Enemies

Love gives to those who don't deserve it. Jesus Christ did not come as a hero or as a king; He came as a carpenter's son under circumstances that made his legitimacy look suspicious.[27] Jesus's

---

[24] Deuteronomy 6:5
[25] Mark 12:31
[26] 1 John 4:7-12, 20-21
[27] In those days, having sexual relations (never mind a baby) before marriage was a

birthplace, race, occupation, and circumstances of birth marked Him as the lowest of the low—born in a stable, raised in a seedy town, accused of blasphemy and lawlessness, rejected by His own people, and finally executed in excruciating pain in the company of criminals who mocked Him. Why did He do it?

Because He loved us.

He certainly had no reason to love us. We are not naturally godly and good—in fact, quite the opposite![28] Even our best actions are done with selfish motives. Even our best kindnesses are tainted with wrong attitudes. Even our best intentions fail. Even our best gifts are imperfect.[29] The Bible calls us "dead in our trespasses."[30] To a God who is perfect and pure, we were like the most diseased, ugly, and filthy person you can imagine. We were unclean, without hope of finding a cure, facing living death because of our separation from the holy God who made us.[31] God could have destroyed the whole world and made it new the way He intended it to be. Instead, He did something totally unexpected.

For when we were yet without strength, in due time Christ died for the ungodly. For scarcely for a righteous man will one die: yet peradventure for a good man some would even dare to die. But God commendeth his love toward us, in that, while we were yet sinners, Christ died for us.[32]

Talk about love! We might die for someone we really love, but would we die for our worst enemy? That's what Jesus did when He died for us; He died for His worst enemies.

For if ye love them which love you, what thank have ye? for sinners also love those that love them. And if ye do good to them which do good to you, what thank have ye? for sinners also do even the same. And if ye lend to them of whom ye hope to receive, what thank have ye? for sinners also lend to sinners, to receive as much again. But love ye your enemies, and do good, and lend, hoping for nothing again; and your reward shall be great, and ye shall be the children of the Highest: for he is kind unto the

---

crime worthy of death.
[28] Romans 3:12
[29] Isaiah 64:6
[30] Ephesians 2:1
[31] Ephesians 2:13
[32] Romans 5:6-8

unthankful and to the evil. Be ye therefore merciful, as your Father also is merciful.[33]

"That's great," we might say. "But no matter how much I try to love my enemies, I can't do it. I feel absolutely no affection for them. I want to love them, but they sure are hard to love!"

I understand that feeling. It seems impossible. But there *is* a way to love our enemies.

Love: An Attitude and an Action

Many people think of love as a feeling of affection, fondness, attraction, or passion. I used to think of love as "the step above liking someone." Actually, love at its most basic level has nothing to do with affection, fondness, attraction, passion, or liking. All of those things depend on our tastes and preferences, and how physical features, personality, character traits, and mannerisms are compatible with our expectations of what is worthy of our attention and affection.

Love is independent of how we feel about someone. Love can love without affection, fondness, attraction, passion, or liking. How is this possible? Because love is not a feeling or an emotion. Love is an *attitude* and an *action*. Love is not what we feel; it is what we *do*. Love is acting in a way that shows concern for the other person's well-being, regardless of whether that person deserves your concern. When Jesus said, "Love your enemies," He did not tell us how to feel more loving toward them. Instead, He immediately followed up His commandment to love our enemies with instructions on *how* to do so: Do good to them. Give them good things without expecting anything in return. Pray for them. Bless them when they curse you.[34] If your enemy is hungry, feed him. If he is thirsty, give him a drink.[35]

Be not overcome of evil, but overcome evil with good.[36]

Notice that, in most of the other places in the Bible when we are encouraged to love one another, we are given examples of specific ways in which to show love, ways that essentially come down to

---

[33] Luke 6:32-36
[34] Matthew 5:44
[35] Romans 12:20
[36] Romans 12:21

our attitudes and our actions.

For example, in Jesus's day, a Roman soldier had the legal authority to make a Jew (or any other random subject) carry his armor for a mile. The Roman armor was heavy and difficult to carry, so this practice was not very popular amongst the subjects who might be grabbed by a Roman soldier and forced to carry his armor for a mile. To make matters worse, the Romans and the Jews were bitter enemies. Jesus, however, gave an example of a loving reaction to this hated practice: Carry the armor for another mile.[37] This is where we get our phrase "going the extra mile" for someone. Carrying the armor for the first mile must have been tiring and difficult; carrying the armor for a second mile must have been exhausting and perhaps even painful. Yet that is what love endures. Love doesn't do the bare minimum; love goes beyond, *even for an enemy.*

Feelings and emotions change. We might like someone one day and dislike him the next day. But love never changes, because it does not depend on our emotions or feelings. Love says, "I will do what is best for others, not because they necessarily deserve it or because they'll even appreciate it, but because that is the right thing to do."

Often, when we act out love even when we don't feel it, we eventually begin to feel loving toward that person. Corrie Ten Boom, a Christian woman who lived through the horrors of the infamous Ravensbruck concentration camp during World War Two, told a story about how God enabled her to love one of her greatest enemies. The horrors she had suffered in the concentration camp included watching the deaths of innocent women (including her sister), facing starvation and sickness and fear, and walking naked past the eyes of the cruel guards. Many years later, she unexpectedly found herself face to face with one of those same guards. He told her that he had become a Christian, asked her forgiveness, and held out his hand. She knew that she needed to forgive him—even to love him—but she could do neither. She prayed for God to help her shake this man's hand. As soon as her

---

[37] Matthew 5:41

hand met his, God gave her overwhelming love and compassion for the man, and she was able to forgive him with all of her heart and to count him as her brother in Christ.

The feeling of love doesn't always instantly catch up with the duty of love, as it does in this true story. Sometimes it takes years or even a lifetime, yet whether or not the feeling is present, the duty is the same. We must love with the love of our Lord— unconditionally, through our hands as well as our hearts. Love does not just *say* "I love you" but *does* "I love you."

The Sacrifice of Love

For God so loved the world, that he gave his only begotten Son...[38]

God didn't give something He could replace or something that was second-best. His gift was worth everything to Him, and was irreplaceable and perfect. He showed us how true love gives the best it can possibly give. Love cost our Lord *everything*.

The Lord does not call us to comfortable love. He calls us to show a love like His own—radical, self-sacrificing love, love that will love to the point of death. We are called to sacrifice our desires, dreams, fears, past, present, future, and even life to follow the call of Love Himself.

The Enemy hates Love, and those who are part of his kingdom hate love also. When they met Love Himself, what did they do? They nailed Him to a cross. When they see Love Himself blazing through our lives like a beacon, they will hate us too. If they beat, cursed, and persecuted Love Himself, they will do the same to us.

If ye were of the world, the world would love his own: but because ye are not of the world, but I have chosen you out of the world, therefore the world hateth you. Remember the word that I said unto you, The servant is not greater than his lord. If they have persecuted me, they will also persecute you; if they have kept my saying, they will keep yours also. But all these things will they do unto you for my name's sake, because they know not him that sent me.[39]

Love comes with a cost. We may not see the cost now, but if we are faithful to the Lord and to His Love, be certain that we *will* pay

---

[38] John 3:16
[39] John 15:19-21

14

that price.[40] Can we love even when we know it will hurt?

God promises that He will comfort us when we suffer for Love, and that our suffering will make us more able to minister to those who are suffering. He promises that if we take part in His suffering, we will take part in His consolation.[41]

Beloved, think it not strange concerning the fiery trial which is to try you, as though some strange thing happened unto you: But rejoice, inasmuch as ye are partakers of Christ's sufferings; that, when his glory shall be revealed, ye may be glad also with exceeding joy. If ye be reproached for the name of Christ, happy are ye; for the spirit of glory and of God resteth upon you: on their part he is evil spoken of, but on your part he is glorified.[42]

Best of all is this:

The Spirit itself beareth witness with our spirit, that we are the children of God: And if children, then heirs; heirs of God, and joint-heirs with Christ; if so be that we suffer with him, that we may be also glorified together. For I reckon that the sufferings of this present time are not worthy to be compared with the glory which shall be revealed in us.[43]

If we are true Christians, then at some point each of us will have to say: "I love my God. When I see Him face to face, I know it will be worth every moment of pain I've had to suffer for Him. The price is worth the prize. I have met Love."

---

[40] 2 Timothy 3:12
[41] 2 Corinthians 1:3-7
[42] 1 Peter 4:12-14
[43] Romans 8:16-18

15

♔ 2 ♕

Authority in Relationships

For years, I have studied what it means to be a woman and how I should relate to the Lord and to others specifically as a woman. During my studies, I became aware that the fear of the Lord was intimately connected with the practice of Biblical womanhood. The deeper I delved into my study, the more convinced I became that the fear of the Lord is a crucial concept which lays the foundation for a woman to understand her role not only in her Heavenly relationship but also in her earthly relationships. Quite simply, I had to understand authority before I could understand womanhood.

People describe the fear of the Lord in many ways: a profound awe and reverence that recognizes His greatness and His goodness; a deep respect for His authority; a sense of complete submission to Him because of His sovereignty. After much study, I believe that the fear of the Lord incorporates all of these ideas, but is most importantly a literal fear, approaching at times even a holy terror. Here is the (very short) explanation:

1. When you see "fear of the Lord" or "fear of God" in English, the original Hebrew or Greek word for "fear" carries the idea of fear, awe, reverence, trembling, even sometimes terror. Overwhelmingly, these words are translated with fear-related meanings, not simply as awe or reverence.

2. The same word used for the fear of the Lord is used for fear of human enemies and fear of bad circumstances. *Fear not them which kill the body, but are not able to kill the soul: but rather fear him which is able to destroy both soul and body in hell.*[44]

    Scholars agree that the one who destroys soul and body in Hell is God, because only He has the ultimate authority to do

---

[44] Matthew 10:28

so. In this passage, we have contrasting fears—fear of man and fear of God. Here's the clincher: The word used for fear of God was exactly the same word used for fear of human enemies. If we translate the word as reverence, we have to be consistent and apply it to both uses. "Reverence/respect/honor not them which kill the body, but are not able to kill the soul: but rather reverence/respect/honor him which is able to destroy both soul and body in hell." It doesn't sound the same, does it? There are many similar cases in the Bible that confirm that the fear of God is a *literal* fear, parallel to other fears.

3. In the Bible, when people encountered God (or even just a messenger from God), their reactions included fear. When God spoke to the Israelites from Sinai, the people begged Moses to speak to God for them because they were scared to death.[45] When the Angel of the Lord appeared to Joshua before the battle against Jericho, upon discovering the angel's identity, Joshua immediately fell on his face.[46] When the Angel of the Lord appeared to Samson's parents to tell them that Samson would be born, Samson's father was terrified that, having seen the Lord's face, he and his wife would both die.[47] When a being from God appeared to Daniel, Daniel shook with fear and lost consciousness.[48] When the Angel of the Lord appeared to the shepherds, they trembled and were "sore afraid."[49] These are reactions of fear, not simply of reverence.

4. In the Bible, the fear of the Lord is always shown to be a good thing. "Those who fear the Lord" always refers to righteous believers. In contrast, "those who do not fear the Lord" always refers to wicked people. Over and over, we are told that the fear of the Lord is good and beneficial:

---

[45] Exodus 30:18-21

[46] Joshua 5:13-15

[47] Judges 13:20-23. The fear of Samson's father was consistent with Exodus 33:20, in which God warns Moses, "Thou canst not see my face, for there shall no man see me, and live."

[48] Daniel 10: 5-10

[49] Luke 2:8-16

> *The secret of the Lord is with them that fear Him, and He will shew them His covenant.*[50]
>
> *Blessed is everyone that feareth the Lord, that walketh in His ways.*[51]

If we look deeper into this topic, we will find many, many reasons to believe in a literal fear of the Lord. I have only listed very few. But why is it important not only to respect and revere the Lord, but also to fear Him?

The Purpose of the Fear of the Lord

I believe (based on my study of the Bible) that the fear of the Lord has three main purposes:

1. **To turn us away from sin.** God is a good Father and He raises no brats. Those who fear Him avoid sinning because they fear His punishment. The Bible includes examples of His punishments—and they aren't pretty.

   David was called "a man after God's own heart,"[52] yet when David killed off one of his friends in order to take the friend's wife for himself, the child that resulted from David's adultery died, according to the word of the Lord by the prophet Nathan. Later, just as David had turned against his good friend, David's own loved ones turned against him.

   When Israel, God's special and set apart people, went after other gods, God sent them to exile, slavery, and death. When Ananias and Sapphira, members of the early church, lied to the apostles and to God's Holy Spirit, God struck them down so that they died.[53] These punishments happened to people who were *within* the chosen people; these weren't just outsiders.

   My son, despise not thou the chastening of the Lord, nor faint when thou art rebuked of him: For whom the Lord loveth he chasteneth, and scourgeth every son whom he receiveth. If ye endure

---

[50] Psalm 25:14
[51] Psalm 128:1
[52] Acts 13:22
[53] Acts 5:1-11

chastening, God dealeth with you as with sons; for what son is he whom the father chasteneth not?[54]

God's punishments hurt, and only pride keeps us from fearing them. The fear of the Lord is meant to make us run away from sin the way we would run away from a raging fire or a charging bull. God is willing to inflict the hurt of punishment in order to keep us from the greater hurt of severely damaging our relationship with Him. It is like a father who punishes his child for wandering too close to the road; the temporary hurt of punishment will prevent the life-threatening hurt of being hit by a passing car. So God punishes us because He *loves* us.

2. **To keep us walking in righteousness.** Often the commandment to fear the Lord is accompanied by a commandment to serve Him or to follow His law.

    And now, Israel, what doth the LORD thy God require of thee, but to fear the LORD thy God, to walk in all his ways, and to love him, and to serve the LORD thy God with all thy heart and with all thy soul, to keep the commandments of the LORD, and his statutes, which I command thee this day for thy good?[55] (emphasis added)

    Therefore, the fear of the Lord not only diverts us away from sin, but it also points us in the way in which we should go. For those who desire to know God's will, the fear of the Lord is the signpost to the destination to which God desires to lead us.

3. **To help us to recognize His lordship.** Ultimately, fearing the Lord comes down to recognizing His complete authority. Often, when God gives a command to fear Him, He follows up with this statement: "I am the Lord." "I AM" is the highest reason God gives for His authority. We fear because HE IS. We fear the forces of nature; should we not fear the One who made those forces, forces that show only an inkling of His power? We fear death; should we not fear the One who has power over death? The Lord is worthy of fear simply because He is Himself.

---

[54] Hebrews 12:5b-7
[55] Deuteronomy 10:12-13

Fear and Love

How can we love God if we fear Him? If fear seems like the exact opposite of love, let me tell you a story.

I grew up in a Christian family and the head of my family was my father. He threw us up in the air and caught us on the way down, he played Tickle Monster with us, he sang us songs and read us stories, he taught us about the plants and the animals, and he let us climb all over him like he was a jungle gym. But Dad had a stern side too. He dealt out judgments and punishment when an offense was brought before him. We all feared the rod of Dad. Mom's discipline was bad enough; Dad's discipline was something to be feared. All of us dreaded to hear the words, from either Mom or from each other, "I'm telling Daddy when he gets home!"

Dad worked long hours away from the family, so when we saw his truck arrive, our hearts leaped for joy. Daddy was home! Our first instinct was to leap into his arms and tell him all about what we had done that day. Then we hesitated. Wait—had someone promised that day to tell Daddy about something? Had Mom disciplined us and might she tell Dad about the offense? Was there anything we had done, or failed to do, that might catch Dad's watchful eye and demand punishment? If our consciences were clear, we ran excitedly to Daddy. If our consciences were heavy, we dreaded the impending confessions.

Yet no matter how frightening Dad's wrath became, we never once doubted that Dad loved us. The discipline hurt but we knew that it hurt him too, because sometimes we saw him cry afterward. Our fear never overpowered our love, but neither did our love fully overpower our fear.

My relationship with my dad was my first glimpse of the fear of the Lord. Can fear and love coexist? Absolutely. We may fear God's punishments (which is not the same as fearing His ultimate judgment) but we also know that He loves us. His love requires punishment and His punishment requires love. *Whom He loves He chastens.*[56] The two cannot exist without each other. That is why I believe that we cannot truly love God until we truly fear Him.

---

[56] Hebrews 12:6

The Benefits of Fearing the Lord

1. The Lord promises that those who fear Him will have wisdom and knowledge and understanding; they will even be taught the secrets of the Lord.

The fear of the LORD is the beginning of wisdom: and the knowledge of the holy is understanding.[57]

And unto man he said, Behold, the fear of the LORD, that is wisdom; and to depart from evil is understanding.[58]

The secret of the LORD is with them that fear him; and he will shew them his covenant.[59]

2. Those who fear the Lord will have long life: *The fear of the LORD prolongeth days: but the years of the wicked shall be shortened.*[60]

3. The Lord will provide for those who fear Him: *O fear the LORD, ye his saints: for there is no want to them that fear him.*[61]

4. The Lord will deliver them and protect them: *The angel of the LORD encampeth round about them that fear him, and delivereth them.*[62]

5. God pays special attention to those who fear Him and promises that He will remember them for good:

Then they that feared the LORD spake often one to another: and the LORD hearkened, and heard it, and a book of remembrance was written before him for them that feared the LORD, and that thought upon his name. And they shall be mine, saith the LORD of hosts, in that day when I make up my jewels; and I will spare them, as a man spareth his own son that serveth him.[63]

God makes it clear that He gives special insight, privileges, and blessing to the people who recognize Him as the one and only God, the righteous God worthy of fear and reverence.

---

[57] Proverbs 9:10
[58] Job 28:28
[59] Psalm 25:14
[60] Proverbs 10:27
[61] Psalm 34:9
[62] Psalm 34:7
[63] Malachi 3:16

21

The Fear of Authority

The fear of the Lord translates into our human relationships. God set up a pattern of authority in our human relationships that mirrors His authority over us, even using terms of earthly authority to emphasize His divine authority:

A son honoureth his father, and a servant his master: if then I be a father, where is mine honour? and if I be a master, where is my fear?[64]

The first four of the Ten Commandments deal with how we treat the Lord. Then, immediately after that, we learn the rule about our first earthly authorities: our parents.

Honour thy father and thy mother: that thy days may be long upon the land which the LORD thy God giveth thee.[65]

This commandment is echoed in the New Testament as well: *Children, obey your parents in all things: for this is well pleasing unto the Lord.*[66]

In Ephesians, the apostle Paul even points out that the command to honor our parents is the first commandment accompanied by a clear promise, the promise of long life.

Children, obey your parents in the Lord: for this is right. Honour thy father and mother; which is the first commandment with promise; That it may be well with thee, and thou mayest live long on the earth.[67]

In today's society, children scream and yell at their parents. Movies and television shows depict parents as incompetent morons and their children as bratty geniuses. Children openly make fun of their parents, backtalk their parents, talk to their friends about how stupid their parents are being, respond in a cocky or smart-alecky way toward their parents, and even have the audacity to say to their parents' faces, "I hate you." The Bible says: *Cursed be he that setteth light by his father or his mother.*[68] That word used for the phrase "to set light by" means "to treat with contempt or dishonor, to despise, to treat shamefully, to lightly esteem." In God's law, a child that continually rebelled against his or her parents and cursed

---

[64] Malachi 1:6a
[65] Exodus 20:12
[66] Colossians 3:20
[67] Ephesians 6:1-3
[68] Deuteronomy 27:16a

them would be stoned to death outside the camp.[69]

Dishonoring parents appears in the same list as all kinds of sexual sin, lying, pride, and other sins that God hates, and the Bible adds that "they which commit such things are worthy of death."[70] Disobedience to parents is an invitation to be judged by God.

Honoring our parents is directly linked in the Bible to honoring God, because our treatment of our earthly authorities translates into our treatment of our Heavenly Authority.

The fear of the LORD is the beginning of knowledge: but fools despise wisdom and instruction. My son, hear the instruction of thy father, and forsake not the law of thy mother: For they shall be an ornament of grace unto thy head, and chains about thy neck.[71]

Immediately after we're told that the fear of the Lord leads to wisdom but fools despise instruction, we are given a command to listen to the instruction of our parents and we are given a promise that their instruction will be like expensive ornaments. In this way, we are shown that the fear of the Lord is linked to obedience to parents. If we will not listen to our parents, why would we listen to the Lord?

Ye shall fear every man his mother, and his father, and keep my sabbaths: I am the LORD your God.[72]

That word for "fear" is the exact same word used of the fear of the Lord. Again, it literally means "to be afraid" as well as "to honor and revere." This word is most often used to indicate how we should react to the Lord and to His holy things. Think about how we should interact with God. The Lord indicates in His word that the way that we treat Him is the way that we are supposed to treat our parents: with reverence, honor, respect, and fear.

For those who wonder if there are exceptions to the rule: Yes, there are exceptions, but there are also two important things to keep in mind. First, just because there is an exception does not mean it is good. When the people of Israel begged for a king, God knew they did not need one, but He gave them one anyway.[73] Because of

---

[69] Deuteronomy 21:18-21
[70] Romans 1:28-32
[71] Proverbs 1:7-9
[72] Leviticus 19:3
[73] 1 Samuel chapter 8

ungodly kings, the people were led astray and suffered many things. Sometimes the exception that God allows is worse than the rule, however difficult the rule may seem. Secondly, if we seek for the exceptions before we have learned the rules, we only prove that we have no intention of truly obeying the rules. The young woman who applies as much of the rule to her life as possible, despite difficult circumstances, is better off than the young woman who instantly seeks for an exception for her situation.

Are there times where a parent (particularly an unsaved one) might require us to do something that is wrong? Absolutely. However, there is a big difference between saying, "I cannot obey you because you are directly contradicting God's Word" and saying, "I cannot obey you because I think you're being unreasonable." Nowhere does God let us squirm from under authority because we think our authority is unreasonable. Only when that authority stands between you and God do you have a right to say, "I must obey God rather than man."[74] I see no other Biblical basis for defying authority. If we must defy authority, the manner in which we do so is also important. There is a great difference between saying, "I cannot obey you because you are directly contradicting God's Word" and "You're telling me to disobey God and as far as I'm concerned you can go to H-E-double hockey sticks!" Yes, there are tough cases where a perverted parent requires or forces evil things upon a child, and those are cases where the child must disobey and seek safety from others, but for the vast majority of us, that is not the case, yet we still make excuses. God makes no excuses for us. He expects us to obey whenever humanly possible, and to disobey respectfully if we must make a choice between God and parent.

An Unmarried Daughter

A woman's first relationship with a man is her relationship with her father. What are the Bible's guidelines for that relationship? What are the evidences of a father's authority over his daughter?

According to the law that God gave Moses, a man has the power to nullify the vows of either his virgin daughter or of his

---

[74] Acts 5:29

wife.[75] A vow is a very sacred thing. A man who makes a vow is expected to follow through on that vow, no matter what the cost, and no one can nullify it for him (release him from his vow).[76] Furthermore, a woman who is no longer under the headship of a man (specifically, a widow, a divorced woman, or a fatherless virgin) is held to the same standard as a man in this respect; when she vows, she must do what she has vowed and cannot be released.[77] But when an unmarried daughter vows and her father disagrees with the vow that she has made, the father can nullify her vow. This is an example of a father's Biblical authority over his daughter and her decisions.

Also, in the Biblical culture, a father is expected to be able to guarantee his daughter's virginity to her future husband. If he cannot and if she is found not to be a virgin, the shame not only falls on the woman but on the father as well, because he was responsible for her.[78]

Furthermore, fathers have the power to bless their children. In the story of Jacob and Esau, we see that Isaac's blessing had an effect not only on the future of his son Jacob, but also on the future of Jacob's descents. Likewise, Jacob's blessing on his twelve sons had an effect not only on his sons' futures, but also on the future of their descendants. These are just a few examples of a father's power to bless his children.

The Bible also gives examples of what happens when women rebel against their authorities (fathers or husbands). Miriam and Aaron, Moses' siblings, got ticked off because Moses had an Ethiopian wife. God was sick of the way they treated Moses and He struck Miriam with leprosy. When Aaron begged God to heal Miriam from this terrifying disease, God used this example to show the shamefulness of her rebellion against Him: "If her father had but spit in her face, should she not be ashamed seven days? Let her be shut out from the camp seven days, and after that let her be received in again."[79] Imagine—if a woman made her father angry

---

[75] Numbers 30:3-8
[76] Numbers 30:2
[77] Numbers 30:9
[78] Deuteronomy 22:13-21
[79] Numbers 12:14

enough for him to spit on her, she would be humiliated and out of favor for a whole week! This shows the importance of a father's relationship with his daughter. It is a serious offense to God Himself for a woman to dishonor her father.

Michal was the wife of King David. When David returned the Ark of the Covenant to Jerusalem, he humbled himself before the Lord. He was willing to look like a complete fool to glorify God, so he danced before the Lord wearing a linen ephod. We don't know exactly how much a linen ephod covered, but we do know that the Bible doesn't mention that he wore britches, and he was dancing pretty exuberantly. Michal saw this and "despised him in her heart." She scolded him for uncovering himself shamelessly, even in front of the slave girls.

David's answer: *It was before the Lord, which chose me before thy father, and before all his house, to appoint me ruler over the people of the LORD, over Israel: therefore will I play before the Lord. And I will yet be more vile than thus, and will be base in mine own sight: and of the maidservants which thou hast spoken of, of them shall I be had in honour.*[80]

The Bible makes no comment about David's behavior, but it adds that because of this incident, Michal had no children until her death. She despised her husband for humbling himself before the Lord, and God considered her attitude against David so serious that He took away her greatest gift as a woman—the ability to have children. As my father commented on David's immodest dancing, "Was David right to do so? I don't know. But I know he was a lot more right than Michal."

It is important to realize that the authority of fathers and husbands isn't just a cultural concept. God laid down these rules Himself, in His law. His law still stands because Jesus said that He had come not to abolish the law, but to fulfill it.[81] If any law could have made us righteous, it would have been that law.[82] When taken as a whole, the Bible's message is clear: Fathers have authority over their daughters, but they also have tremendous responsibility. Whether or not they do well in that responsibility, God will hold

---

[80] 2 Samuel 6:21-22
[81] Matthew 5:17-19
[82] Galatians 3:21

them accountable. I have a feeling that the day of accountability will be a terrible one for many fathers.

On the flip side, daughters should respect their fathers' God-given authority, despite their father's failings. Unfortunately, I have a feeling that the day of accountability will also be a terrible one for many daughters—myself included. Ladies, let us do what we can to honor God by honoring our fathers, so that we will not be ashamed on that day.

A Married Woman

When a woman has moved out of her parents' home and has moved into her husband's, is she still under authority?

The answer is a resounding YES.

I am not married, so I have no authority to teach in depth about this concept, but here are several passages that clearly outline a woman's relationship to her new authority: her husband.

1. **A husband's authority over his wife is directly linked to Christ's authority over His Church:** *For the husband is the head of the wife, even as Christ is the head of the church: and he is the saviour of the body.*[83]

   But I would have you know, that the head of every man is Christ; and the head of the woman is the man; and the head of Christ is God.[84]

   There isn't much wiggle room in these statements. If the husband is not the head of the wife, then Christ is not the head of the Church and God is not the head of Christ. The whole analogy falls apart if we view this passage as just a "cultural" statement.

2. **A woman's submission to her husband is directly linked to her submission to the Lord:** The wife is told to submit herself to her own husband, in the same way that she would submit herself to the Lord.[85] The word for "submit" includes the ideas of yielding, subordination, obedience, subjection, and to be put

---

[83] Ephesians 5:23
[84] 1 Corinthians 11:3
[85] Ephesians 5:22, Colossians 3:18

under another's control. It is used in passages where Christ puts all of the world under His feet, where we are told to obey the ruling authorities, where the younger person is reminded to submit to the elder person, where servants are encouraged to be subject to their masters, and where believers are taught to yield to God.

Therefore as the church is subject unto Christ, so let the wives be to their own husbands in every thing.[86]

The wife is also told to "be in subjection to" her own husband, even a husband who is a nonbeliever, so that he will see the work of Christ in her life. A woman who does this is compared favorably to holy women and to Sarah, Abraham's wife: *After this manner in the old time the holy women also, who trusted in God, adorned themselves, being in subjection unto their own husbands: Even as Sara obeyed Abraham, calling him lord: whose daughters ye are, as long as ye do well, and are not afraid with any amazement.*[87] Notice that she called him "Lord" which literally means "lord, master, owner, possessor." The word for *lord* here, *kurios*, is the same word used multiple times in the New Testament for God Himself. This does *not* mean that man and God are on the same level, but it does indicate something about the Biblical authority that a man may have over his woman.

3. *A woman's submission to her husband is directly linked to her fear of the Lord*: A newly-married friend once asked me, "When Ephesians 5:33 says that a woman should 'reverence' or 'respect' her husband, what does that mean?" My study showed that the word used in that passage for "respect" was *phobeo*, the same word used for "fear" (fear, alarm, to be afraid, to be frightened away, terror, to venerate, to reverence). This word occurs in passages that talk about the fear of God, the fear of man, and the fear of bad circumstances.

Likewise, ye wives, be in subjection to your own husbands; that, if any obey not the word, they also may without the word be won by the conversation of the wives; while they behold your chaste conversation

---

[86] Ephesians 5:24
[87] 1 Peter 3:1-6

coupled with fear.[88] Again, this is a literal fear.

Interestingly, as I researched the uses of "fear" concerning a wife's relation to her husband, I noticed that my source often gave the translation of the word for fear (*phobos* or *phobeo*) like this: "(1) fear, terror, something terrible or terrifying; (2) a woman's reverence for her husband." Nowhere could I find validation or explanation for this sudden switch from *fear* to *reverence* as soon as the matter concerned a wife's relation to her husband.

Studying Biblical Fear

In our culture, fear is taboo, but in the Biblical culture, fear has an important place in worship and in revering earthly authority. Significantly, both Old and New Testament books agree that proper and holy fear of earthly and heavenly authority is essential to all relationships.

Even if you don't agree with me, it is worthwhile to study the topic of holy fear in the Bible. I challenge you to do what I have done. Outline a Biblical argument for why you believe what you believe. Find both Old and New Testament passages. Pray and think about it. Approach the question from the opposite point of view, to see what possible objections could be raised to your arguments. Only once you have explored the topic for yourself are you qualified to declare which beliefs you do or do not support. If your mind is open, the Holy Spirit will reveal the truth.

Who shall not fear thee, O Lord, and glorify thy name? for thou only art holy: for all nations shall come and worship before thee; for thy judgments are made manifest.[89]

---

[88] 1 Peter 3:1-2
[89] Revelation 15:4

ജ 3 ൫

Future Relationships Start Today

This is obvious, but many people don't consider this aspect seriously. They cultivate lukewarm or strained relationships with their parents, their siblings, and their friends, yet they expect that as soon as they get married, they will know how to keep a relationship sweet and growing. If someone points out their inconsistencies, they'll explain that the problems with the relationships are the fault of the other people, not themselves.

Relationships that grow and become more beautiful with time (especially marriage relationships) begin with wise, committed relationship habits today.

How do our current relationships impact our future ones?

First, our current relationships are practice for our marriage relationship. We get a chance to practice patience, service, humility, forgiveness, and encouragement on our parents, on our siblings, and on our friends. Our family relationships are especially important because these are the people whom we know best, who raised us, or who grew up with us. If our relationships with our families are strained, what is the reason? Is there anything we could do better? Is the way we treat them now the way that we plan to treat our husbands or our children?

Furthermore, we need practice in getting over significant obstacles in our relationships, and our families offer those opportunities. Even if we have the seemingly perfect family, we know about the things that go on behind the scenes. Things that aren't pretty. Things that hurt. Things that make us very angry or upset. How do we deal with those things? Do we grow resentful or bitter? Do we allow those things to damage our relationships? Or do we struggle through the hard times and decide that we're going to make these relationships work?

It's tempting to look at someone else's life and think, "It's easy for her to love her sister. Her sister's a sweetheart. She doesn't know what *mine* does." But if things are going on behind the scenes in your family that she doesn't know about, what things might be going on in her family that you don't know about? Comparing your inner reality with someone else's outer image is like comparing apples and oranges.

Many women make excuses for why they can't make their other relationships work, yet they expect that they'll be able to make marriage work. Then, when they face similar obstacles in their marriage as they faced earlier in other relationships, they have no strategy to put into action. A past pattern of failure or of never fully mastering the problem is not practice for future victory.

On the bus trip home after a sports event, my sister and I were exhausted and a little chilly, so it seemed natural to just snuggle up next to each other on the bus seat and lean against each other as we dozed. Some time later, I became aware of a whispered commotion and of brilliant flashes. Our teammates were taking pictures of us and whispering, "Oh, it's so cute!" and "Aw, how sweet!"

"Wow," one guy said later. "You guys have an awesome relationship. That's amazing."

Two thoughts went through my head. My first was this: *We just dozed off together. No big deal. That's what sisters do.* My second thought was this: *You have no idea what we've gone through together to get this kind of relationship.* I remembered the times we had fought each other; it seemed that nobody could make me as angry as she made me. Yet we always managed to forgive each other one more time. We always found a reason to give the relationship another shot. Even when we *really* didn't like each other, we never gave up on each other.

I finally turned to my teammate and said, "It takes a lot of work to get a relationship like this. It doesn't happen overnight."

I was in my mid-teens, but already I knew that relationships take commitment and hard work. My sister and I had never allowed ourselves to think, "Man, this relationship is more trouble than it's worth!" As a result, we had an imperfect, yet beautiful, relationship, which prompted other young women to ask us for advice on how to have a healthy sisterly relationship.

Some young women feel that marriage is the most important relationship in life (aside from our relationship with the Lord, of course). I agree that it is the most exclusive relationship and that it is the one that you should work the hardest to maintain. However, *all* relationships are important, because all relationships teach us and expose our hearts. The Bible indicates that the relationship between a married child and his or her parents are still important. For example, God made a mind-blowing promise to the Rechabites, to reward them for faithfully following a command given by an ancestor.[90] The paternal blessing of Isaac was important in the case of his sons Jacob and Esau, even though Esau was already married at that time.[91]

Relationships between relatives are important. For example, Jacob and Esau (brothers) healed their broken relationship with each other.[92] Absalom and Tamar had such a strong brother-sister relationship that Absalom avenged Tamar when she was harmed, and even named his daughter after her.[93]

Friendship is also important; for example, David's love for Jonathan was said to "exceed love for women,"[94] and the apostle Paul loved the runaway slave Onesimus and pleaded that his master would receive him with mercy.[95]

Yes, marriage is a relationship that requires a priority position, but it is not the only relationship we have in our lives. If we allow other relationships to crumble, we can sabotage our marriages too—even *before* we get married! Furthermore, we can sabotage our witness. People aren't just watching to see how we treat our husbands. They're watching to see how we treat our family, our friends, our co-workers, our acquaintances, and the strangers we meet. Their observation of our relationships influences their opinions of our faith and our God. What do our relationships say about us? What do our relationships say about the God that we serve?

---

[90] Jeremiah 35
[91] Genesis 27
[92] Genesis 33:1-16
[93] 2 Samuel chapter 13, also 14:27
[94] 2 Samuel 1:26
[95] The book of Philemon

The Impact of the Father-Daughter Relationship

In one of the autobiographical stories by Scottish veterinarian James Herriot, he describes how he courted a beautiful young woman named Helen. Jim was impressed with Helen's kindness toward her aging and lonely father, whose wife had died some years before. Jim then reminded his young male readers that, when they consider a woman for marriage, they should take a passing glance at how she treats her father, because that is how the woman will treat her husband someday. Jim's instincts were right, because the kindness, respect, and skill that Helen had given to her father were brought into her marriage with Jim.

Our relationships with our parents, and particularly our fathers, are especially important. There are two main reasons. The first reason (which we've explored in a previous chapter) is that God has made fathers the head of the home and He has made them responsible for their daughters in a special way. The second reason is that some aspects of the father-daughter relationship are similar to some aspects of the husband-wife relationship. For example, our fathers are our God-given authorities. If we cannot respect the authorities to whom we were born and who gave us life, how can we respect the authorities whom we marry? Furthermore, our husbands are likely to be just as fallible and frustrating as our fathers in some way. Our current reactions to our fathers set up a pattern for our reactions to our future husbands.

I know that fathers are hard to live with. I know there may even be some cases where fathers are simply not safe to live with. I can understand that, and I am deeply grieved that significant barriers stand between these fathers and their daughters. However, in the vast majority of cases, the rule applies far more than the exception. Are we judging ourselves as critically as we judge our fathers?

We may see something as a problem when it is really not a problem, or when it is a smaller problem than we imagine. Looking back, I realize that I have been oversensitive at times about my father's habits. We should ask ourselves: Is this truly a significant issue? Does it show a bad character or is it just annoying? Is this a sin issue or not? And, if so, how can I appropriately deal with it while continuing to honor my father?

I've had some struggles with this myself. My father is not a

33

perfect man and I am not a perfect daughter, so the two of us together can make a head-butting team! When I was going through a difficult time in my relationship with Dad, I thought hard about why the relationship with my father was going sour. After being honest with myself, I realized that I had not treated him according to the criteria of Biblical love and I was therefore disrespecting him, even when I didn't realize it. I finally asked myself: Was this how I wanted to view or treat my husband? Was I practicing as a daughter the attitude that I would want to show as a wife?

No matter why we "have issues" with someone, we can't change other people. We can (and should) pray for them, but we can't fix their end. The only thing for which we are responsible is our response to the situation. Do we respond in a way that demonstrates love or in a way that demonstrates lack of love? Is this the way we want to respond to our husbands' idiosyncrasies and faults someday? Is this the way we want others to respond to *our* failings? Do we believe we can respond in a Biblical and loving way in our marriage relationships without practicing in our current relationships? If we don't practice on the hard cases, how will we know the capabilities of true love?

Show Your SMARTS

Here is your six-step tutorial on how to show godliness in your relationship with your male authority and to prepare for your future husband. Show your SMARTS in the way that you interact with the men in your life!

1. Submission
2. Modesty
3. Appreciation
4. Respect
5. Trust
6. Strength

1. Submission

In a Biblical society, God makes it very clear: Every daughter in her father's household has a responsibility to submit to her father's authority and every wife has a responsibility to submit to her husband's authority. The father is responsible to protect his daughter's virginity and to raise her as a godly woman. Do fathers do that perfectly? No. Even so, God expects daughters to do their utmost to submit to their father's authority, whether he is a good father or not. God doesn't tell us to honor our fathers' authority only if our fathers are honorable, respectable, and kind, just the same way He doesn't tell fathers to protect and teach their daughters only if those daughters are lovable, respectful, and appreciative. Are there exceptions, such as fathers who are unsafe for their daughters? Sure, but they account for only a small percentage of fathers, and for the rest of us, it's easy to make excuses.

Obedience and submission are a choice. Sometimes I feel that my father's commands are unreasonable and unfair. However, when I cheerfully submit to him and obey him, I usually learn that the tasks aren't as bad as they at first seemed and I discover a joy that does not depend on the circumstances. I know that I am training for my future marriage as well. As a wife, it will be my job to submit to my husband in all things, in the way that I would submit to the Lord Himself.[96] I cannot expect that I can practice frustration or disobedience toward my father and later demonstrate cheerfulness and obedience to my husband.

I used to think of submission like this: "If push comes to shove, he should win." That's not the definition of submission. Submitting to my father means that I acknowledge his authority over me and find joy in obeying him. It means that I make a conscious choice to trust his judgment and leave the results up to God.

Submitting to my father doesn't mean that I'm under his thumb all the time. If I have an objection or a concern, I respectfully tell my father how I feel. It's helpful to suggest a solution or a compromise to the problem, rather than to simply say, "I don't like your idea." Often, I find that my father is willing to listen to a respectful request. On those occasions when he hasn't, guess what? I have somehow managed to have a happy and fulfilled life despite having to sacrifice some things. Submission is a choice and so is

---

[96] Ephesians 5:22, Colossians 3:18

happiness. When we choose both, God is well pleased and I believe He will bless the results of our submission.

2. Modesty

"I had no idea." Those words described my feelings the first time that I realized that men really *are* wired totally differently than women. Guys are wired so that a woman's body exerts a powerful attraction to him. If a guy sees even part of a woman's body, he rarely forgets it, even if he desperately wants to! Long after a woman is gone, he still remembers what she was wearing—or not wearing. Images of women he's seen may pop up into his head at random times of the day. The temptation to fantasize is very strong and if he doesn't shut down on it at once, he is tempted to mentally undress her in his mind and… Well, you get the picture.

When a guy says that a girl is "hot," I always thought he meant that she had a pretty face. Actually, a girl's face is often *not* part of the evaluation; decent guys have to remind themselves to look at her face—not the rest of her. I once overheard a high school boy tell his buddy, "Well, her face isn't that attractive. I could take it or leave it. But that *body*! Wow!"

Almost all guys struggle with this, even the guys we most admire, even the guys in happy relationships. Even the best of guys agree that they have a daily, sometimes hourly, sometimes minute-by-minute struggle to honor and respect women in their minds—and these men are strong Christian men. This kind of temptation is *normal* for guys! A guy once said that the average male thinks about something sex-related once a minute. If a guy is awake for 15 hours, that's 900 times a day that he has to refocus his mind. Even if the occurrence is only once an hour for some guys, that's still 15 times in a day that he must fight the same fight over and over again—every day. Talk about exhausting!

Job was a righteous man of God. He stated that he had made "a covenant with his eyes" to keep from looking at a woman with lust.[97] Jesus also said that if any man looks at a woman to lust after her, then he has committed adultery with her in his heart already.[98]

---

[97] Job 31:1
[98] Matthew 5:28

In the very next sentence, Jesus said that if anyone's eye "offended" him (caused him to be tempted), that he should pluck out his eye.[99] This is serious. Even a conspicuously righteous man like Job was tempted by a woman's body, and even Jesus Himself warned men that if they lusted, they were adulterers and were better off being blind. Think about what it would mean if guys took these verses very literally. What if 99% of the men in our world were blinded just so they could think about women in a righteous context?

Over and over in the Bible, we see women being used as traps for men. Satan didn't go to Adam when he tempted the first humans to sin; no, he went to Eve. Adam chose his wife over obedience to God. Ever since that day, men have struggled to place obedience to God above their attraction to women. Samson, the strongest man on earth, was finally overcome by his enemies—because of a woman. David, a man after God's own heart, had one sinful blot on his record—because of a woman. Solomon, the wisest man on earth, was turned away from God—because of women. Ahab, one of the wickedest kings in Israel, was stirred up to do evil—because of a woman. Satan is still using women like bait for guys and the guys are still falling for it. Of course the guys are ultimately responsible for their sin—and should be—but sometimes women fail to see the ways in which they invite the problems. For example, Eve should not have second-guessed God's words, thereby tempting her husband to sin with her, and Bathsheba shouldn't have been bathing where she could be seen. Even Christian women unknowingly go along with the enemy's program and become weapons that are used against their brothers in Christ.

Let's break the chain. The world is filled with bombs for a guy's mind. Magazines, movies, commercials, random women walking by—all of these can be traps to even the nicest guy. We are being cruel and unkind if we simply think, "Well, that's a guy's problem! He needs to get over it!" Yes, guys are ultimately responsible to God for their thoughts and they will *not* be able to blame women when they must give an account of themselves before God. However, we women will have to answer to God for how we have or have not taken responsibility for how we have affected our

[99] Matthew 5:29

37

brothers in Christ.

When I shared these thoughts in a group of my young adult friends, one of the young men in the group, who tended to be quiet and reserved, agreed strongly with me. "Yes! Ladies, please remember us! Remember that what you wear *does* affect us."

It is important to practice modesty even around your father and brothers, because it influences your character and (in some cases) may also have an impact on them. They are still men, after all. Furthermore, if you marry, remember that, if it was inappropriate to wear publicly before marriage, it is inappropriate to wear publicly afterward. What you wear in private with your husband is between you and him, but your public wardrobe must continue to be modest. If a woman dresses immodestly after marriage, her husband's male friends may gradually abandon him, because they cannot be in the presence of the wife without feeling tempted.

True Christian men—the type who would make good husbands—are on the look-out for women who have enough respect for the Lord, themselves, their future husbands, and even the future husbands of other women not to make themselves eye-candy to be devoured by any random guy who passes by. True Christian men appreciate women to whom they can talk without fear of being teased by tempting images. True Christian men value women who sacrifice their clothing preferences in order to wear things that are feminine and attractive, but not tempting or revealing in any way. True Christian men respect women who behave with dignity and self-control, not flirting or trying to attract attention to themselves. True Christian men will pass by the "hot" girls and marry the women who show, through their appearance and their attitudes, that they respect and encourage men's purity. Let's protect the men in our lives.

3. Appreciation

There was a time in my life when I struggled to honor and respect my father. I battled anger and disappointment, and I asked God to change my father. Through a series of very difficult and painful exposures, God showed me that I was approaching the problem backwards. I was not my father's keeper; God was. I was not responsible for my father, but I was responsible for myself. I begged the Lord to help me to reverse the trend, to honor and respect my father no matter how provoked I felt. In answer, God pointed out two areas that needed work in my life.

First, He showed me that I was keeping a record of wrongs. I had memorized all the times when Dad had done or said something that frustrated me. I had stewed over them and grumbled about them to God and to others. I realized that, if love covers a multitude of sins and thinks no evil, then love keeps no record of wrongs. I determined that I would no longer write, speak about, or deliberately recall the things that fed my anger toward my father. Instead, I kept a record of rights. Whenever I was tempted to think angrily toward Dad, I thought of one reason why I loved him: "I remember the time when he danced with my little cousin who has Down's Syndrome. Many men would feel intimidated by a 'different' child, but he just loved her as she was. I love my father for loving children."

As my record of rights began to grow longer than my record of wrongs, something incredible happened. First, Dad's faults stopped annoying me so much. I began to see that I had become sensitive and I had even overreacted much of the time. Second, I began to love and appreciate my father as I had not loved or appreciated him in years. That little girl love and trust of my Daddy returned. Third, a completely unrelated sin in my life began to lose its power over me. You see, when we treasure one sin, we feed another one. My liberation from my anger toward my father resulted in my liberation from other sins as well.

The second change came when the Lord taught me to speak positively to and about my father. I learned how to treat my father appreciatively even when I did not feel like it. I did not allow myself to grumble or speak negatively about my father to others; instead, I determined that I would make my dad look awesome to other people. When I honored my father through my words, I found that my heart followed my words. I tried to show appreciation for my father by obeying him and by noticing when he did something that I liked: "Dad, I know how angry my thoughtlessness made you. I just want you to know that I am very sorry for how much I inconvenienced you and I really appreciate your patience with me." Or "Hey, Dad, I saw that you fixed my car.

I know fixing cars isn't your favorite hobby, but I appreciate the time you spent on it. Thank you so much!"

A year after praying that God would heal our relationship, I realized that He had answered my prayer profoundly. Significantly, the prayer had been answered not so much by a change in the situation or by a change in my father, but by a change in *me*.

Ladies, you have no idea how much men thrive on our praise and appreciation. Even a man who seems to take little notice of our praise remembers our appreciative words; he just may not know how to respond. A man who hears that his daughter or wife talked positively about him to others practically bounces with joy! When a man comes home to a family that shows appreciation for his hard work to provide for the family, he feels at peace in his home. Our words and actions have tremendous power to encourage and to build up the men in our lives.

A word fitly spoken is like apples of gold in pictures of silver.[100]

Wherefore comfort yourselves together, and edify one another, even as also ye do...[101]

4. Respect

In the books *For Young Women Only* (by Shaunti Feldhahn and Lisa A. Rice) and *Love and Respect* (by Dr. Emerson Eggerich), the authors reveal an astonishing fact: Most men would rather be respected than loved. I decided to investigate this claim. I asked men that I trusted: "Would you rather be respected or loved?"

My dad: (with emphasis) "Respected. Definitely. No question."

My male cousin: (without hesitation) "Respected. For sure."

A guy friend: (giving me a look that asked "What are you up to now?") "I'd rather be respected."

Wow, I thought. *It must be true!*

The Bible states that husbands must focus on loving their wives, while wives must focus on respecting their husbands:

Nevertheless let every one of you in particular so love his wife even as himself; and the wife see that she reverence her husband.[102]

---

[100] Proverbs 25:11
[101] 1 Thessalonians 5:11
[102] Ephesians 5:33

Many women feel like me: "I know I'm going to make stupid mistakes, but if I know that I have someone who doesn't care about the mistakes, who simply loves me no matter what, then I feel happy and secure." On the other hand, guys want to be loved, but they also have an intense inner drive to be successful, to be a hero, to be a *somebody*. They struggle with secret feelings of inadequacy and so they set out to prove themselves. More than anything, they want to prove themselves to their women—their wives, their daughters, their sisters, and their girlfriends. When a man is respected at work but not in his own household, he feels like a failure. He would rather bury his head in work than come home and feel inadequate.

One day, my brother (who was 11 at the time) ran across the yard as I was chopping wood.

"You're doing it wrong!" he yelled. "Let me show you how to do it!"

Irritated, I told him to go away and mind his own business, and my brother finally stalked off in a huff. After a few minutes of trying to restrain my temper, I realized with chagrin that the little twerp had actually been right; his method was safer and smarter than mine. Plus, I had treated him unkindly. I eventually scraped up the humility to apologize to my brother. As he told me what he felt about my actions toward him, I realized with astonishment that his words of frustration were guy-code for "I want to be respected!"

Someday, I thought, *My brother will be the leader of his own home. How am I, as his sister, training him to respond to his wife? How am I building him up for that heavy role of responsibility?*

I began to find ways to show my respect to the men in my family. Here are some ways to show respect:

Treat your father like the president or a king and treat your brother like a prince. When a man of authority walks into a room, no one ignores him. He is greeted with respect and shown special attention. Try this sometime: When your dad comes home from work, give him a smile and a greeting. Meet him at the car door and carry in his lunchbox. Be aware that he may not want to talk; he may have had a bad day. If so, show him that you love him and then give him space. I have seen my father come home tired and discouraged, but when my mom says, "Hi, honey!" and we kids

41

echo, "Hey, Daddy!" some of the weight is gone. He may still need time to unwind, but he knows that he is valued.

Give your father the head place at the table. Serve him first. Offer to take his dirty dishes. Take special care of his things (even if they're scattered around the house). Obey him. Do things the way he likes them to be done. Help to make foods that you know he enjoys. Just as a woman who is treated like a queen often blossoms, so a man who is treated like a king often develops the graciousness of a king.

When he speaks to you, stop what you are doing, turn, and face him. Listen attentively. I find that the men in my household often interrupt me at the most inconvenient times. After I have listened for a few minutes, I politely say, "You know, I have a lot to do. What you're saying is very interesting and I'd like to hear more about it, but can we finish this discussion later?" Once he has wrapped up, I respond, "Thank you for sharing that with me," and I smile at him as I get back to work. Guys are surprisingly positive when this method is used.

Show interest in his hobbies or projects, even if you're not that interested initially. One time my father was working on a project in the basement and I came down simply to watch him.

"I'm so excited about the new bunk-bed!" I said. (I was being truthful, by the way.) He looked at me in surprise. "Really? You're excited?" His body language changed a little. He was more sure of himself, more cheerful, and more ready to talk with me as I sat nearby and told him about my week.

Sometimes my brother corners me (at the most inconvenient times) and shows me a contraption he made out of LEGO bricks. I am not always interested in his newest creation, but I ask him questions about it and make suggestions and thank him for showing me. It is amazing how happy this makes him. Surprisingly, I grow fonder of my brother and prouder of his engineering skills!

Respond to every provocation respectfully. Sometimes he will push your buttons, make assumptions, or lose his temper. One day, my father and I had a misunderstanding. He thought I had done something deliberately but I had been unaware of my mistake. It took me a few minutes to figure out what he was talking about, but during those few minutes, a mental voice kept telling me, "Respect, respect, respect." I looked him straight in the eye (without defiance), answered calmly, physically relaxed my body, and tried to understand his point of view. When we finally figured out that it was simply a misunderstanding, the tension faded away. A respectful response *does* make a difference.

Apologize promptly. One day my sister said to my brother, "Hey, I know that Mom assigned you and so-and-so as a team to work on that project. Your teammate has already started. Shouldn't you be helping?" My brother hunched his shoulders, didn't answer, and his whole body communicated frustration. My sister realized that she had made an assumption that implied that he was untrustworthy and inadequate. She needed to inspire him and give him the benefit of the doubt. She immediately apologized. "I'm sorry, that was rude of me. I know that you understand what you need to do." My sister watched in amazement as our brother's frown cleared away magically. A few minutes later, he was working on the assigned project cheerfully.

Sure, this method doesn't work all the time, but it can't hurt. Often we don't realize that our words communicate distrust or discouragement to a guy. When we become aware that we have done this, we should apologize quickly. Guys don't like to hear "I'm sorry, but..." or "I'm sorry I made you feel..." A girl will accept that (maybe), but a guy won't. Guys need to hear a simple "I'm sorry, I was wrong for..." It's humbling for us ladies, particularly if the guy was wrong too. However, we are responsible only for ourselves, not for our men. In the long run, our humility strengthens the relationship.

5. Trust

A man wants to be a hero. More than anything he wants to be a hero to the women in his family—his wife and his daughters. We women often have a hard time giving up control and trusting a man's judgment, but this is an important part of being a good daughter or a good wife.

When my family (plus a guest) went to see a movie, it was important to get seats in the cinema early if we wanted to find seating for all of us together. I handed over the tickets to my father, but he didn't immediately head to the growing line. Instead, he continued a discussion with one of the other family members. Some of us girls began to dance with impatience. Didn't he know seating nine people was difficult? Couldn't he see the line? Didn't he realize that the theater was filling up? Wasn't this the whole point of pre-buying tickets to this showing?

A little voice whispered in my mind. *If we get separated into little groups or miss out on this showing, so what? It will be inconvenient and disappointing, but in a year we probably won't even remember it. Are you going to demonstrate distrust of your father over a movie?*

When Dad finished his discussion and we finally got into the theater, we found to our surprise that there was plenty of seating. We found the perfect row, settled down, and enjoyed the film.

Another time, we were driving through an unfamiliar city in two vehicles, heading for the interstate. Dad's vehicle led and I drove the following vehicle. Dad made a turn onto a street that the rest of us were certain we had never taken before. Predictions of being "lost forever" began to circulate, when suddenly we came in sight of the interstate. With wonder and delight, we gasped, "Dad's a genius! He knew a shortcut!" Later we discovered that Dad had indeed taken a wrong turn and had arrived at the interstate by accident. We had a good laugh, but we learned something. Sure, we could have gotten lost, but so what? We had the choice to murmur against Dad and distrust his judgment, or to cheerfully follow his meandering trail and trust that he would lead us home eventually.

Sometimes men really *will* misjudge or make a big mistake. Surprise! They're human, just like us! The question is not, "Is my trust in him perfectly justified all the time?" The question is, "Will I trust God enough to trust the man whom God placed in my life as my authority?" We need to give our men the chance to prove themselves to us, not just once but over and over. We need to keep believing in them. If we don't, who will?

A strong relationship must be built on trust. Just as we need to give men a chance to show themselves to be trustworthy, we need to demonstrate our own trustworthiness. There are many ways to do this, but here's an important one: Guard your lips. Men are seldom very communicative, but when they open up, they need to know that their information is safe with you. A newly-married friend of mine did not realize that her husband considered some things private which she felt were fair to discuss with others. Out of respect for her husband's desires and out of an effort to demonstrate trustworthiness, she learned to be careful what kind of information she revealed to others.

As I mentioned before, men like to know that their women are talking positively about them to others. Consider how your words will make him look to others, or affect his job or his reputation. Consider what he might think if he knew you were sharing this information. In a world where social media and other avenues of communication make it easy for us to tell all, we need to learn how to keep silence. Learn to be a keeper of secrets for the men you have in your life now—and you may be entrusted someday with the deepest secrets of your beloved.

6. Strength

A man has a very heavy responsibility: He must answer directly to God Himself for how he leads his family. He is compared to Christ in the marriage relationship, and he is called to live up to Christ's sacrificial standard.

Husbands, love your wives, even as Christ also loved the church, and gave himself for it; that he might sanctify and cleanse it with the washing of water by the word, that he might present it to himself a glorious church, not having spot, or wrinkle, or any such thing; but that it should be holy and without blemish. So ought men to love their wives as their own bodies. He that loveth his wife loveth himself.[103]

Whether or not a man does a good job, or even cares, he will have to be accountable to God. The Bible says that a man who does not provide for those of his own household has denied the faith and is worse than an unbeliever.[104] I believe this includes providing for his family materially and spiritually. All throughout the Bible, we see that the father is ultimately responsible to teach his family about the Lord, to manage his household well, and to be an example to his family.

Women do not have the same heavy responsibility as men. The

---

[103] Ephesians 5:25-28
[104] 1 Timothy 5:8

Lord gives women only one main responsibility: To strengthen and support the men that He ordained as their authorities. For an unmarried daughter, she must answer to God for how she obeys and respects her father. For a married woman, she must answer to God for how she obeys and respects her husband.

In the old days, when knights prepared to do battle, they could not lace up the heavy and awkward armor on their own. The job of dressing the knight for battle fell to the squire, who placed and laced the various pieces. We women are the squires of our men. It is our job to recognize the sacred calling that God has given to our men and to serve them in ways that best encourage them and prepare them to do battle with the dark spiritual forces at work in the world.

When I was six or seven, my dad faced an extremely difficult situation. He knew what he had to do, but he was very afraid to do it. In my high-pitched little-girl voice, I said, "Daddy, it's got to be done. You know what you have to do. So go and do it!" My daddy saw my child-like trust in him, prayed to the Lord for strength, and went and did it—successfully. I forgot all about the incident, but my dad never forgot and he reminded me years later.

Importantly, my mother had modeled that trust for me; she had stuck by my dad's side when he had faced multiple battles in many contexts. Dad learned to trust Mom's wisdom and to draw strength from her encouragement. There were many times when she wanted to shield him and to make him take the easy road, but she knew that she should not quench the warrior's strength in my father.

Do men sometimes pick the wrong battles? You bet. Do men sometimes overreact to things? Absolutely. Do men sometimes drop out of the fight when they should stay in it? Sure. Do men sometimes behave in a way that doesn't seem spiritual? Definitely. But it's not our job, as women, to evaluate their progress.

Who art thou that judgest another man's servant? to his own master he standeth or falleth. Yea, he shall be holden up: for God is able to make him stand.[105]

In the end, God is going to judge the men for what they did or

---

[105] Romans 14:4

did not do. In the meantime, He did not place us as overseers over our men; He made us to be "suitable helpers" to them. Yes, we can tell our men (respectfully) when we think they're wrong, but sometimes we have to let them make their own mistakes. My mother taught me as a teenager that sometimes my father's or future husband's mistakes would hurt not only himself, but also me. I had to be ready and willing to bear those consequences with him and not to add to his shame by showing an angry or vengeful attitude. Saying "I told you so" to a man who has made a world-class blooper is the same as saying, "I didn't trust you all along, and guess what? I was right not to trust you. You're a loser." Can you imagine anything more discouraging for a man? Why would he even want to pick himself up and try again if he knows he never measures up?

Sometimes, even when he is *right*, his decisions will result in suffering for the family. When Richard Wurmbrand made a bold stand for Christ against the Communist regime of Romania, he went to jail for 14 years, while his wife worked in the unspeakable conditions of a work camp and his son lived like an orphan. His wife, despite her suffering, showed only love and support of her husband when they were finally reunited. After all that he had cost her, she was still proud of him.

We have the power to bring out the best or the worst in our men. I am ashamed to think of the ways in which I have weakened my father's heart in the past and I have determined that, with God's help, I will become a daughter who will strengthen and encourage my father to live the life God gave to him. Someday I hope to accept the even more difficult job of strengthening and encouraging my own husband. We have a choice: Will we take the control into our hands when we see our men struggling or will we strengthen and support our men as God calls us to do?

Purity

℘ 4 ∝

Marriage

In any discussion of purity, we need to first understand the institution which purity was designed to protect and strengthen: marriage. It is important to understand what marriage is, and what God meant to be.

What is Marriage?

To put it in a nutshell: Marriage is an exclusive, life-long relationship between a man and a woman. I have broken this definition down into three parts so that we can look at the Bible verses that back up each part of the definition.

1. Marriage is a relationship between a man and a woman.

The Bible's teaching about marriage is very clear: Marriage is between *only* a man and a woman. God makes very strong statements about those who form relationships outside of His order.[106] The benefits of marriage and of God's blessing can only come to those relationships that are within God's natural order.

The creation account specifically demonstrates that marriage must be between a man and a woman. After God had created all the creatures and commanded them to fill the earth with their offspring, Adam was created in the image of God. Although every other creature had a mate, there was no mate for Adam.

And the Lord God said, It is not good that the man should be alone; I will make him an help meet for him... And the Lord God caused a deep sleep to fall upon Adam, and he slept: and he took one of his ribs, and closed up the flesh instead thereof; and the rib, which the LORD God had taken from man, made he a woman, and brought her unto the man. And Adam said, This is now bone of my bones, and flesh of my flesh: she shall be called Woman, because she was taken out of Man. Therefore shall a man

---

[106] Genesis 13:13, Leviticus 20:13, 1 Timothy 1:10, Romans 1:26-27, and Genesis chapters 18 and 19

leave his father and his mother, and shall cleave unto his wife: and they shall be one flesh.[107]

2. Marriage is an exclusive relationship.

God made marriage to be a union between just the man and his wife—no one else. If marriage were not exclusive, then it would have no meaning, just like there would be nothing special about a professional sports team that let just anybody play. If marriage included just anybody, what would be the point of getting married at all?

When a man unites to his wife, he commits to never unite with anyone else but his wife. When a woman unites to her husband, she commits to never unite with anyone else but her husband. In this special relationship, nobody else but God is allowed in that relationship.

Some people use the Bible to defend polygamy, the practice of having more than one wife. I'm not here to say whether that is or isn't Biblically allowed. No matter what we believe about polygamy, we all agree that God's original intention was for marriage to be between a single man and a single woman: "And the *two* shall become one flesh..."[108]

3. Marriage is a life-long commitment.

This concept may hit a nerve with some of us, because we come from broken families or we know people who have divorced. The wound is deep and I do not wish to cause unnecessary pain, but we can't ignore God's feelings about divorce.

Jesus was once directly challenged about divorce. Listen to his response in this passage:

And the Pharisees came to him, and asked him, Is it lawful for a man to put away his wife? tempting him. And he answered and said unto them, What did Moses command you? And they said, Moses suffered to write a bill of divorcement, and to put her away. And Jesus answered and said unto them, For the hardness of your heart he wrote you this precept. But from the beginning of the creation God made them male and female. For

---

[107] Genesis 2:18, 21-24
[108] Mark 10:8

*this cause shall a man leave his father and mother, and cleave to his wife;
And they twain shall be one flesh: so then they are no more twain, but one
flesh. What therefore God hath joined together, let not man put asunder.*[109]

Although God allowed divorce under specific circumstances
(only for infidelity),[110] divorce was never part of His original design
for marriage. In fact, He hates divorce.[111] Even when divorce is
Biblically allowed, it is as destructive, in God's eyes, as tearing a
single body in half. When so much injury and scarring results from
divorce, it is no wonder that God meant marriage to be for life.

What Is Marriage For?

We have studied what marriage should be; now we'll study what
marriage is for. There are four reasons for marriage:
companionship, children, physical intimacy, and presenting a
shadow of Christ and His church. This list is not necessarily in the
order of importance.

1. Marriage is for companionship.

*And the LORD God said, It is not good that the man should be alone; I
will make him an help meet [a helper suitable] for him.*[112]

Some people say that we should only desire a relationship with
God and that earthly relationships are a distraction. While the Bible
clearly indicates that our relationship with God is more important
than all other relationships, I see nothing in the Bible to indicate
that relationships with other human beings—especially marriage
relationships—are "unspiritual." If that were the case, it would
have been all right for Adam to be the only human being on earth,
or Adam would have asked God for another human being and God
would have said no.

God Himself realized that there was something incomplete
about Adam's place on earth. Even though Adam had a perfect and
sinless relationship with the Lord, it was important for Adam to
have a relationship with another human being too. That's where

---

[109] Mark 10:2-9
[110] Matthew 5:32
[111] Malachi 2:16
[112] Genesis 2:18

Eve came in, as his companion and helper. If God has marriage in your future, that's what you're meant to be too—a companion and a helper.

Neither men nor women are meant to be alone. They need each other. Of course there is a place for Godly singleness (which we will talk about later), but in general, marriage is meant to be a relationship in which a man and a woman may find healthy companionship.

2. Marriage is for the procreation of children.

When God created the first man and woman, He gave them a specific command, the same command that He gave to the creatures that He had made earlier.

So God created man in his own image, in the image of God created he him; male and female created he them. And God blessed them, and God said unto them, Be fruitful, and multiply, and replenish the earth, and subdue it...[113]

I am surprised by the number of Christians who want few children or no children at all. Yet having children is the first command that God gave to the first married couple! One of the greatest curses in the Bible was the inability to have children; for example, several stories in the Bible tell how God used infertility as a punishment.[114]

This is what God says about children:

Lo, children are an heritage of the LORD: and the fruit of the womb is his reward. As arrows are in the hand of a mighty man; so are children of the youth. Happy is the man that hath his quiver full of them.[115]

I can't think of anyone who does *not* want a gift or a reward from God. Why wouldn't someone want children, who are specifically called gifts and rewards from God? Why is it that children are a blessing from the Lord that we intentionally try to prevent?

People in Jesus' day were afraid that little children would bother Jesus; after all, if someone important like the president came to town, it would seem rude to allow children to climb all over him!

---

[113] Genesis 1:27-28a
[114] 2 Samuel 6:16-23, Genesis chapter 20
[115] Psalm 127:3-5a

But Jesus didn't send the children away. He welcomed them, took them in His arms, and blessed them.

And they brought young children to him, that he should touch them: and his disciples rebuked those that brought them. But when Jesus saw it, he was much displeased, and said unto them, Suffer the little children to come unto me, and forbid them not: for of such is the kingdom of God. Verily I say unto you, Whosoever shall not receive the kingdom of God as a little child, he shall not enter therein. And he took them up in his arms, put his hands upon them, and blessed them.[116]

Jesus was gentle and patient with the children. He loved and valued them. We should follow His example and should desire, love, and value children. Admittedly, some of us may not be able to have children of our own. Although we should accept God's will if He chooses that for us, we should always consider children to be blessings and be ready to have them if God will give them.

3. Marriage is a way of fulfilling natural sexual desires.

God created physical intimacy to be a crucial part of a healthy marriage relationship. For example, the book of Song of Solomon describes the physical and emotional satisfaction that spouses should have in their relationship. God loves to see a healthy, intimate relationship. Marriage was designed to be that special and God-ordained outlet for natural desires for sex.

Now concerning the things whereof ye wrote unto me: It is good for a man not to touch a woman. Nevertheless, to avoid fornication, let every man have his own wife, and let every woman have her own husband... I say therefore to the unmarried and widows, it is good for them if they abide even as I. But if they cannot contain, let them marry: for it is better to marry than to burn.[117]

The King James version of the Bible often uses the phrase "he knew his wife" to mean that he had relations with his wife. I like this wording, because it shows that physical intimacy involves knowing each other in a deep and powerful way. God desires for spouses to know each other intimately and to find joy in that special knowledge of each other. [118]

---

[116] Mark 10:13-16
[117] 1 Corinthians 7:1-2, 8-9
[118] Proverbs 5:19

4. Marriage is an earthly picture of Jesus Christ's relationship with His Bride, the Church.

When the Apostle Paul writes (by divine inspiration) about marriage relationships, he frequently refers to Christ's relationship with the church and he compares earthly marriage with our Heavenly marriage. Christ's relationship with His church is exclusive; He has no other Bride. Christ's relationship with His church is also life-long; no matter how wayward she might be at times, He never leaves her or cheats on her. Earthly marriage that is exclusive and life-long hints at the full beauty of this Heavenly relationship. That is why the Bible spends so much time explaining how husbands and wives should interact with each other, because their relationship is a powerful symbol for our relationship with Jesus Christ.

Wives, submit yourselves unto your own husbands, as unto the Lord. For the husband is the head of the wife, even as Christ is the head of the church: and he is the saviour of the body. Therefore as the church is subject unto Christ, so let the wives be to their own husbands in every thing.

Husbands, love your wives, even as Christ also loved the church, and gave himself for it; that he might sanctify and cleanse it with the washing of water by the word, that he might present it to himself a glorious church, not having spot, or wrinkle, or any such thing; but that it should be holy and without blemish. So ought men to love their wives as their own bodies. He that loveth his wife loveth himself. For no man ever yet hated his own flesh; but nourisheth and cherisheth it, even as the Lord the church: for we are members of his body, of his flesh, and of his bones.[119]

This idea that earthly marriage is supposed to mirror Heavenly marriage is not some new thing that God thought up when Jesus Christ had finished His mission on earth. The Bible states that it was part of God's design from the beginning.

For this cause shall a man leave his father and mother, and shall be joined unto his wife, and they two shall be one flesh. This is a great mystery: but I speak concerning Christ and the church.[120]

This means that when Genesis talks about spouses becoming one body, that passage applies to Christ's relationship with His

---

[119] Ephesians 5:22-30
[120] Ephesians 5:31-32

54

church. Even though Jesus did not come until thousands of years after Adam and Eve were created, God had already created marriage as a parallel to His Son's relationship with His Bride!

Of course it doesn't take a genius to see that earthly marriage can never be as perfect as the Heavenly marriage. Earthly spouses are not always Christ-like in their love toward one another. Marriage is not a piece of heaven on earth; it is a weak, trembling shadow cast on the earth by the form of God Himself. We cannot see the true, detailed, three-dimensional form that it should be, but we can see the shadow and we can work toward making the shape of our marriages more like the reality of Christ's marriage.

ఴ 5 ಞ

What is Purity?

Because marriage is so significant on both the physical and spiritual level, the devil hates marriage with a passion. So he attacks one of the three important parts of marriage: exclusiveness. If he can damage the purity of either the man or the woman, he can damage the marriage before it even starts. Every day, we see evidence of the vicious, bitter war over purity. What is purity? Although people disagree about the specifics, the *spirit* of purity is very clear from what the Bible says.

Purity Honors Marriage—Before Marriage

When God gave Moses the law, He gave very specific instructions about intimate relationships. Adultery (having a sexual relationship with someone else's spouse) is strictly forbidden in the Ten Commandments. [121] Fornication (having a sexual relationship outside of lawful marriage) is also forbidden; a woman was expected to be a virgin when she married, or suffer dire consequences. The punishment for violating these laws ranged from paying a fine to receiving a severe beating to being put to death,[122] depending on the nature of the offense.

Many verses also deal specifically with the value of purity.

Now concerning the things whereof ye wrote unto me: It is good for a man not to touch a woman. Nevertheless, to avoid fornication, let every man have his own wife, and let every woman have her own husband. But if they cannot contain, let them marry: for it is better to marry than to burn.[123]

Flee fornication. Every sin that a man doeth is without the body; but he that committeth fornication sinneth against his own body.[124]

---

[121] Exodus 20:14,17; Leviticus 20:10, Deuteronomy 22:22, Numbers 5:12-31
[122] Deuteronomy 22:13-29
[123] 1 Corinthians 7:1-2, 9
[124] 1 Corinthians 6:18

God not only requires His people to keep intimacy within marriage, but He also does not want His children "playing at" marriage by touching each other. After all, that shows disrespect for the exclusiveness of marriage; if two people touch each other romantically but end up marrying other people, they have shared something between each other that they should have reserved for their spouses.

Remember, marriage is a life-long, exclusive relationship that is supposed to mirror Christ's relationship with His church (the body of those who trust and believe in Him). Purity is not simply a matter of avoiding pregnancy and sexually transmitted diseases; it is a matter of preserving the value and worth of marriage.

Purity Does Not End When We Marry

We may have heard some people say, "I'm going to stay pure until I am married." Although that is a great decision to make, it's a little inaccurate, because we don't stay pure until we're married— we stay pure for our whole lives. You see, purity does not mean "abstaining from an intimate relationship," which many people mistakenly take it to mean. Purity only means "abstaining from an intimate relationship *outside of lawful marriage.*" Purity is all about having a relationship within the right context. An intimate relationship exclusively within marriage *is* purity.

Let me put this idea another way: Purity does not equal virginity. Virginity is that part of purity that comes with godly singleness. Therefore, purity does not end as soon as we are married; we do not stop being vigilant about our physical or mental purity. In marriage, our goal will be focused upon defending our marriage from any outside temptations, and on keeping our minds and bodies pure for our husbands alone. We will *still* be saving ourselves for our husbands.

Purity is a Continual Decision-Making Process

A lot of young women say, "Well, I have made a commitment to purity." That's great; I believe that the Lord is truly pleased. However, we do not commit to purity just once. Purity is a decision that we make every morning when we get up, every time a tempting situation arises, and every time we go to bed. We don't make *a single* commitment to purity; we make a *lifetime* commitment to purity. It is a work that is always under construction. In a sense, we are not saying "I decided to be pure." Rather, we are saying, "I am continually deciding to be pure."

If we think that being married will take away any temptation to be impure, we are very mistaken. Often, once people get married, they forget that they need to guard themselves. The men may struggle with pornography and the women may expect a romance novel type of marriage. Both men and women compare their spouses with other peoples' spouses. They let themselves read, watch, and listen to things that they would have avoided as "impure" during their virgin singlehood. They trust that because they have an outlet for their physical desires, they will no longer have sexual temptations. That is not true. If the Enemy can't destroy marriage before it even starts, he certainly will not quit after the vows have been made.

ᔥ 6 ᨀ

Why Does Purity Matter?

Even if you think you don't need to read this section—even if you think that you know it already or that you're unlikely to be tempted—I'd encourage you to read through it anyway. When we find ourselves in tempting situations, we sometimes need more than "Because it's a good idea" or "Because it's right" or even "Because God said so." Sometimes, we wonder if God comes up with random laws to keep us from being happy, like He's some kind of cosmic kill-joy.

If you have sex outside of marriage, the truth is that you will pay—physically, mentally, emotionally, relationally, and spiritually. God intends for purity to ensure that we have the best possible chance at happiness and, more importantly, that our lives glorify Him.

Purity Protects Our Bodies

Outside of marriage to an uninfected spouse, there is no such thing as safe sex. Forty years ago, there were just a few sexually transmitted diseases; today there are over twenty-five. The Center for Disease Control and Prevention estimates that there are almost 19 million new people infected with sexually transmitted diseases every year in the United States. Almost half of those cases involve sexually active young people, ages 15 to 24. These statistics reflect only the cases that are reported; many cases are not reported because the infected people do not even know they have an STD.

Some sexually transmitted diseases can be passed through contact with infected skin—not even through actual sex. Many people do not even know that they have an STD, because the symptoms don't show up for years, sometimes for several decades. This means that someone isn't necessarily lying if he says he doesn't have a disease; he just may not know that he has it. Even though symptoms may not be present, an infection can damage internal organs permanently. Women are especially vulnerable to damage from sexually transmitted diseases, and the consequences can be very serious if the infections are not treated as soon as possible. For instance, chlamydia (the most commonly reported STD), if left untreated, can result in infertility and repeated miscarriage. Fortunately, once the infection has been identified, treatment for chlamydia is usually effective.

Unfortunately, some STDs are not so easily dealt with. Human Papilloma Virus (the most common STD) cannot be cured, but treatment can address some of the symptoms. HPV can cause cervical cancer and other cancers; in fact, almost all cases of cervical cancer are caused by HPV, of which there are over 30 types. Gardasil, the new vaccine for HPV, only protects against the four strains most likely to cause cancer, and its duration of protection is still unknown.[125]

Some people mistakenly believe that contraceptives will keep them safe from STDs. That is not true. Some methods offer absolutely no protection. Some products can offer *some* protection, but only if they are used consistently and correctly, and only if they cover the infected areas.

Consider this: Many people consider birth control and contraceptives to be safe and effective, but the truth is that many women become pregnant *even while using birth control*. The Food and Drug Administration lists the failure rates of various birth control methods as anywhere from 1% to 30%.[126] Since women are generally most fertile only a few days out of each month and since we can get pregnant even while using birth control, how much more likely are we to get a sexually transmitted disease, which can be contracted at any time?

Finally, the evidence is overwhelming that the more partners you have, the higher your risk. As someone once said, when you sleep with a person, you're sleeping with everyone that person has ever slept with, and everyone *they* have slept with, and on and on.

---

[125] "Common Questions Answered." *www.gardasil.com*. Gardasil. Web. 1 February 13, 2013. <http://gardasil.com/what-is-gardasil/information-on-gardasil/index.html>

[126] "Birth Control Guide." *www.FDA.gov*. U.S. Food and Drug Administration. 18 June 2012. Web. 1 December 2012. <http://www.fda.gov/ForConsumers/ByAudience/ForWomen/ucm118465.htm

You may have had sex with only a few people, but you may have been exposed to dozens of people.

Sometimes, even that first time changes your life forever. Barbara Wise never had clear sexual boundaries and had sex with six men before she decided to remain sexually inactive until marriage (this is called "secondary virginity"). When she finally met Rick, the man of her dreams, she decided it would be a good time to get tested for sexually transmitted diseases. She was devastated when she learned that she had HIV, a virus for which there is no cure and which eventually results in death. By a process of elimination, she learned that she had contracted the disease from her very first partner—and had therefore exposed all her other partners to HIV as well. Despite this news, Rick chose Barb as his bride, demonstrating Christ-like love and forgiveness. Today, Rick and Barb lead an organization called Wise Choices, which uses their powerful story to remind young people that their sexual choices have lifetime consequences.[127]

The Center for Disease Control and Prevention sums up the situation very aptly on its website:

The most reliable ways to avoid transmission of sexually transmitted diseases (STDs), including human immunodeficiency virus (HIV), are to abstain from sexual activity or to be in a long-term mutually monogamous relationship with an uninfected partner.[128]

Purity Protects Our Children

Few women envision raising a child without the father's presence and emotional support, yet this is a reality for many single mothers today. This is not to say that having a child outside of marriage results in only pain and hardship. Crisis pregnancy centers often observe that pregnant young women who choose to carry their babies rather than aborting them become more confident, more healthy, more responsible, more mature, and more joyful than they were before. Still, the life of a single mother is a hard one for both herself and her child.

---

[127] www.wise-choices.org
[128] "Male Latex Condoms and Sexually Transmitted Diseases." *www.CDC.gov.* Center for Disease Control and Prevention, n.d. Web. 1 December 2012. <http://www.cdc.gov/condomeffectiveness/latex.htm>

Not all unmarried mothers are single parents, however; some women choose to cohabit with the fathers of their children. Even in these situations, marriage offers distinct advantages. Some studies have suggested that cohabitation before marriage, as opposed to living separately before marriage, increases the chances of divorce, of child abuse, of child learning disabilities or socialization problems, and of other negative consequences.

Some women decide to avoid parenting altogether by having an abortion. This option carries its own consequences. Abortion can cause physical, emotional, and spiritual damage to the woman.[129]

Physically, immediate risks of abortion include heavy bleeding, infection, damage to the uterus and other reproductive organs (such as perforation of the uterus or scarring of the fallopian tubes), and, in rare cases, death. Long-term physical risks include increased possibility of having a future ectopic pregnancy (a life-threatening condition), infertility, and breast cancer.

Emotionally, abortion can increase the woman's likelihood of experiencing depression, guilt, anger, difficulty bonding with her sexual partner, difficulty bonding with children, emotional numbness, suicidal thoughts, abortion-related flashbacks, and other negative consequences.

Spiritually, abortion is devastating, because it ends the life of a child. The Bible states that God knows children before they are even conceived, that He is intimately involved in their development in the womb, and that He can set them apart for a particular purpose in life before their birth.[130] The life that He forms with such care is not ours to take.

God designed sex to make babies. When people engage in sexual activity, pregnancy is *always* a possibility, despite contraceptives. Many women have had to make difficult choices because they thought that they could have sex outside of marriage without consequences—and now their choices affect not only themselves, but also the new life inside them.

---

[129] I recommend visiting www.abortionrisks.org to learn more about the medical studies and incidents that document these risks and complications.

[130] Jeremiah 1:5, Psalm 139:13-16

Purity Protects Our Emotions

Consider two different girls. Both have boyfriends, and both entered the relationship as virgins, but now one is sexually active and one is still a virgin. Both relationships end. Which of the two girls do you think feels the most hurt? Answer: The girl that was sexually active with her boyfriend. This answer is not just a guess or a hunch; it has something to do with how brain chemicals affect emotions when two people are intimate.

God designed physical intimacy to bond the husband and the wife together, physically and *emotionally*. During intimacy, the female body releases special chemicals and hormones (dopamine and oxytocin in women) that trigger emotional bonding.[131] Whether or not the woman wishes to bond to her partner, these chemicals influence her subconscious mind to bond with him during sexual activity. When she continues to have sex without the commitment of marriage, she conditions her mind to become addicted to sex itself, instead of to her partner, which damages her ability to emotionally bond with any future partners when she decides that she wants to bond.

Women have a strong craving to be loved, and some believe that sexual intimacy is a way to feel valuable and desirable. Even though hormones promote bonding, physical intimacy is *not* love. It is very powerful physical contact that has tremendous physical, spiritual, and emotional implications. When this kind of bonding is part of a relationship that is not committed or life-long, it can become a source of emotional pain, not emotional security.

Studies indicate that sexually active teen girls are more likely to feel depressed and to contemplate or attempt suicide.[132] Women may also feel guilt that they let other people down (such as their

---

[131] This is discussed more in depth in the section entitled "The Power of Physical Contact."

[132] Rector, Robert E.; Kirk A. Johnson; Lauren R. Noyes. "Sexually Active Teenagers are More Likely to be Depressed and to Attempt Suicide." A Report of the Heritage Center for Data Analysis. *www.ERIC.ed.gov.* Education Resources Information Center. 2 June 2003. Web. 1 December 2012.
http://eric.ed.gov/ERICWebPortal/search/detailmini.jsp?_nfpb=true&_&ERICE xtSearch_SearchValue_0=ED476392&ERICExtSearch_SearchType_0=no&accno=E D476392

parents), anger at a partner who gave them an STD or who cheated on them, and many other negative emotions.

Purity effectively protects a woman's heart from serious emotional damage. In general, marriage offers significantly more emotional security than non-marital sexual relationships offer.

Purity Protects Us From Regrets

Many studies show that women often wish they had delayed their first sexual experience or saved it until marriage. One study indicates that two-thirds of young women who have been sexually active wish they had waited.[133] That's a significant regret, since loss of virginity can't be reversed or wished away.

Many women have entered marriage and wished that they could honestly tell that special man that he was the very first man to win them, heart and body. Conversely, many women who have entered marriage as virgins have been glad they chose abstinence. They had no fears that they were bringing unknown sexually transmitted diseases into their marriage, no secrets to hide or confess, no wounds left by other men, no reason to feel less valuable or less desirable than they could have been. Virgins do not bring sexual memories of other partners into their marriage. They are less likely to compare their husband to their former boyfriends, to cheat on their husbands, or to feel emotional separation from their husbands.

This does not mean that non-virgins cannot have good and beautiful marriages. Barb Wise is an example of a woman whose marriage is beautiful despite her past. I personally know women who did not do things God's way, but whom the Lord has blessed with beautiful marriages. Our God is the God of the impossible; He purifies and gives us a second chance. Yet, if we have the choice, why would we not want to choose God's best from the beginning?

---

[133] National Campaign to Prevent Teen and Unplanned Pregnancy. "Not Just Another Thing to Do: Teens Talk About Sex, Regret, and the Influence of their Parents." *www.thenationalcampaign.org.*
<http://www.thenationalcampaign.org/national-data/pdf/teenwant.pdf>
27 April 2000. Web. 22 February 2013.

Purity Protects the Specialness of Marriage

Imagine that you are a little child with a big bag of candy—all types and flavors. First, you pick out a candy bar. That first bite fills your mouth with the delicious taste of chocolate. It's pure indulgence. After finishing it, you eat a candy whose fruity flavor is a nice contrast to the chocolate. Then you eat some candy corn, followed by sour candy, mint candy, strawberry candy... Soon your stomach begins to churn. Furthermore, you notice something else. The more candy you eat, the less you can taste the unique flavor. In fact, the particular piece of candy that left the most impression on you was that first chocolate bar, because you ate it when everything was still fresh and new and exciting, and because the taste hadn't been obscured by all the previous tastes.

People who have sexual experiences outside of marriage can have this type of reaction to their relationships. It's special and wonderful in the beginning, but as more partners come and go, the experience loses its potency and allure. Soon sex is more a habit than anything else, and true happiness remains elusive. It is difficult to form real friendships, since friendship usually turns into sexual activity—and ends there.

Let's take the analogy one step further. After you have eaten all that candy and felt ill and unhappy, your friend drops by with your favorite dessert—dense chocolate mousse cake. (You can tell I love chocolate!) But at this point, even though you desperately want to eat that cake, you can't stand the idea. You know it will make you sicker and you know you won't be able to taste or enjoy it the way it should be tasted and enjoyed. Indulging in that other candy created a situation in which you can't enjoy the one thing you really, really want.

This is what some people realize when they finally *do* find that one special person with whom they want to spend their whole life. "What did I waste my time with all those other people for? Why didn't I save it all for that person? He is so worth it!" Now bonding with that special person is difficult, because regrets, fears, diseases, emotional withdrawal, and other effects of the past tend to creep into the relationship.

It is possible to have a healthy relationship, but it requires much unpleasantness. Let's go back to the candy analogy. Having eaten all that candy and felt so sick, the only way that your stomach can handle the overload is to get rid of it, quickly and painfully. After being sick, there is still a bad taste in your mouth and a curdled feeling in your stomach. You need time to get back to normal, but when you are back to your healthy self, you can eat that chocolate mousse cake. Returning from a life of impurity is very hard and much more unpleasant than being sick, but the rewards are much more worthwhile. It takes confession, repentance, and the beginning of a new life to turn an unhealthy pattern into a clean life ready for that special person. There will be scars and regrets from the past, but with the Lord's help, it is possible to find healing and to experience fulfillment in that one special lifetime relationship. God truly is a Healer; many lives are proof of His healing love.

Purity Helps a Marriage to Last

The amount of evidence is overwhelming: Marriage offers significant benefits that other types of relationships simply cannot provide. Many studies suggest that, when compared to marriage, cohabitation (living together while not married) results in more cheating, more divorce, more disagreements, more domestic violence, and more depression, while also involving less emotional and sexual satisfaction and less financial security.

Marriage isn't perfect, but it sure looks better than the alternatives! Our current relationships, especially with family members, are practice for our marriage relationship. If we get into the habit of forming relationships that do not have a strong, lifelong commitment, it will be difficult to keep to such a commitment once we have made it. By making a physical commitment to a relationship before making the full official commitment, a person often loses the accountability, responsibility, and benefits that come with a committed relationship. It's more work to wait for a committed relationship, but it's more worthwhile in the end.

Many women wish they had avoided the pain of past sexual relationships and chosen to save their emotions and bodies for the one man whom they really love, the man who is willing to make that lifelong commitment to them in marriage. Saving it all for marriage and keeping it all within marriage is one of the most profound ways to say "I love you."

Purity Honors Our Heavenly Marriage

Our God is a jealous God; that means that He wants us to save our love for Him and for Him alone. Flirting with idols—anything that bumps Him out of first place in our hearts—is like cheating on Him. God makes this clear in Ezekiel, a book of the Bible in which He repeatedly compares His people, Israel, with an adulterous wife. Chapter 16 tells a figurative story of how God took compassion on Jerusalem, who was like an abandoned baby, ready to die. He took her into His house, washed the blood off of her, healed her, and brought her up as His own. When she was grown, He became her husband, and gave her expensive clothing, beautiful jewels, and a costly crown.

And thy renown went forth among the heathen for thy beauty: for it was perfect through my comeliness, which I had put upon thee, saith the Lord GOD. But thou didst trust in thine own beauty, and playedst the harlot because of thy renown, and pouredst out thy fornications on every one that passed by; his it was.[134]

Then God felt like a husband who had been cheated on, because the beauty that He had given to his beloved wife was used to attract her adulterous lovers. God's language in this chapter is filled with the pain of a husband who has been betrayed by the woman he loves. Relationships are important to God, and His relationship with us is just as important to Him as a husband's relationship to his wife.

Marriage is a symbol of our relationship with Christ. Just as a fiancé would be rightfully upset if his beloved flirted with other men, so Christ will be angry and sad if we love anything or anybody more than we love Him. We might cheat on God by loving things like money, power, hobbies, knowledge, work, recreation, friends, and family more than we love Him. It even counts as cheating on God when we desire a husband more than we desire God. Nothing should ever take the place of Christ in our hearts. Nothing else is worth it.

In a marriage commitment, a man should give all of his love, respect, and life to the woman he loves. Christ did the same thing

---

[134] Ezekiel 16:14-15

for the people He loves; in fact, He chose the most excruciating and agonizing way possible to show how much He loved His Bride. His Bride was not beautiful or valuable, but He chose the ugliest Bride so that He could make her special, and now He is constantly making His Bride more radiant and more perfect than when He first engaged Himself to her.

For when we were yet without strength, in due time Christ died for the ungodly. For scarcely for a righteous man will one die: yet peradventure for a good man some would even dare to die. But God commendeth his love toward us, in that, while we were yet sinners, Christ died for us.[135]

Christ also loved the church, and gave himself for it; that he might sanctify and cleanse it with the washing of water by the word, that he might present it to himself a glorious church, not having spot, or wrinkle, or any such thing; but that it should be holy and without blemish.[136]

In return, we are filled with gratitude and, like a bride on her wedding day, we make a lifelong commitment to love and honor Him for His goodness to us.

We love Him because He first loved us.[137]

That commitment to Christ brings with it a big responsibility. We are promised to Him. He is our fiancé. We must honor His faithfulness to us with the same kind of faithfulness to Him. Like a good fiancée, we can't just do whatever we want; we have to think about what He wants.

Purity is not ultimately about being faithful to our husbands. Purity is about being faithful to God, first and foremost. Even if we never have that earthly relationship, we must remember that we are not our own. We belong to Christ and when He returns to make us His bride, He must find us faithful.

This is the will of God, even your sanctification, that ye should abstain from fornication: that every one of you should know how to possess his vessel in sanctification and honor...[138]

Flee fornication. Every sin that a man doeth is without the body; but he that committeth fornication sinneth against his own body. What? know

---

[135] Romans 5:6-8
[136] Ephesians 5:25b-27
[137] 1 John 4:19
[138] 1 Thessalonians 4:3-4

ye not that your body is the temple of the Holy Ghost which is in you, which ye have of God, and ye are not your own? For ye are bought with a price: therefore glorify God in your body, and in your spirit, which are God's.[139]

---

[139] 1 Corinthians 6:18-20

ଛ 7 ଓ

So Where Do We Draw the Line?

How do we put purity into practice? How do we know what is impure and what is pure? Where do we draw the line?

Many people have tried to define the line and there's a large range of ideas. God does not specifically say "Thou shalt not kiss" or "Thou shalt not hug." Maybe He intentionally left that gap so that we wouldn't try to see how close to the line we could get. For example, if He had said, "No kissing, but hugging and hand-holding is okay," I'd be willing to bet that the hugging and hand-holding would become more and more involved and intimate. We would obey the literal sense of the command without obeying the full spirit of the command. That's our nature as human beings. We're always going right to the edge of the cliff to see how close we can get without falling off. That is why I believe we need to have a clear picture of the spirit of purity, rather than of the particulars.

A Matter of the Heart

The most specific thing the Bible mentions regarding physical contact is this: *It is good for a man not to touch a woman.*[140]

To give you an idea of what "touch" means in that verse, that same word was used for when Jesus reached out to touch a sick person to heal them and for when sick people reached out to touch Jesus. It is interesting to me that the same word was used for something as innocent as touching to heal someone and as suspicious as touching someone with more intimate intent. The word does not even necessarily mean anything intimate in itself, but the context of the verse tells us more: *It is good for a man not to touch a woman. Nevertheless, to avoid fornication, let every man have his own wife, and let every woman have her own husband.*[141]

This context indicates to me that "touching" is linked in God's

---

[140] 1 Corinthians 7:1
[141] 1 Corinthians 7:1-2

mind to fornication; this passage is a warning. That should give us something to consider: It is good to be careful about *any* physical contact between an unmarried man and woman, innocent or otherwise.

Our actions are just extensions of our thoughts. We can't do something without thinking about it first. In fact, the Bible says that our thoughts count as our actions:

For as he thinketh in his heart, so is he.[142]

Whosoever looketh on a woman to lust after her hath committed adultery with her already in his heart.[143]

That means if we think any impure thoughts, God counts it as if we had actually *done* those impure things. That's a frightening reality. In fact, if we're honest with ourselves, that means no one is really, totally, 100% pure—not you, not me. This shows us just how much we need Jesus and just how quickly and easily we can fail. It also shows us the purity of God; His purity is so complete and so high that thoughts and actions both have the same level of importance to Him.

Let the wicked forsake his way, and the unrighteous man his thoughts: and let him return unto the LORD, and he will have mercy upon him; and to our God, for he will abundantly pardon. For my thoughts are not your thoughts, neither are your ways my ways, saith the LORD. For as the heavens are higher than the earth, so are my ways higher than your ways, and my thoughts than your thoughts.[144]

Purity does not start from a list of "do's" and "don'ts." It starts from a mindset. The Bible says that the evil things we do come from inside our hearts. In other words, purity and impurity are matters of the heart.

But those things which proceed out of the mouth come forth from the heart; and they defile the man. For out of the heart proceed evil thoughts, murders, adulteries, fornications, thefts, false witness, blasphemies: these are the things which defile a man.[145]

Since God looks into our hearts and judges us based on what

---

[142] Proverbs 23:7a
[143] Matthew 5:28
[144] Isaiah 55:7-9
[145] Matthew 15:18-20a

He sees there,[146] then avoiding impure actions is not good enough. We have to avoid impure thoughts too. Even more importantly, we have to replace the impure thoughts with pure ones. It's not enough to just keep from doing what is wrong; we have to keep on doing what is right.

Therefore to him that knoweth to do good, and doeth it not, to him it is sin.[147]

This emphasis on our hearts is linked to what some people call "obeying the spirit rather than the letter of the law." It is helpful to remember that when the Bible speaks of this concept, the word "spirit" in the passage also indicates that our obedience is made possible through the Holy Spirit, the part of God that lives in us and gives us strength, comfort, and hope.[148]

The law—that list of do's and don'ts—was meant to be a guideline, but people like to find the loopholes in the law, so they can still do what they want to do without *technically* breaking the law. Because of that, the Bible explains in Romans chapters 6, 7, and 8 that God gave us the law to give us an idea of what is right, what is wrong, and what kind of behavior pleases Him. The specifics of the law aren't as important as the general idea behind it. Trying to stick to specific rules is not as important to our purity as trying to keep our hearts and minds in tune to God's desires for us. When we are pure inside, it will be easy to be pure outside too.

The Power of Physical Contact

We can't fool ourselves about the power of physical contact. Contact can begin innocently—hugging or holding hands—but it may not end there. Even something seemingly innocent, like tickling, can become passionate embracing in the blink of an eye or can create a situation in which the hands might touch somewhere that's not appropriate. It can happen so easily, even with the best of intentions.

In fact, there are chemical reasons for why physical contact can start something that is difficult to stop. For example, studies have

---

[146] 1 Samuel 16:7b
[147] James 4:17
[148] Romans 7:5-6

shown that pheromones, chemicals released by both men and women, can increase sexual attraction. Pheromones appear to be particularly influential on women, and they generally work through a woman's sense of smell to influence her brain. The smell may be so subtle that she is not even conscious of its presence. If a woman is physically close to a man, even without actually touching him, the pheromones from the sweat on his skin may increase her attraction to him at a subconscious level.

Furthermore, the book *Hooked* by doctors Mcilhaney and Bush,[149] explains that physical contact between men and women—even mild contact such as hugging—triggers the release of the hormone oxytocin. This hormone produces a sense of bonding in the woman, increasing her trust for and her emotional bond with the man. This explains why so many women stay with abusive boyfriends or husbands; the oxytocin reinforcement of sexual contact between a woman and her abuser makes it difficult for her to get out of the situation. This also explains why women who get involved with men on an emotional level, starting out with innocent hugs and hand-holding, find it increasingly difficult to say no to more intimate physical contact. In her book *The Female Brain*, neuropsychiatrist Louann Brizendine adds that behaviors such as emotionally satisfying interaction, prolonged eye contact, touching, kissing, and sexual excitement all stimulate oxytocin release. Oxytocin turns off the brain's sense of caution and anxiety, leaving the woman in a state of impaired judgment.

Women are not the only ones who find it difficult to stop the sexual progression. The book *For Young Women Only* shows that once physical contact is initiated, it's hard for guys to keep from getting more involved. According to the surveys cited in the book, the average man expects the woman to place limits on the physical relationship, because the man knows that he will always want more. That's a lot of pressure for a woman. She might think a kiss is just a kiss; he might think it's a stepping stone to something more, even if she's made her boundaries clear.

We might think we're spiritually and emotionally strong

---

[149] *Hooked: New Science on How Casual Sex is Affecting our Children* by Joe S. Mcilhaney, Jr., M.D., and Freda McKissic Bush.

enough to resist temptation, and then we may get into the situation and find out otherwise. Even if we think we're strong enough to handle a certain situation, how do we know that the other person is strong enough too? Are we willing to trust our purity to someone else's self-control? How much are we willing to risk in order to test the limits of self-control?

A young woman once told me, "I never thought I'd make those choices—never. Then, when I got into tempting situations, I found out that I had much less self-control than I ever imagined. I learned that I wasn't invincible." God doesn't tell us to stand firm against sexual temptation. He tells us to *flee*.[150] In other words, the key to being sexually safe is not to exert more self-control; it is to stay away from compromising circumstances.

Boundaries

When a young woman told me about some purity-related mistakes in her past, I asked her how she had gotten to that place. "Was it something you thought about ahead of time, or did it take you by surprise?"

"There were no plans," she replied. "It just happened as we went along. It was unintentional."

That conversation illustrates one of the most important truths about all relationships, but particularly relationships between guys and girls: Everything about the relationship must be intentional. Why? Because whatever is not intentional is unintentional by default. If you do not have intentional emotional and physical boundaries in your relationship with a guy, you will unintentionally cross those boundaries (which were never really set in the first place). Intention and purpose are not just good ideas; they are necessary.

Therefore, it is critical to have a plan. Consider these questions:

- How would you feel about another woman holding hands with your husband?
- Hugging him?
- Kissing him?

---

[150] 2 Timothy 2:22

- Leaning against him?
- Touching him?
- Would you feel comfortable showing your husband a video of the physical contact you have had with other men?
- Would you feel comfortable giving your husband full access to all of your e-mail, Facebook, Skype, texting, and phone conversations with other men?

You should ask yourself: What are my boundaries? Why have I set those boundaries? If I allow myself to do certain things, where might those things lead? If that relationship doesn't work out, what kind of regrets might I have? Would I be comfortable with my future husband having that type of contact with another woman?

Here is an example of how a plan works. In my family, my parents laid out very specific rules about my physical contact with boys, long before I ever hit puberty. I was allowed to hug boys within my family and extended family, but I was not allowed to hug boys outside of my family. Kissing and hand-holding were also out of the picture. I was not allowed to be alone with any boy. This did not mean that my parents hung over my shoulder during social situations or that I never got to attend events on my own as I got older, but it did mean that my contact with men was almost always in an accountable situation with other people around.

My boundaries have helped me to separate the good guys from the not-so-good guys. The men amongst my friends whom I most trust and admire are the men who are respectful of my space and who treat their female friends like ladies. The men who intentionally try to push my boundaries prove that they are not respectful of me, and therefore I knew that they are not worthy of my time. A respectable guy would not push a girl into a pool or put her in a headlock, even in fun; he would treat her with honor and dignity. If you want to know if a guy is respectable, give him boundaries. He will show his colors quickly.

As far as being alone with a guy, I also ensure that I stay in social situations, whether with my family, at work, at church, or with other friends. I will not carpool alone with a guy. One time, I stuffed my brother (who was eleven at the time) in the back seat when I went to pick up a guy friend who needed a ride. Avoiding alone time with a guy is not simply helpful in avoiding sexual temptation; it is also helpful in avoiding rumors. Even the best of friends may be tempted to speculate if a guy and a girl often hang out alone together. Since our reputations reflect on God, it is important to have as spotless a record as possible.[151]

Contact over the phone or through social media is one of the most common pitfalls. Young women who would be discreet in person might be quite indiscreet through Skype or Facebook or texting. I know some young women whose contact with young men was very secretive and exclusive. Their parents did not know that things were spiraling out of control until damage had already been done. The damage was largely emotional, not physical, but these young women were thrown into depression and self-destructive thoughts as a result of unsupervised contact with young men through private phones, social media, and unsupervised meetings. We should be just as vigilant online and in our phone conversations as we are in person.

Sneaky Attraction

If we're attracted to a particular guy, we probably have plenty of sneaky ways to deceive ourselves into thinking that we're not having any problems with temptation.

Suppose your family invites another family over to dinner. Your guests include a young man to whom you feel attracted. When it's time for everyone to hold hands and pray before the meal, who do you make sure you're standing next to? When it's time to arrange the seating, who do you make sure you're sitting next to (or across from)? When it's time to play a game, whose team are you on? When it's time to do an activity, who do you make sure you're near? It's all very innocent and above-board; you're just praying and eating and playing, right?

Wearing certain clothes, doing certain activities, or acting in certain ways in hopes of impressing someone can be a way of temptation. We can be tempting ourselves to expect some kind of reaction from him. We can be tempting ourselves by day-dreaming

---

[151] Ephesians 5:3

about the possibility of some romantic spark igniting. We can be tempting ourselves by simply being physically near someone we like.

This doesn't mean we can't hang around people we like. It just means that, if we like someone, we have to be especially careful about how we react to that person in thought, word, and deed, because stronger attraction is accompanied by stronger temptation. After their engagement, my father moved away from my mother until the wedding day. The temptation of being so close to their future spouse made my parents take special precautions, even though they were engaged. If it's too much to handle being alone with someone or being physically close to someone we like, then why in the world would we put ourselves in that situation?

I strongly recommend designing a boundary plan with your parents, because then you have your parents' support for the plan, you are clear about their expectations, and you are honoring their God-given responsibility for your purity. Furthermore, they can help to hold you accountable. As a rule, remember this: If you feel that you have to hide something from your parents or make a situation sound like less than it is, then you are stepping beyond your Biblical boundaries as a daughter and as a future wife, and you are likely stepping beyond your physical boundaries too.

When you make a plan, remember that the main point of having a plan is not so that you have a ruler by which you measure everyone else; it is the ruler by which you measure yourself. For example, my personal plan allows little physical contact until my wedding day. I do not expect that everybody will make the same choice as I have made. Even so, any choice should be made well ahead of time and should be kept. A young woman once remarked, "I would like to save my first kiss for my wedding day but...well, we'll see how it goes." My response: "If you really want to save your first kiss for your wedding day, you have to make that your goal now and make sure to follow through."

If something happens and we're not sure if it crossed the line or not, chances are that it *did*. We wouldn't even be wondering about it if we were perfectly comfortable with it. The plan then is to make it clear that such a thing will not happen again and to take steps to make sure that it doesn't. Just because we've made a mistake once does not mean that we can't prevent the next mistake.

Make sure that you create specific boundaries; general boundaries do no good and are not enforceable. When you make your plan, base it on the Word of God, and, when possible, have Biblical reasons for your boundaries. Write down your reasons for each specific boundary, so that you have something to which you can refer when you are tempted to lower your standards. Finally, create a plan to enforce your boundaries. Boundaries are useless unless you have established a way to make sure that they are kept.

Finally, if summed up into a single sentence, you might think of the mindset of physical boundaries in this way: "Treat every Christian man like a brother in Christ, and every man like another woman's husband."

What if I know he's the one?

Most people are not married to the very first person that they thought was "the one." They have been in serious relationships with a special someone, or have even been "engaged to be engaged," and found out that the relationship was a dead end. Even some people have been engaged—actually wearing a ring on their finger—and endured the pain of a broken engagement.

The only person who has a right to touch your body—and whose body you have a right to touch—is your husband's. If a man is not your husband, regardless of whether he is a friend or a fiancé, then he has no right to your body. Only "I do" gives you permission to override the boundaries.

Having a special relationship or being engaged offers *more* temptation, not less. I heard of a young engaged couple who let down their guards too soon, and who ended up sleeping together before the wedding. Even though they were each other's first and only partners, their pre-marital sex created baggage that they brought into their marriage. You might think "I would never do that!" Yes, and they thought so too. What makes you different?

Even in an engagement, boundaries are necessary. Some engaged couples may choose to express their love with mild physical contact—hugging, for example, or hand-holding. I still strongly advise that both the man and the woman lay down clear sexual boundaries for their engagement period, and that they build control and accountability into the situation. The boundaries must be enforced and guarded just as much as before the engagement. I plan to maintain certain physical boundaries until my wedding day; this is my way of making that day even more special. Again, this is my preference, but whatever you choose must be decided upon long before you get into the situation, it must be communicated to the young man, and it must be enforced.

Parental Parameters

Do you know how your parents expect you to deal with potentially romantic situations? Most parents, especially Christian parents, have expectations for their children when it comes to relationships, engagement, and marriage. We need to take our parents' expectations, commands, and advice very seriously.

We tend to make excuses for why we don't have to obey or honor our parents—"They don't understand" or "They don't care"—but God doesn't say "If your parents are reasonable" or "If your parents are kind." He just said: "Honor your father and your mother."[152] Having said that, I realize that some young women think: "Yeah, my parents are Christian, but they avoid the topic like the plague. They barely had 'the talk' with me when I hit puberty." Or perhaps some young women think: "My parents are not Christians. How can I obey them when they might advise me to do something opposite of what God teaches?"

I know young women from all of the above situations. I feel blessed that my parents started teaching me about relationships when I was young. They laid specific physical boundaries and they kept communication open and comfortable. As I grew older, the explanations became more frequent and detailed. I know that my situation is much better than the situations of many other people. Maybe you're one of those people.

If you are, please remember this. Our parents are still our parents, even with all their faults. We owe it to God, to them, and to ourselves to know what they think about relationships and how they want us to behave in a relationship. We should keep trying to open the communication. They might shut us out, but we should

---

[152] Ephesians 6:1-3

never shut them out. The only side of the equation that we can control is our side, and we need to make sure that our side continues to do what God expects. We should honor our parents as much as we can.

Some parents may not give you Godly advice. You can still have an honest dialogue with them about the kind of relationship you are looking for (a committed marriage relationship) and the way you feel is right to pursue it. Ultimately, you need to follow God's ways, but follow your parents' wishes as much as possible. If you behave in a Godly, humble way while trying to be an obedient daughter, your nonbelieving parents might get curious about the confidence and peace they see in you, and you'll have an opportunity to share with them about Christ.

๛ 8 ๛

Commitment to Purity

Making a commitment to purity, either formally or informally, is a big decision in a woman's life. Therefore, it is important to understand the types of benefits and drawbacks that we might see when we make this commitment.

The Purity Movement and Its Results

Purity is making a comeback these days. Some of my friends wear purity rings with messages like "True Love Waits." Some have gone to purity groups. Purity balls, father/daughter events in which the girls pledge to their fathers to remain pure, are becoming more common. Websites abound with purity rings, purity certificates, and purity pledge cards. Speakers such as Mike Long and Pam Stenzel remind young people that "everyone is NOT doing it" and that "free love" carries a cost, while events such as Silver Ring Thing encourage abstinence.

It is very encouraging to me to see that purity is being given the respect it deserves. Although the purity movement has empowered many young people to make better choices, there is also a sobering side to the story. Many studies on the effectiveness of abstinence education show conflicting results. I don't know the true answers, but I have to wonder: Out of all the people who decide to save sex for marriage, how many keep that vow? I *know* that the success rate is not 100 percent. I am familiar with stories of young women who said, "I had always planned to save sex for marriage, but I wanted to secure our relationship. So we did it."

This is not to say that the purity movement is ineffective; I think that would be very unfair. But why doesn't abstinence work for everyone who plans to remain pure? Perhaps, for some people, the purity movement does not strike at the root of the problem—the heart. In the following two sections, I want to present some thoughts that I think explain why some people involved in the purity movement don't see better results.

Purity Vows

Many young women make pledges such as this one:

I acknowledge that my body is the Temple of God and that, because He has redeemed me, I am not my own. I desire to honor God with my mind and body. Before God and these witnesses, I (name) pledge to remain completely pure and to save myself wholly for the man whom God is preparing for me.

These vows emphasize the authority of God and the importance of purity. I am proud that young people are willing to take this commitment so seriously. However, God never asks us to pledge our purity to Him; He simply expects us to be pure. When we pledge our purity to the Lord, we are obligated to follow through on that promise or we risk being guilty before God.[153] That does not mean that He cannot forgive us, but it is a very serious thing to break a pledge to God. We cannot take a vow lightly. I know our culture is rife with broken words, but God still expects the same commitment to accompany a vow as He did in the Old Testament days. If we break a purity vow, then we have just committed two sins, one by damaging our purity and another by breaking our vow to remain pure. With doubled sin comes doubled guilt, and many young women are living with that double guilt.

There is also a temptation to trust in the fact that we made a vow of purity: "Well, I've made a vow so I *have* to keep it." We realize that we can't break it without risking serious guilt before God. While this is all true, there is a tendency to feel this way: "Since I have to keep a vow once I've made it, the fact that I've made this vow will give me the strength to fight temptation."

My question is: If that system works so well, why do so many people fail? We can't assume that we are stronger than anyone else. I've spoken with young women who really struggle with lack of self-control. I've struggled with it too. I thought I had the best defenses any girl could ever have—a strong will, a solid faith, a supportive family, and constant reinforcement. Guess what? I've realized that my strength is often very fragile and very weak, no matter what kind of support I have! We are *all* vulnerable in some way.

---

[153] Deuteronomy 23:21; Ecclesiastes 5:4-5

We cannot trust in a vow to defend us through temptation. It is true that physical symbols and mental or verbal commitments may give us strong reminders to remain pure, but they cannot guard our minds or hold us accountable or stop us when we can't take the pressure anymore. A vow is just a tool; it is not a Savior.

Yes, if we fail, God can create a clean heart in us again.[154] But, before we vow, we should think carefully. Is it necessary to vow? Shouldn't we remain pure whether we vow or not? Why do we need a vow to remind us that we should obey God's expectations? After all, God expects honesty and kindness too; should we pledge to remain honest and kind? Focusing on a purity vow seems (to me) to set purity apart from other necessary virtues and to emphasize its difficulty. Rather than acting as if purity is an especially difficult virtue to develop, perhaps we should simply include it amongst the other expected virtues and encourage the godly mindset that develops those virtues.

If you have pledged already, I'm not saying that you've sinned. I just want you to realize that the pledge must be kept and that it cannot protect you. Only God can do that.

Emotional Purity Vows

Sometimes young ladies take what is called an "emotional purity vow," which is a promise to the Lord (and sometimes to the parents) that she will keep her mind completely free of sexually tempting thoughts.

While we may be able to abstain from physical sin, we are extremely vulnerable when it comes to "mental" or "spiritual" sin. I have asked women, old and young, married and single, to tell me honestly whether they think anyone has yet been able to remain 100% pure in the mind. Their answer is always the same: "No." In short, I believe that any young woman who makes a vow of emotional purity will eventually break it. This is a tragic situation for a young woman who really wants to do the right thing.

Although Jesus took the penalty of our sins, our earthly bodies (and minds) are still influenced by sin. Even as Christians, we still commit sin. Compared to God's perfect goodness, even the good

---

[154] Psalm 51:10

things we do are dirty with sin.[155] Until Jesus comes again and gives us new bodies, our polluted minds will still struggle against sin, even when we have the power of God in our lives.

No woman wants to set herself up for failure. If we should be pure no matter what—vow or no vow—what is the vow worth to us? If you have already made a vow, keep it. If you have made an emotional purity vow, talk to your parents and ask God about an appropriate way to deal with the situation. I can't really say what would be the best thing to do in that situation, but I do believe that God will understand your desire to please Him and will take that into account.

Keeper of the Commitment

I have had lots of good intentions over the years. For instance, I once had the intention to write 500 words a day, every day. I was able to keep it up for several months, but then it petered out and I was back at square one. Great intention, poor end results. It is easier to write 500 words a day than to remain pure. So if I fail at something easy, what kind of result can I expect when I try to do something hard?

We cannot trust in our good intentions to keep us pure. Sometimes all the reasons for remaining pure are just not convincing at that moment of struggle. So what's left when our good intentions seem weak? Although the following passage is speaking about the final fulfillment of salvation, it can also be applied to anything with which we struggle spiritually:

But if we hope for that we see not, then do we with patience wait for it. Likewise the Spirit also helpeth our infirmities: for we know not what we should pray for as we ought: but the Spirit itself maketh intercession for us with groanings which cannot be uttered.[156]

It is the Lord, not our good intentions, who will make us able to keep our commitment to purity. We cannot trust in a certificate, in a ring on our finger, in a purity ball we attended, in a promise that we made, or in a mental or verbal intention to be a virgin. But we can trust God to help us do what He expects us to do. Our only

[155] Isaiah 64:6
[156] Romans 8:25-26

84

hope lies in seeking God wholeheartedly. A good relationship with Him is our *only* safeguard against impurity (or any other sin, for that matter). Purity, along with other virtues, will fall into place when our relationship is right with Him.

To reiterate: Purity does not produce godliness. Godliness produces purity. The relationship comes *first*; the rest will follow. So, in a sense, it is best not to focus on being pure. Instead, we should focus on loving and fearing and pleasing the Lord. Then *He* will make us pure.

ঙ 9 ন

The War Against Purity

Choosing a life of purity is not easy. I thought that because I grew up with the benefits of a Christian home, a homeschooled education, strong and supportive parents, responsible siblings, like-minded friends, and a strong faith, I wouldn't have problems like "most people." Turns out, I'm just like "most people." It doesn't matter what our situation in life may be; once we make that commitment to purity and seek for a love and a life that's really worth it, there's no end to the things that will attempt to steal that from us. Because of this, I've devoted a whole chapter to how do deal with purity issues when the going gets rough. I do not focus on just the negative things; there are some tremendous positives that come out of the struggle to follow God.

Also, much of this information can relate to other areas of temptation and sin. Even if you are not tempted sexually, I hope that you find that the ideas in this chapter are helpful to you in the other areas of temptation you may face.

Defining Temptation

Defined in the Biblical sense, temptation is an examination, a test, a way to prove that we really mean what we say. It's persecution from an enemy and an attempt to provoke or entice us to do wrong things. How do we stand up to all that pressure? Ultimately, our true defense lies in strengthening our love for the Lord and in keeping a close relationship with Him. Please don't lose sight of that truth as I try to share some of my experiences and tips. Of course there are many types of temptation, but the one that I'm going to focus most on is sexual temptation, because that seems to pop up a lot in young people—yes, even young women!

I do not believe that all thoughts about sex are necessarily wrong or even tempting. For example, it is not wrong to think about physical intimacy if we are studying what the Bible has to say about it, or honestly evaluating society's reactions to sexuality, or learning about intimacy and pregnancy in relation to a job or ministry. That is not necessarily a temptation or sin (although it could be); that's just like trying to understand how our digestive system works. Sexual temptation comes when we are tempted to think about or do something that gives us a feeling of sexual excitement or satisfaction outside of the Biblical context of marriage. By that definition, we might cross the line from thinking acceptable thoughts into tempting ourselves.

For example, I volunteer at a crisis pregnancy center. It's part of my job to understand how physical intimacy affects women emotionally, mentally, physically, and spiritually, because intimacy is obviously a part of all my clients' lifestyles. But if I start seeking after information about intimacy, not just so I can help my clients, but so I can feed my own desires, then that is wrong, because I will be indulging in fantasies outside of the Biblical context for intimacy (marriage). I have to identify my motives and distinguish between what is okay and what is tempting. If there comes a point where the demands of my ministry become too confused with my own desires, I have to step back so that I can get my motives right. No one can serve in a Christ-like way with mixed motives.

Understanding Temptation

When I was going through a hard time with a particular temptation, my good friend sent me an e-mail with this reminder:

Being tempted is not a sin. I know that sounds obvious, but think about it. The second a wrong thought crosses my mind, I feel guilty, which, I believe, is what Satan loves: to take away my joy, and my trust in God. The fact is, unless I allow those thoughts to take control, I haven't sinned. Jesus was tempted. All sorts of evil thoughts from Satan bombarded Him, but because those thoughts never took control, Jesus never sinned. I know I do allow sinful thoughts to take control too often, but, I also think that guilt is one of the devil's tools. Sometimes, the devil tries to make us think we have sinned, when we haven't! Of course, when we have sinned, the only Biblical response to failure is repentance. However, since the Bible says that when we confess our sins, He WILL forgive us and cleanse us from all unrighteousness, if we continue to dwell on our failure (including, I think, groveling in remorse), we are evidencing a lack of faith and trust. Do you believe the Bible is God's inerrant word?

And does the Bible say that He is faithful and just to forgive you when you repent? All right then! We need to act like we believe what we say we believe! Stop groveling, stop feeling sorry for ourselves, stop wondering how God could forgive us AGAIN. Get up—take the offered forgiveness—act in faith—we will not be tempted beyond what we can bear.

My friend wisely pointed out a very important Biblical truth: Temptation is *not* sin. The Bible says we must take every thought captive for Christ.[157] This verse probably has many meanings, but one of the meanings is that we should evaluate our thoughts and see if they line up with what we know to be true, honest, right, pure, lovely, praiseworthy, or God-pleasing.[158] If the thought is prompting us to do something wrong, then we should mentally flush it down the toilet.

At the point where we decide to cuddle the thought and dwell on it and make up imaginary scenarios from it, then that temptation becomes sin, because we are allowing the thought to have access into our minds. It came knocking and, instead of telling it to go away, we invited it in and made it welcome.

Some temptations are so shocking or so obviously wrong that we feel dirty for even having that temptation, but that's how Satan tries to make us feel guilty, even if we haven't sinned. He tries to make us dwell on our temptation: "Oh my goodness! That was a horrible thought! I can't believe I thought something like that! It makes me feel so disgusting! Oh, God, I'm sorry, sorry, sorry."

The best defense is to brush the ugly thought away casually: "Ew! Sorry, Lord. I'm going to think about something good now." The prayer has to be quick and the temptation should immediately be flushed away and forgotten, otherwise Satan will try to make us feel guilty for something we didn't even do!

My dad sometimes quotes Luther: "You can't keep the birds from flying over head, but you can keep them from making a nest in your hair." We don't choose which temptations we will have to face in our lives, but we do choose how to deal with them. Our lives are not defined by our particular temptations, but by the strength of God in overcoming all temptations.

---

[157] 2 Corinthians 10:5
[158] Philippians 4:8

Why Jesus Understands Temptation

When we think about Jesus being tempted, we often doubt that He actually understands temptation. Being God, didn't He have an unfair advantage over us when faced with temptation? Didn't He have all the power in the universe to resist? So how can He really understand what we go through when we face temptation in our puny human power?

Suppose that a person with no prior swimming experience decides that he wants to become an Olympic swimmer. When an Olympic swimmer offers to teach him how to swim, he replies, "No, I can't connect with someone who is superior to me in skill. I'd rather learn from someone who daily experiences the difficulty of swimming and who can sympathize with my struggle. In short, I'd rather learn from a peer than from an expert."

Jesus is the only person qualified to help us because He is the only person who successfully resisted temptation. If we want to learn how to do something, to whom do we look: The person who is still learning or the person who has succeeded?

For we have not an high priest which cannot be touched with the feeling of our infirmities; but was in all points tempted like as we are, yet without sin. Let us therefore come boldly unto the throne of grace, that we may obtain mercy, and find grace to help in time of need.[159]

For consider him that endured such contradiction of sinners against himself, lest ye be wearied and faint in your minds. Ye have not yet resisted unto blood, striving against sin.[160]

It makes sense to learn about enduring temptation without sinning by looking to someone who was successful at that endeavor. Jesus can sympathize with us, because He went through it all too. He also went to the greatest extreme to overcome temptation; He actually resisted temptation to the point of death. When we are faced with strong temptation, He knows exactly what we are going through—and He knows exactly how to help.

---

[159] Hebrews 4:15-16
[160] Hebrews 12:3-4

Jesus: Our Example in Temptation

In Matthew chapter 4, we are given a glimpse of how Jesus Himself responded to temptation.

Temptation One

The Holy Spirit had led Jesus into the desert, where He stayed for forty days and forty nights without anything to eat. Satan took advantage of Jesus's weakened condition.

Satan: If thou be the Son of God, command this stone that it may be made bread.

Notice that Satan is starting with "If you're the Son of God..." In other words, he's daring Jesus. "Prove yourself! You say you're the Son of God. Well, the Son of God has whatever power He wants. So prove your power to me and get a tad to eat in the bargain."

It can happen the same way for us; Satan will try to make us prove ourselves. He might try to break our faith: "Prove you're a Christian by withstanding all the pressure I'm going to throw at you. If you break, too bad! Better know it sooner rather than later!" Or he might try to distract us from Jesus Christ: "Prove you're a Christian by concentrating so much on not sinning against Him that you forget to simply love Him. And you'll still think that you're pleasing God! What a laugh!"

Jesus: It is written, That man shall not live by bread alone, but by every word of God.

Notice Jesus's answer. He didn't say, "I'm not hungry." That would have been a lie. Similarly, when we're tempted to sin, we can't say, "I don't care about that stuff!" because we *do* care and that's why we're vulnerable. It's a temptation because we *want* it.

Jesus didn't say, "You're trying to test my power and I'm not falling for it." Likewise, we can't think, "You're trying to test my strength and I'm not falling for it!" Our gestures of defiance don't impress anybody, even ourselves, because deep down we know we are weak. Jesus knew it too. Sure, He was the Son of God, but He was in human form, and therefore made weak like us. Temptations hit Him just as hard as they hit us. Pretending that we're strong is not the answer.

Jesus also didn't say, "That's a waste of my God-given power. I can't be irresponsible like that!" Satan could argue *that* one any way he chose. Jesus needed an answer that would stop Satan completely and put Satan on the defense.

So Jesus went to the root of the problem. Satan was trying to make Jesus satisfy Himself with earthly things, but Jesus knew that real satisfaction comes from godly things. God Himself was enough for Jesus. This is an important lesson for us. Many women have believed that if they could only get married, be successful in their chosen field, become beautiful, or (insert your desire here), *then* they would have everything they want. Not so. No human being is enough. No stuff is enough. No success is enough. When God is enough for us—really and truly enough—what can Satan answer to that?

Temptation Two

Seeing that he'd lost the first argument, Satan took Jesus to the top of the temple in Jerusalem.

Satan: If thou be the Son of God, cast thyself down from hence, for it is written, He shall give his angels charge over thee, to keep thee: and in their hands they shall bear thee up, lest at any time thou dash thy foot against a stone.

Satan was getting even sneakier now. He was quoting the Bible at Jesus. After all, who can argue with the Bible? Jesus had just indicated that the Word of God was more important than anything else; very well, here was the Word of God, telling Jesus that God would protect Him if He jumped off the roof.

That's a good lesson to us. We know that God will look after us and protect us, but that doesn't mean that we can put ourselves in tempting situations. It's like Satan's little whisper in our ear: "If you're really a Christian, you can withstand temptation because God will give you a way to escape it, like He says in 1 Corinthians 10:13. He'll also give you strength to do the right thing, like He says in Isaiah 41:10. So you don't have to worry about how those situations or movies or books are affecting you; God will make sure that you're ultimately safe."

91

God's power is not meant to save us from our stupidity! It's meant to help us to overcome obstacles in our relationship with Him. There's a big difference, but Satan makes it all sound like the same thing.

Jesus: It is said, Thou shalt not tempt the Lord thy God.

Again, notice Jesus's answer. He didn't say, "You're taking Scripture out of context. We're talking basic hermeneutics here!" It wasn't an issue of how Satan was misapplying the passage based on issues X, Y, and Z. Satan already knew that Jesus was quite capable of applying Scripture properly. So what was Satan after?

Jesus identified that Satan was trying to make Him test God— would God really do what He said? It was the same question that Satan had posed to Eve in the Garden: "Did God really say you couldn't eat the fruit?" Jesus replied (very appropriately) with another Bible verse: "Don't test God."[161]

Temptation Three

Satan switched tactics—and got quite a bit bolder. He took Jesus to a high mountain and showed Him all the kingdoms of the world and all the great things of those kingdoms.

Satan: All this power I will give to thee, and the glory of them: for that is delivered unto me; and to whomsoever I will I give it.

Satan wasn't disguising his sneakiness anymore. Instead of being the wolf in sheep's clothing, piously quoting Bible verses, he threw off his sheep's skin, bared his teeth, and violently attacked. Where sneakiness failed, brute force would have to win.

I wonder if Satan was playing on Jesus's human weaknesses at that point. He knew that Jesus was mistreated, misunderstood, despised, and lonely. I'm sure Jesus had the very human longing to be loved and respected. For an obvious attack, this is still hard to overcome when we face it in our real lives. Who wants to be lonely? Despised? Sneered at? Shunned? Misunderstood? Hated?

Satan tells us the same thing today. "I have bad news and good

---

[161] Deuteronomy 6:16

news. Bad news: If you do things God's way, you'll give up oh-so-much good stuff! Everybody else will think you're a snob and a goody-two-shoes (even when you're not). What are your chances of finding a friend, never mind a spouse? You're so weird and radical and Jesus-freaky, who'd want you? The good news: You can still have it all. You can be popular! Rich! Happy! Kiss your insecurity and negative feelings goodbye! Live the life you've always wanted! Get your best life now!"

When we're not being tempted, it's easy to answer a sales pitch like this. When we *are* being tempted, the sheer pressure of the idea is crushing. We start to wonder: *Is my relationship with God really worth all the stuff I have to give up to make Him happy? Why is God so picky anyway? If He wants me to be happy, as He says He does, why does He make it so hard to do what He says?* Suddenly God isn't good enough and we want to turn to other things—other "gods" and idols—to make ourselves feel better about being such a loser.

There's another possibility: Satan may have been trying to use Jesus's good motives against Him.

"If you controlled the whole world, you could do something about all the ugliness and misery. You could fix the problems, and the world would be like You always planned it to be—perfect. Paradise on earth! A glory to your Father!"

That would have been a case of doing the wrong thing for the right reason. When we face temptation, Satan often tries to get us to do the same thing. He makes it seem like our deeds are so Christian, but his real intention is to distract us from the main goal, which is to follow God without compromise.

"Hey, you should get really rich so that you can help people who are less fortunate than you. You'll be doing something noble by establishing that charity organization and donating to this program! That little dishonest dealing—ah, don't worry about it. It was all for the greater good, believe me!"

Or how about, "Hey, you can afford to lighten up about purity. After all, if you make a few slip-ups, you'll be able to minister all the more effectively to all the young women who slip up too. You could reach them so much better for Christ!" Then we fall into the trap of believing that the good thing we desire to do is worth a little shady business.

93

Jesus: Get thee behind me, Satan, for it is written, Thou shalt worship the Lord thy God, and him only shalt thou serve.

Jesus could have said, "I'll get power over the world whether you give it to me or not, because my Father has promised the world to me already!" Why didn't He just remind Satan that Satan was going to be the loser soon? The issue wasn't the fact that God wins in the end; God's ability to win is obvious.

Instead, Jesus didn't think of Himself at all. He didn't think of Satan's evil goals or how the tempting proposition affected Himself. He thought about how Satan's idea would affect God's glory. If Jesus worshiped Satan, that would be the ultimate betrayal of God. Jesus cared most about His Father, not Himself. He reminded Satan forcefully that there is only *one* God and that He is the *only* one who should be served. I imagine He hurled these words at Satan with all His might.

We should respond that way too. We should think first of the Lord and how our choices affect His reputation, His glory, and His honor. If we represent God, as the Bible says we do, what do our actions show about God Himself? When we are most concerned about God and not about our comforts or desires, it is easy to see through Satan's lies and tricks. Like Jesus, we should shout back at the lies, "I SERVE ONLY GOD!"

You Are Not Alone

If Satan can't make a young woman feel like she's sinned when she's only been tempted, he'll try to make her feel like she is the only person who's ever had such impure thoughts, motives, or desires: "No one who really loved the Lord would be so strongly tempted. If your relationship with God were as strong as it ought to be, you would have a much easier time dealing with temptation."

That's such a LIE!

I can't say it strongly enough. It's a lie straight from the pit and don't you believe it!

Do you really think that Satan attacks just the people who are already weak? Aren't the strong people more of a threat to him? The Bible says that Jesus was tempted *in every way*, yet without sin. In *every* way. That means He was tempted with lust too. That's probably shocking, since we usually assume that Jesus would never think about sex. Nobody has ever been closer to God than Jesus Christ, and He was still tempted. Being tempted has absolutely nothing to do with how close or how far we are from God spiritually. It has everything to do with the fact that we are human beings in a sinful world. Everybody is capable of being tempted.

When I first encountered sexual temptation, I thought I must be weaker than everybody else. All my Christian friends seemed to be dealing with temptation so well. I believed that only immature, backslidden, or "loser" Christians experienced real temptation. Then God opened my eyes and I saw the truth.

I wasn't alone. Everybody else whom I thought was "doing so well" had his or her private moments of doubt and failure and—yes—even sin. Temptation was just as difficult for others as it was for me. Just like me, these people felt ashamed of it and they didn't want to show it. That's why, up until that point, I almost never heard anything about their struggles. Of course it's disturbing to think that even strong Christians are so vulnerable to temptation, but it's also encouraging to realize that you're not the only one who struggles with sexual issues!

There hath no temptation taken you but such as is common to man: but God is faithful, who will not suffer you to be tempted above that ye are able; but will with the temptation also make a way to escape, that ye may be able to bear it.[162]

Sometimes we feel that things are unbearable and we ask God, "Isn't marriage the 'way of escape' for this kind of temptation? But I can't get married until You make it possible, so isn't this a Catch-22?" Not very spiritual, but I'm trying to be honest. This is how it can feel when we're on the front lines of the spiritual battle.

The more we learn about God, the more we realize that Jesus is meant to be our way of escape. God knows that we are weak, so He gave us Jesus to strengthen us. How does Jesus strengthen us? By showing us good and godly ways to deal with the temptation. Just as He was able to see Satan's real motive behind the temptation, He allows us to also see the temptation for what it really is.

---

[162] 1 Corinthians 10:13

The Cycle

There will be good days and bad days. Sometimes I don't really want to marry and other times I feel like I've got to marry or bust! That's natural. Shifting emotions are not an indication of immaturity, doubt, or spiritual weakness. These problems only come on the scene if we allow the hormonal-spiritual-emotional cycle to damage our relationship with Christ. It's like having PMS; we have no control over whether or not we get PMS, but we can (and should) control how we respond to it.

We shouldn't be discouraged if we feel like we are so strong and content and trusting during one week, and then the next week we struggle with temptation, discontentment, and frustration. That will happen. The important thing is to recognize that it's just a phase (even, perhaps, a long one). The best response at that point is to obey God whether we feel like it or not. Remember the definition of love that we reviewed earlier? This is our love for God in action: obedience regardless of our feelings. In the end, I believe God cares less about the consistency of our emotions than about the consistency of our obedience.

One of the Hardest Things You'll Ever Do

Defending your purity will be harder than you think and it doesn't get easier with time. Just as strength and weakness go in cycles, so there will be times when you will wonder in a daze, "If I am doing the right thing, why is it so hard? Why doesn't it feel right?" The right thing doesn't always feel right, but we have to take God at His word even when nothing else makes sense. Even when our emotions and our understandings change, *He* never changes.

People will misunderstand us. They'll think we're trying to be a goody-two-shoes. They'll say that we're being legalistic about purity. They'll even try to tempt us. They'll say we must be special to withstand temptation, that somehow we're not as strongly tempted as they are. This shows they don't understand temptation very well. Who feels the pull of the current more, the person who is swimming against it or the person who is swimming with it? Those who give into temptation do not realize how strong the temptation really is, while those who fight it realize its strength much more clearly. Those who give in after a short period of struggle have no concept of the bitterness of a long struggle. That is why those who yield to sin actually know less about it than those who fight it. When someone says, "I could never do what you do!" you can reply, "Yes, you can. You are no weaker than I am. It's simply a matter of choice. What do you choose?"

Unfortunately, in my experience, the temptation doesn't get better with time. It often gets worse, especially as more of our friends develop relationships. I know that sounds discouraging, but I say it because it is easier to expect hardship than to be surprised by it.

We are in a battle against a sinful world that has rejected God's way of doing things. But, as Christ said, be comforted—He has overcome the world.[163] We are also in a battle against ancient evil forces with powers that are far beyond our imagination, Satan and his demons. I know that sounds like science fiction, but it's real.

Finally, my brethren, be strong in the Lord, and in the power of his might. Put on the whole armour of God, that ye may be able to stand against the wiles of the devil. For we wrestle not against flesh and blood, but against principalities, against powers, against the rulers of the darkness of this world, against spiritual wickedness in high places. Wherefore take unto you the whole armour of God, that ye may be able to withstand in the evil day, and having done all, to stand.[164]

In the end, it's not about our purity. Satan only wants us to be impure for one main reason—to separate us from God. It's like the story of Balaam. The Israelites showed up in the neighborhood of the Midianites, and the Midianite king freaked out, because he'd heard that the Israelites had beaten all their enemies. He knew that the Israelite God was stronger than any other god, so he asked the prophet Balaam to curse them.[165] After a few adventures, Balaam eventually said he wouldn't curse the Israelites, but he gave the Midianite king a tip on how to get the Israelites to curse themselves. All the king had to do was to encourage the Israelites to marry with

---

[163] John 16:33
[164] Ephesians 6:10-13
[165] Numbers 22:5-6

the pagan Midianites, to make alliances with idol-worshippers.[166] Then God would get mad at His people and punish them. Voila! Israelite impurity would separate them from God and, once separated, they would be easy pickings.

It's the same here. Satan will use greed or pride or lust or vanity or anything else as a weapon to separate us from God. He often chooses purity because that is where we tend to have a lot of weakness. But we know this: We're not fighting alone. Jesus is fighting for us too.

When we are overwhelmed, the only way we can deal with temptation and our own desires is to keep our eyes fixed on true love. When we clearly see the nature of true love, we will not be interested in lust. We must understand not only *what* true love is but also *Who* true Love is.[167] When we have real Love, who wants anything less?

---

[166] Numbers 31:16, Revelation 2:14
[167] 1 John 4:8

ஒ 10 ௧

Common Sources of Temptation

Okay, we've got the overview; now let's get specific. I'll try to be delicate, because I don't want to give anyone tempting ideas, but we also need to identify areas where we are weak so we can protect ourselves.

If we were soldiers and we were going to fight the enemy, we would first have to understand three things: (1) what the enemy looks like, (2) how the enemy fights, and (3) how we can defeat him. We've already identified sexual temptation: A thought, situation, or other thing that prompts us to think or do something that excites or satisfies us sexually in ways outside of the Biblical view of marriage. Now we need to explore how the enemy fights; in other words, how Satan tempts us to sin.

Here are some common sources of temptation:

Internal Desires

We are rarely tempted by things we dislike. Temptation is strong because it teases us with something that we *do* want. Let's face it: We want to have fulfilling intimate relationships. Until we marry, that desire can drive us crazy. *But every man is tempted, when he is drawn away of his own lust, and enticed.*[168]

Temptation is further complicated by this little fact: Our desires are actually *good*. God created that desire to be part of a healthy, satisfying marriage relationship. Sexual temptation does not involve Satan simply presenting us with desires to be intimate, because these desires are good and God-given. No, sexual temptation involves Satan presenting us with desires to be intimate *in a context outside of God's rules*. The good desire is twisted and perverted to become something diseased and poisonous to us, or the good desire is used to make us discontented and frustrated with

---

[168] James 1:14

our God-given singleness. The very thing that God designed to make our relationships beautiful is used like a weapon against us.

You probably desire a fulfilling marriage relationship. God has placed that desire within you. Do not confuse the desire with the temptation; simply be aware that the good thing that God has placed inside of you can—and probably will—be used against you. Praise God for the goodness of the desire and ask Him for deliverance from the twisted, counterfeit version of the good thing.

Peer Pressure

"I feel like I don't have much in common with my friends anymore. When we were younger, we could connect about our favorite activities. Since sex has become their favorite activity, there's nothing to talk about anymore. I'm losing my friends."

"The girls act like it's no big deal. In fact, they act like it's the cool thing to do. You start feeling like it might be okay."

"If you aren't sexually active like the other girls, they tease you and call you a prude and a goody-two-shoes. But if you *are* sexually active, they call you a slut and treat you like you're dirty."

Can you hear the confusion and the hurt in these statements? We ladies don't like being alone. Especially when we're trying hard not to form tempting relationships with young men, we naturally turn to young women to be our good and supportive friends. If we don't get support from them, we feel abandoned.

Satan uses loneliness or fear of loneliness to entice us to do things we would never consider doing otherwise. We worry about what people think of us, what we might be missing, what we might have to face on our own. Fear and loneliness are great motivators toward sin. If we fear, then we are not trusting God, and if we are lonely to the point of being willing to sin, then our relationship with God is not as important to us as our relationships with other people. Most importantly, when we give fear or loneliness control of our lives, then we are emphasizing our selves and our needs, instead of God's glory and goodness. We must overcome our fear with the power of God's perfect love.[169]

---

[169] 1 John 4:18

Peer Envy

Sometimes even when friends mean well or when they're supportive, we feel overwhelmed. For example, I had some good friends who had always encouraged me to follow the Lord and do things the right way, but then they started forming relationships. I heard about their developing romances, I celebrated their engagements, I went to their bridal showers, and I attended their weddings. For the most part, marriage did not change our friendships, but I was always aware that they were married and I wasn't. I felt left behind. This was peer pressure of a different kind; I call it *peer envy*.

If this feeling is not carefully controlled, it can result in a lot of discontentment. It can make us doubt ourselves ("Is there something wrong with me that I'm not married yet?") and doubt God ("Does He really care about my marriage desires?"). It can make us frustrated and dissatisfied with our lives. It can even make us decide we'll take matters into our own hands.

Comparison often creates frustration. *She's* married, but *I'm* not. Why do guys like *her* and not *me*? Did God think *she* was more ready than *me*? The truth is that we are all different. It's not necessarily a matter of being unready, unattractive, or unlucky. It's a matter of God having a different life for each of us. If God had a routine love story for everyone so that no one would feel left out, wouldn't we feel cheated of our individuality? Would we ever have a reason to learn trust and patience?

Images

Most guys are more visually-oriented than women and, therefore, they are most affected by the things they see. That does not mean that we ladies are not affected by images. For example, today our society feels that the "ideal woman" is slim, tall, long-legged, and large-bosomed. So how do many young women try to look today? Slim, tall, long-legged, and large-bosomed. Eating disorders such as anorexia or bulimia are the direct result of trying to look like the ideal woman. Even the most sensible of us are still strongly attracted to being considered "beautiful" by other people.

When I was involved in high school sports, I remember looking

101

over my friend's shoulder casually one day on the bus. To my surprise, I noticed that she had a magazine open to a page with a young man in a suggestive pose. The readers (women) were asked to rate the male model for "hotness." I've seen posters of male celebrities in young women's bedrooms (from Legolas the Elf to Justin Beiber) and I've heard the locker room conversations about whether a guy's body is hot or not. Roughly a quarter of women are visually stimulated like guys. In fact, women can and do become addicted to pornography, just like guys. I think I have a pretty compelling case that women are very influenced by images.

We need to be careful not to feed ourselves with tempting images—whatever those images might be. Sometimes these things trigger lustful feelings, sometimes just discontentment or frustration. It's different for different people, but the principle is the same: We need to recognize and avoid images that are tempting or discouraging to us.

Music & Poetry

Music is a part of every culture. So is poetry, which is a kind of "word-music." If we try to memorize a whole list, it can be very difficult, but if we put that list to music or poetry, we usually find that the memorization process is a lot easier. For example, which do you think you would remember more?

The message of music can creep into your subconscious mind without you knowing exactly what you are learning. You must be careful to make sure that your mind is protected from ideas that may be harmful.

Music seeps into the bones;
It filters through the skin.
Beware! You may not know just what
Ideas you've let in.

Music and poetry have been used for centuries to ignite or to continue romances. From Shakespeare and John Donne to movie soundtracks and pop albums, our lives are filled with musical or poetical references to love. We can't assume that we are not affected by what we hear. Studies have even linked certain types of music to various types of behavior, because messages that we hear over and over again through music and rhythmic speech can eventually worm their way into our subconscious minds. We have to be on our guard continually.

Dreams

Sometimes, a young woman admits to me that she is frustrated by her dreams, which might present tempting scenarios. While she's awake, she feels that she has more control over her thoughts and is better able to guard against discontentment or lust. When she's asleep, she feels that she loses that conscious control. I've been asked many times: "Can I control my dreams?"

I wish I had a real answer to that, but honestly, I've asked the same question myself. Although I have no complete answers to this questions, here are some thoughts:

Our dreams are often linked to our real lives. I'm not going to "go Freud" on you and claim that your suppressed or subconscious desires are expressed in your dreams. I'm just saying that if we make sure that, during the day, we continually turn our thoughts toward the Lord, we stand a much better chance of having dreams that are more godly.

Furthermore, I believe that dreams *can* actually intersect with real life. For example, many people in the Bible experienced real encounters with God or real prophetic visions through dreams. In my life, I have experienced times when the choices that I made in my dreams were as deliberate and conscious as if I were awake. I was aware of the reality of those choices even after I awoke. I don't claim that this happens all the time; I just know that it is true some of the time. Therefore, I believe we can sometimes control our dreams.

I also believe that some dreams are direct attacks from the enemy, to put ideas in our heads or to discourage us. Even though some dream situations are out of our control, they are not out of God's. I once experienced bad dreams on two consecutive nights. I asked God fervently that I would have a good dream on the third night. God sent it to me. It wasn't what I expected (it was a lot weirder, as dreams often are!) but when I woke up, I felt refreshed and relaxed and comforted. If God knows our thoughts, He knows our dreams too, and He cares about how these things affect us. We shouldn't be afraid to ask for His help if we face troubling dreams.

Discontentment

This is one of the primary reasons for sin, whether we're old, young, male, female, Christian, or non-Christian. People just plain aren't content with what they already have. If they're young, they wish they would hurry up and get older. If they're old, they wish they could shed the years. If they're married, they wish they had more freedom or that their spouses were different. If they're unmarried, they wish they were married. God was hitting at the root of a lot of problems when He put "Thou shalt not covet" in the Ten Commandments.

Discontentment, often accompanied by envy, has a variety of triggers. A story: "I wish I had a love story like the people in the book!" A song: "I wish I could say that those words are true for me!" A couple at church: "They're married and I'm not!" A real-life courtship story: "It worked for them, but how about me?" A good-looking or desirable guy: "I wish he'd pay attention to me just a little bit!"

Discontentment is the falsehood that our current possessions or situations are not good enough; we want something more and we have a right to expect it! That expectation sets us up to feel discontented with the blessings that we have currently. When our expectations aren't met, we feel cheated. Whether we admit it to ourselves or not, we feel cheated *by God*, as if He owes us something. Then we are tempted to take matters into our own hands or to find ways, even sinful ways, to make ourselves feel better.

God owes us nothing. We owe Him *everything*. Discontentment equals ingratitude: "God hasn't done enough for me." Contentment is the fruit of a grateful and loving heart: "God has blessed me greatly already and He is enough for me."

Nighttime/Tiredness

When I have talked with other women about temptation, all of them have said the same thing: Night, and especially bedtime, is one of the worst times to face temptation. We are tired, so our defenses are down. Little problems suddenly seem like big ones. The weight of the next day's stresses are already piling on, while the weight of the past day's stresses haven't yet disembarked. We have time to think, uninterrupted, especially about anything that has been simmering inside of us all day long. It's no surprise that this is the perfect time for Satan to launch a temptation attack. When preparing for bed, I find it helpful to turn off all music, to do something relaxing to unwind, and to pray or read my Bible. I have also trained myself to consciously shut away any thoughts about stressful or frustrating things at that time of the night, because I know that my perspective is not always clear when I am tired. Often I tell myself, "I know I'm just feeling this way because I'm tired. Lord, I am going to turn my attention to You now."

Being alone/Boredom

If we're alone with no unexpected distractions—just doing homework or working—we can face strong temptation. We might have plenty to *occupy* us, but nothing to *distract* us. Without some kind of pressure or demand, we can easily let our minds wander. That's why the old adage says "Idleness is the devil's tool"; if we don't have enough to do or enough motivation to stay focused and get it done, we can easily leave ourselves vulnerable to temptation. Motivating ourselves; making ourselves charts, deadlines, or schedules; or asking others to help to motivate us can be great tools in defeating this trigger.

Stress/Frustration

You might be having a bad day, something may have interrupted your plans, you might have been trying to fix a problem or meet a deadline, your siblings or parents may have been grumpy... Frustration is one of the greatest triggers for a lot of young women. Unless there's a good outlet for the frustration, it can simmer inside of us until it comes out in a wrong desire or a wrong reaction to temptation. For example, during college, I had very little time to write creatively. Writing is my outlet for a lot of mental energy and pent-up stress. Without that outlet, I felt strong pressure to relieve stress by making foolish choices or by flirting with temptation. So I learned how to add writing into my schedule, even a little bit, to help me cope with frustration. Find an outlet for your frustration and build helpful activities into your schedule.

Unhealthy Diet

Don't laugh; I'm completely serious when I include this in my list of triggers. What we eat *can* affect our spirits. For example, certain foods cause gastrointestinal problems for me. If I eat a "trigger" food, I feel sick, anxious, and frustrated for hours, if not days. Much modern research suggests that certain nutrients and vitamins can have positive or negative effects on our moods. Many people go to certain foods whose taste or smell reduces their anxiety and many people also find that certain foods, such as those high in empty calories (like fast food), can make them feel more depressed. It's important that we should not underestimate the effect that our bodies can have on our moods and on our spirit. Although our bodies are not eternal, they are also the temples of the Lord.[170] Anything that affects this temple can affect our spirits too. It doesn't have to, but it *can*. If we have physical defenses available to help us deal with spiritual battles, why not use those defenses?

Improper Exercise Habits

Exercise is one of the biggest factors for me, and others agree with me. Exercise, like diet, influences both the mind and the body. We know that a lot of our sexual drive is fueled by hormones, which can give us a surge of energy. Finding ways to constructively use that energy can be a great defense. Exercise produces endorphins, chemicals which make you feel happy and satisfied— great substitutes for the raging hormones we can experience during sexual temptation.

Exercise has other benefits when it comes to beating temptation. Exercise helps us to deal with some of the triggers that I've already talked about: tiredness, stress, frustration, discouragement, and anxiety. Through exercise, we can cultivate healthy bodies that are

---

[170] 1 Corinthians 6:19

more resilient to both physical and emotional stress. Exercise improves sleep and digestion, boosts the immune system, quickens the healing process, strengthens the muscles, improves flexibility, regulates our moods and our hormones, increases energy, improves concentration, and gives us more satisfaction in our daily activities. If it sounds like I'm exaggerating the benefits of exercise, I'm not. Regular exercise is one of the natural tools that God uses to help us deal with the many stresses and difficulties of life. We should take advantage of that tool to whatever extent we can.

Summary

We can't just cut out every source of temptation from our lives. Some people eliminate a great number of things in an attempt to avoid all possible triggers, but I believe that this extreme can be just as dangerous as foolishly ignoring the effect of possible temptations. The key is not elimination but habit. It is impossible to avoid all temptations or to control all situations. Therefore, it is wiser to train your character and to develop godly responses that can be applied to all circumstances, even unforeseen ones.

❦ 11 ❧

Resisting Temptation

As they say, an ounce of prevention is worth a pound of cure. If we know our triggers, we should consider ways to deal with them before they become major problems. Temptation does not have to lead us into sin. We can fight back, but we have to be willing to do what it takes.

Submit yourselves therefore to God. Resist the devil, and he will flee from you. Draw nigh to God, and he will draw nigh to you.[171]

We don't have the power to resist Satan unless we submit to God. That is the purpose of this chapter—to show us what it means to resist the devil and to come near to God in submission.

Dealing with temptation can feel like an impossible task. The temptation is too strong, it keeps coming back, and it tries several different tactics to get us to fail. But every time you want to yell at God, "This is impossible!" remember two things: (1) With God, nothing is impossible,[172] and (2) Jesus was tempted in every way but without sin.[173] Jesus showed that it *is* possible to overcome temptation, even when it's really strong or lasts a long time. If it's possible, why don't we at least try?

I don't know exactly how God gives us the power to overcome temptation, but I can give you some examples that I've seen in my life. These are not things that I "drum up" by trying to be good. When precisely the right encouragement or distraction shows up at just the right moment over and over and over, it is too purposeful to be coincidence. It cannot be the result of my own efforts. It has to be something—or Someone—fighting for me.

Whether or not you find the following examples helpful, I would encourage you to find your own methods to deal in a godly way with your temptations.

---

[171] James 4:7-8a
[172] Luke 1:37
[173] Hebrews 4:15

Focus on Christ

Our first line of defense is God Himself. We tend to focus on ourselves, or (even worse) on our temptations. Instead, we must focus our attention on the Lord, His expectations for us, His goodness to us, and the fact that He loves us too much to let us face temptation alone.

When we love the Lord, we don't want to hurt or disappoint Him, or do anything that would make Him look bad. This mindset of love influences our attitude toward every sin.

Flee fornication. Every sin that a man doeth is without the body; but he that committeth fornication sinneth against his own body. What? know ye not that your body is the temple of the Holy Ghost which is in you, which ye have of God, and ye are not your own? For ye are bought with a price: therefore glorify God in your body, and in your spirit, which are God's.[174]

If God's Holy Spirit lives in us and if we are His body on earth, then why would we ever dare to cause our hands to do something that He would never do? Why would we ever say something His lips would never say? Why would we ever think something His mind would never consider? How could we dare to sin when the Holy Spirit lives in us?

For he hath made him to be sin for us, who knew no sin; that we might be made the righteousness of God in him.[175]

When the Bible says that Jesus became sin for us, it was as if He had done and said and thought all the wrong things we had done and said and thought. He became *us*, in all our sinfulness. Sometimes God places a vision in my mind of Jesus on the cross— bloody, battered, in excruciating pain—and He reminds me, "This sin that you're about to commit, He paid for that one too. This sin put Him here on the cross. This sin killed My only beloved Son." It's a terrifying thought: Our sin murdered Someone. We have to take our sin seriously before we can even understand God's incredible, awesome mercy. When we realize what our sin cost Him, we should feel like shouting with joy that He loved us so

---

[174] 1 Corinthians 6:18-20
[175] 2 Corinthians 5:21

much to suffer so deeply for us! We should love Him with all our hearts, and our gratitude should make us want to please Him.

Focus on True Love

Because temptation often makes us confused about the difference between love and lust, the Lord brings us back to the true definition of love when we face temptation. When we know the real thing, we won't be fooled by the fake thing. The Lord reminds us that the motivation of love is selflessness and a desire to do what is best for another person; He reminds us that the motivation of lust is selfishness and a desire to do what is best for ourselves.

It is similar to food. When a person is used to eating wholesome food, she can't stand the idea of eating junk food. She knows that the junk food will not nourish her body the way it needs to be nourished. She also loses her taste for junk food; the wholesome foods actually taste better to her! In the same way, Jesus Christ feeds us with a "diet" of real love so that we can taste the difference between love and lust. When we are used to true love, we don't want lust. It is not as satisfying, it is not as nourishing, and it is not as sweet. *O taste and see that the LORD is good: blessed is the man that trusteth in him!*[176]

Pray

Often, our first reaction to temptation is to pray for strength to resist it. Whether we know it or not, the very act of praying is a way of resisting temptation. Instead of trying to deal with things on our own, we are going to someone who cares about us and who has the power to help. It's ineffective to focus on the temptation in prayer; rather, the best defense lies in asking for the strength to do the right thing and in praising the Lord for His goodness. So instead of praying, "O Lord, please take away this horrible temptation. Give me strength to kill it..." try praying, "O Lord, thank You for this beautiful day and for how good You've been to me..." Take your mind off of your sin and yourself and put it on the only One who

---

[176] Psalm 34:8

deserves your attention.

It is also helpful to pray for other people whenever we face temptation. When we pray for other people, we are getting our minds off of ourselves. We must be more concerned with others' needs—their illnesses, spiritual condition, and other needs—than with our own. Who will pray for all those people if we don't? Let's not fight defensively; let's fight offensively and bring the battle back to the Enemy. Let's not take whatever shots he gives out; through God's help, let's respond with hits of our own as we fight for God's glory!

The effectual fervent prayer of a righteous man availeth much.[177]

Read the Bible

If you face strong temptation, whatever you do, don't take a break from regular Bible-reading. *Stand therefore, having your loins girt with truth.*[178] Often I have asked myself, "What went wrong?" Then I remember that I have not spent time reading God's Word and talking to Him that day. To focus on my Bible-reading and not to just zip through it, I keep a notebook to jot down one interesting verse that I read that day, to write down a question that occurs to me as I read, or to summarize my reading of the day.

Reading the Bible regularly and memorizing a new verse periodically are not just good exercises in diligence. No good soldier goes into battle without his weapon, yet this is *exactly* what we do when we neglect to fill ourselves with God's words. We leave ourselves wide open to the enemy's lies, because we are no longer familiar with the truth.

For the word of God is quick, and powerful, and sharper than any two-edged sword, piercing even to the dividing asunder of soul and spirit, and of the joints and marrow, and is a discerner of the thoughts and intents of the heart.[179]

Leave no opening to the enemy. Come with a sword that is ready for action. This is a *real* battle and we need to get serious, because, believe me, our enemy is deadly serious.

---

[177] James 5:16b
[178] Ephesians 6:14
[179] Hebrews 4:12

Use Distraction

Sometimes as we listen to a radio station, another radio station cuts in. That second radio station may not be very strong or clear, but it chops up the airwaves from that first station and makes listening very frustrating. We lose the full pleasure of listening to the first radio station.

That can happen when you are allowing a tempting thought to have control of your mind. God jams the temptation airwaves by sending a distracting thought. In my experience, the distracting thought is often in the form of a song and, significantly, it's almost always a worship song. It's hard to indulge in an impure thought when some mental radio is blaring out, "A mighty fortress is our God, a bulwark never failing..."

Sometimes *any* kind of distraction will do. For example, a little sibling will barge in the room with a petty request. "Can you braid my hair? I can't do it right. It keeps coming out all bubbly." (Yes, I have heard this one before!) Or the cat might decide that it's the perfect time for you to pat her. Or your mother might call for help to make dinner. Who knows? The distractions might not arrive wearing halos or be accompanied by angelic strains of music, but they could be God-sent distractions during your time of temptation.

Truthfully, we sometimes get annoyed by the distractions and wish they'd stop interrupting us. But when we recognize them for what they are—God's way of getting our minds off of a temptation—we should seize those distractions and hang on until we are in the safe zone.

Other helpful distractions include singing at the top of your voice, quoting a memorized Bible verse, striking up a conversation with a nearby person, or intentionally putting yourself in a situation where you are in the midst of distracting activities.

"Sure, hon, how do you want me to braid your hair? Regular braid or French braid?"

Serve Others

The best distraction is to serve others. The moment of temptation is intensely self-centered. We are tempted to focus on the temptation and its effect on us, rather than on God and on His will. What is His will? To be like Christ in all things. As much as Christ taught the mysteries of God, He also worked in a very earthly sense. When people were sick, He healed them. When people were hungry, He fed them. Every spiritual lesson had a practical application. The hermit who abandons humanity in order to meditate himself into a "pure" state of mind has missed the very core of Jesus Christ, which is unflinching service to others.

Our best defense is a strong offense. Temptation is meant to make us focus on ourselves. Let us turn the attention to God first, and to others secondly. Temptation is meant to paralyze us; let it instead mobilize us and thrust us into action! Let temptation goad us to write letters to young women who need encouragement, to make meals for struggling families, to sing songs for lonely elderly people, to lovingly nurture little ones in the Lord, or to cheerfully share work with our family members. At the moment when temptation is strongest, let its own strength be converted to a pair of hands and a pair of feet that are eager to do the will of God.

Don't Compromise

Ben Franklin was known for his wise sayings. This one about temptation hits the nail on the head: "'Tis easier to suppress the first desire than to satisfy all those that follow it." If we give in once, we will be tempted to give in again. We will find excuses for why it wasn't so bad. Do not compromise! Sin is bondage. Why flirt with bondage?

When Joseph was sold into Egypt, he became the manager of the household of Potiphar, a rich Egyptian official. Potiphar's wife thought, "Woah, Joseph is one hot dude!" So she tried to tempt him to commit adultery with her. Joseph told her "No way" and when she persisted, he ran—fast—in the opposite direction![180] He didn't try to explain any more. The time for persuasion was over.

In the same way, we have no right to flirt with temptation. Put a sign on the door of your heart that says "No Admittance to Temptation!" Then, when temptation comes knocking, stand firm. Don't even crack open the door. If it gets a foot in the door, slam the door on its foot!

---

[180] Genesis 39:6-12

Be Accountable

Just as it was not good for Adam to be alone, so it is not good for us to be alone, especially when we're facing a spiritual battle. The Lord encourages us through other people to continue to "fight the good fight"[181] and "run the race with endurance."[182] They might be parents, siblings, relatives, friends, pastors, mentors, teachers, speakers, or some random people that God throws in our path. Those people will encourage us to stay on track, to remember the importance of Biblical purity, and to keep seeking the Lord.

Often they are people that we know, respect, and trust. Sharing our struggles reminds us that we are not alone in the fight, helps us to admit our weaknesses to ourselves, and allows other people to step in and help. People might be able to help simply by listening and praying, or they might be able to offer strong Biblical advice. The advice might hurt, but the Bible says that wounds from a friend can be trusted, but an enemy multiplies kisses.[183] In other words, be more ready to hear "I have a bone to pick with you" from your best friend than "You are such a sweet person" from a flattering acquaintance or enemy.

Sometimes, our helpers are people who are willing to keep us accountable. This means that they get tough on us when we can't get tough on ourselves. They remind us continually of God's Word. They pray for us and help us to take one step at a time. Just knowing that people are keeping an eye on us can help us to make right choices when we face temptation.

However, if we want to be held accountable, we must not wait for others to check in with us all the time. Making others responsible for our accountability gives us the excuse to blame them if we fail; taking responsibility for our own accountability forces us to face the battle ourselves. Our accountability partners are our supporters, but they cannot fight for us.

My parents were the first people to whom I went. Over the years, they have listened when I tell them my struggles, and they have dealt with my spiritual needs and given me practical ways to

---

[181] 1 Timothy 6:12
[182] Hebrews 12:1
[183] Proverbs 27:6

deal with temptation and sin. Best of all, my parents recognize that neither they nor I can ultimately win this battle, so they bring me to the Lord in prayer. I am convinced that the prayers of my parents have been shields for me.

My siblings are also great listeners. They encourage me constantly, keep themselves available to me, and pray for me. My siblings also don't accept my excuses. "Yaasha, you said you want to do things God's way. That isn't doing things God's way. Honey, I've been praying for you, but you've got to put some effort into things too. Stop being so easy on yourself. Get tough! Live without compromise!" They let me have the benefit of listening to their struggles too. Being able to both listen and share is a great encouragement, especially for women. We ladies like to know that we are wanted and valued, and sharing our thoughts with others helps us to do that. One of my sisters has been especially helpful and committed to hold me accountable and to pray for me constantly. During a particularly difficult time in my life, I heard her cheerful voice: "Checkin' in!" Knowing that I would have to tell her my tales of the day helped me to refocus when I faced temptation. I did not want to tell her that I had failed, so I fought harder.

Finally, I have friends who are tremendous encouragements to me. One friend shares a lot of the same struggles but, most importantly, she loves the Lord with all her heart. If I share something with her, I know that she will give me advice based not on her own opinions but on Biblical truth. We can admit our faults to each other without worrying that the other person will either be judgmental or tempted to "rescue" us from shame that we should rightly feel. We still pray for each other and ask each other regularly how we are doing. "Heart check! How are you doing? Anything I can pray about specifically?"

At another time, a married friend listened to me when I had a bad day, told me her own struggles, and prayed for me often. We usually ended up praying together for the Lord to answer my prayer for a husband and her prayer for a baby. The Lord answered her desire; she is now a mother to a beautiful little boy!

If we need people to hold us accountable or to encourage us, we should consider three main things.

1. I am strongly of the opinion that our parents should be the first place to which we should turn for help. After all, they are the ones who know us best and who are the most concerned about us (whether they show it or not). More importantly, they have to answer to God for us, because He placed us in their care. They deserve to know if anything is endangering us spiritually, physically, or in any other way. I know that communication can be uncomfortable, but believe me, our parents would rather know than not know. The Lord says: "Children, obey your parents in the Lord, for this is right."[184] God specifically mentions in the Bible that we should listen to the advice of our parents.[185] He also tells the older generation to teach the younger generation.[186] How can they do all the things that God requires of them if their children will not communicate with them?

2. We need to go to people who are Christians and who show evidence of God at work in their lives. It is best if we go first to older women. They need to know their Bibles well enough to give us godly advice. Sometimes when we are in the middle of a situation, it is hard to see everything clearly because there are so many details and so many emotions. Others can help to clarify the situation for us because they can step back and divorce their feelings more easily from it. Older women can look back on their experiences, see the big picture, and share that with us.

Our peers can be helpful because they often struggle with the same temptations that we do. For that very reason, however, we need to take what they say with a grain of salt. A soldier under heavy fire may do one of two things: act above and beyond the call of duty, or grow tired or discouraged and drop out of the fight. In other words, our friends can be an extremely valuable resource if they are maintaining a godly focus and a great hindrance if they aren't. I'm sure our friends would never mean to mislead us, but it can happen. It is worthwhile to find friends whom we know are strong in the Lord. When we do find friends like that, we ought to keep 'em!

---

[184] Ephesians 6:1
[185] Proverbs 1:8
[186] Titus 2:3-5, Deuteronomy 11:19

3. We should find people that we know well and personally trust.
When it comes to sharing issues about our deepest desires and
maybe even our worst sins, we need to know that our information
is not going to be used against us or shared with other people. We
need to know that our accountability partners care about our entire
well-being—spiritual, mental, emotional, and physical. We need to
know that they are giving advice because they love us, not just
because they like giving out advice. We need to know that they will
not shun us or treat us badly because of our sins, but we also need
to know that they will not take sin lightly. We need people with
realistic, Biblical mindsets who will tell us the hard truth with love.

ৡ 12 ল

Dealing with Sin

Despite the fact that we can prevent much pain if we say "no" to temptation, we're all going to face times when we fail or when we simply don't *want* to do the right thing. No matter what type of failure we face, we need to respond to it in a Biblical way.

Recognize and Hate Sin

Until we have recognized something as a sin, we will not be able to take steps to get rid of it. Sometimes, people notice the sin and point it out, but sometimes our sin is secret. Sometimes *we* are the ones who have to identify the sin. We recognize sin because of the Bible's message and because God speaks to our consciences.

We might not want to admit that something is sinful, so we might make excuses for our thoughts or actions. "It wasn't *really* a sin." Or "It wasn't as bad as it could have been!" Here's a good test: Are we hiding anything from our parents? Would we be uncomfortable telling our parents, our best friends, or God about our activities? Remember, God sees our hearts. What is He seeing?

After we recognize our sin, we need to hate it. This is the hardest part, because, like I said before, we are tempted by things we want. When we fall to temptation, our sin separates us from the One who loves us so much. Jesus died to break down that wall of separation; why would we want to put the wall up again?

We cannot fight something we still want and still love. Sometimes, it is impossible to hate our sin because we want something so badly. My sister and I noticed that we prayed: "O Lord, please take this sin away from me," and held out the sin as though to offer it. Yet when God took hold of the sin, we tightened our grip and sweated and strained to keep hold of it, all the time piously praying, "O Lord, I've been asking You and asking You, please take this sin away from me!"

It is humbling, but that is the time when I have to go on my knees and pray this pathetic little prayer: "God, I know that I have sinned, but I'm having a hard time hating my sin. I still want it. Help me, Father, to hate the sin so that I can glorify You fully in my life." It's okay to be honest with God. If we still want our sin, we need to admit it and ask for help. He doesn't want us to pretend we're stronger or more spiritual than we are; He sees our hearts. Remember, we need to hate the *sin*, but not any good desires that the sin may have started from. For example, it's not wrong to want to be married or to want to be physically intimate, but it is wrong to allow our desires to lead us into sin.

We might not get to a place where we truly hate our sin. Sometimes we might hate it and sometimes we might still want it. Whether or not we have our feelings on our side, we still have to obey God.

Guilt v. Repentance

Guilt can influence us in two ways. On the one hand, we can become defiant and frustrated. We want to pretend that we have a right to feel disappointed in God. "What else did you expect? I have no real way to deal with this temptation!" On the other hand, we can wallow in shame and tell God over and over how sorry we are. We would rather punish ourselves with guilt than take the necessary steps to get rid of the *cause* of the guilt! We believe that if we feel sorry (to the point of depression), we will please God more and we will be less likely to sin again. When either of these scenarios occurs, the last thing we want to do is pray. We're too grumpy or too ashamed to talk to God. So we stay in our pit and wallow or stew.

That's exactly what Satan is looking for! If he can make us feel too guilty to pray, perfect! If he can make us too grumpy to pray, great! After all, the last thing he wants us to do is to *talk* to God about the situation. Sin and guilt are all about breaking down communication between us and our Father. We should tell God about our troubles. "Lord, I know I shouldn't continue to feel guilty, because You died to take my sin and guilt away. But I'm still feeling guilty and I need help..." Or, "Lord, I'm really frustrated. I know You expect us to do things a certain way, but it's really hard to do things that way. I need help..."

Remember that He is God; He doesn't owe us anything. At the same time, He wants to know what we're thinking. And He wants to hear the *truth*, not the sugar-coated version, because He already knows what is in our hearts. If our lips are saying something different than our hearts, He knows we're hypocrites. Respect Him, but tell Him the truth. If we can't communicate with our Father, who else is there?

Whom have I in heaven but thee? And there is none upon earth that I desire beside thee.[187]

Lord, to whom shall we go? Thou hast the words of eternal life.[188]

Guilt is meant for only one thing—to bring you to a place where you acknowledge your sin, ask for forgiveness, and turn away from that sin. In other words, when we're really, truly sorry, we do more than just feel sorry. We *act* sorry.

The Bible includes some important examples of repentance. Paul had written a letter to the Corinthians to point out their sins, and when he heard that the Corinthians had listened to him and been sorry in the right way, he wrote this passage in a second letter:

Now I rejoice, not that ye were made sorry, but that ye sorrowed to repentance: for ye were made sorry after a godly manner, that ye might receive damage by us in nothing. For godly sorrow worketh repentance to salvation not to be repented of: but the sorrow of the world worketh death.[189]

The Bible always shows that repentance includes turning your back to sin and shoving it behind you. If the sin was idolatry, the idols were broken up or burned.[190] If the sin was believers marrying pagans, the pagan spouses were divorced.[191] If the sin was unbiblical slavery, then the slaves were set free.[192]

True repentance always follows the same pattern. First, they *said* that they were sorry—"We have sinned, and have done perversely, we have committed wickedness"[193]—and then they

---

[187] Psalm 73:25

[188] John 6:68

[189] 2 Corinthians 7:9-10

[190] 2 Kings 23:24, 2 Chronicles 15:8

[191] Ezra chapter 10

[192] Nehemiah chapter 5

[193] 1 Kings 8:47

showed that they were sorry. In old times, people showed that they were sorry by putting dust and ashes on their heads and dressing in clothes that were scratchy and uncomfortable. I know this may sound hilarious to us (it sure does to me!) but it also shows that people were willing to humiliate themselves to show how sorry they were. They didn't just kneel comfortably in a pew or by their bedside, apologize privately, and then go about their day. No, their hearts were broken! Their spirits cried out, "What have I done?" They recognized that sinning against God was like spitting in His face and that He had every right to punish them. They spoke like the praying man in the temple: "Have mercy on me, a sinner!"[194]

That is repentance. Not only do we recognize our sin, say sorry for it, and turn away from it, but we humble ourselves before God. We realize that sin is serious enough for God to kill His only son. We ensure (with God's help) that the sin will not happen again.

A young woman of my acquaintance once gave a testimony that I will never forget. "I was trying to take baby steps toward God. I was choosing to fix only one of my many problems at a time. My brother told me, 'You cannot take little steps toward God. You have to turn fully around and *run* toward Him with all your strength.'"

If you have ever seen the drama "Lifehouse Everything" (it's on Youtube and GodTube), you have some picture of how this works. During the drama, the girl pantomimes various sins, until she reaches the end of hope and she holds the gun to her head. Just at the moment when she is about to pull the trigger, she throws it away and leaps toward Jesus Christ. Her enemies—wealth, worldly beauty, alcoholism, self-destructive behavior, even the Devil himself—claw at her, tearing the black shirt from her body to reveal a white shirt underneath. She fights like her life depends on it. That's what it is like to repent. It's complete desperation for God.

Guilt is not meant to be a swamp to wallow in. Once you've confessed and turned your back on the sin, *it's all gone.* When we continue to feel guilty after confessing, it is like telling God that Jesus didn't do enough on the cross to erase our sins. To use my mother's words: "The devil would like nothing better than for us to keep feeling guilty for our sin. After all, if we feel guilty for a day,

---

[194] Luke 18:13

why not for a whole week? Why not for a month? A year? A lifetime? Don't we deserve to feel guilty for all the wrong things we do? But that isn't what living for Christ is all about. He's freed us from that guilt. We can go to Him and be clean. Instead of wallowing in our guilt, we should praise God for sending His son to die in order to take away our sin and our guilt!"

As far as the east is from the west, so far hath he removed our transgressions from us.[195]

He will turn again, he will have compassion upon us; he will subdue our iniquities; and thou wilt cast all their sins into the depths of the sea.[196]

The Key to Repentance

Knock, knock!

"Hello, can I help you?"

"Yes, my name is Temptation. Can you let me in, please? I promise to wreak havoc in your home."

"Sure thing. Just step this way, and be sure to wipe your feet on the doormat, please. Now, if you would be so kind, hang out here on the porch. I'm going to step inside and do everything I can to fight you off from there. Okay? I'll tell you when I'm ready."

Sounds crazy, doesn't it? You might be laughing now, but let me ask you this question: Have you ever repented, then sinned the same sin again, repented, sinned, repented, sinned...on and on? If you have, I'd be willing to bet my MacBook Pro that your heart has been the setting of a scene very like this one. How do I know? Because I've been there.

One day, as I wondered why I had so many relapses, it slowly dawned on me that I already knew why. I had heard it spoken years before by my father, in one of his many dinner-table family sermons. He had asked, "Did you know that repentance literally means 'to change your mind'?"

Intrigued, I looked up the word in the various Bible-help books on Dad's shelf. It was true. To repent is to change one's mind. And suddenly I knew why my former repentances had not "stuck." I had been trying to change my behavior without changing my mind.

---

[195] Psalm 103:12
[196] Micah 7:19

Repentance is not behavior modification. If we try to change how we act without changing how we think, we're fighting a losing battle. When Jesus said, "Whoever looks at a woman to lust after her has committed adultery with her,"[197] He was pinpointing this very problem. All wrong actions begin with wrong thoughts. The *real* sin is the sin in the mind. If that's hard to understand, here's an example to help you out.

Suppose that you steal a coveted pencil from your sibling. Now suppose that you steal a CD from a store. Which sin is worse? You're probably tempted to say that stealing the CD was worse. I argue that it's not. The problem is not the type of thing that you stole, or whom you stole it from. The problem is that you stole. You're a thief either way.

In the same way, when it comes to sexual sin, everything from watching porn, to reading erotica, to fantasizing, to full fornication is sin. The sin is not the level of sexual involvement but the practice of the corruption of our character. Fantasizing *seems* to exhibit more self-control than actual physical intimacy, but it doesn't. Why? Because we're really just choosing the version of sexual sin that makes us feel less guilty or that suits our tastes better. Choosing to fantasize rather than to fornicate is *not* proof that we are exhibiting self-control. If we were actually behaving with self-control, we wouldn't be indulging in any kind of sexual sin in the first place. The sin is not based on the *type* of sexual sin; it's based on the fact that it *is* sexual sin.

Let's hit the root of the problem: our minds. When we change our minds, our behavior will follow.

And be not conformed to this world: but be ye transformed by the renewing of your mind, that ye may prove what is that good, and acceptable, and perfect, will of God.[198]

Strangle the Sin

What would we say about a person who desperately fights back a fire in his house, but keeps piling more wood on the fire? That's right: That person is crazy! If we try to fight our sin but we allow

---

[197] Matthew 5:28
[198] Romans 12:2

ourselves to go into situations in which we are strongly tempted to sin, then we are feeding our sin. If a guy struggles with pornography, wouldn't we advise him *not* to look at the sleazy magazine photos at the end of the check-out aisle in the grocery store or to hang out near the lingerie section in the department store or watch movies with nudity? If we struggle to think about sex in a Biblical way, the last thing we should do is read a book or watch a movie that includes scenes with sexual hints or content. If we struggle with contentment, the last thing we should do is compare ourselves to other people. We need to make sure that we don't allow things into our minds that could strengthen our sin. I admit, some situations are out of our control, but we need to take responsibility for those things that *are* in our control.

When we consistently struggle with a sin, we show that don't want freedom from that sin enough. We find excuses for ourselves. If we go to someone for accountability, we can't leave the relationship in their laps, expecting that they will come to us to check up on how we are doing. Instead, we have to take responsibility for our own battle and be active in the accountability process. We only win the battles that we fight.

I once remarked casually that I wanted to be able to identify all of the major constellations someday. My cousin glanced at me and said dryly, "Someday. Ha! Someday means never. If it's important to you, don't tell yourself 'someday.' Do it!" I realized that I needed to apply this mindset to my own spiritual struggles. From that time on, I began to fight as I had not yet fought and pray as I had not yet prayed. I prayed that I would store up strength and resolve during the good times, to be used during the bad times, the way Joseph stored up grain during the seven years of plenty in order to prepare for the seven years of famine. God answered my prayers. Incredibly, I saw bad habits begin to break. I saw huge holes torn in walls that had seemed unbreakable. Did I have bad days? Sure. But I was ready for them. I had a plan and I had God fighting for me. I repeated my battle cries, aloud if I had to, whenever I faced temptation.

"No! I accept no compromise! I will fight!"

Fight to Win

We need to realize that we may always struggle with some things. Some temptations might never go away. This is what it means to be humans in a world that has rejected God. This is what it means to be a descendant of Adam and Eve. Life is always a battle to be holy.

If this were the end of the story, we would despair of ever pleasing God. But this is how it works: First, God loved us even when we were unlovable and sent His son to die for us.[199] In fact, He died for us *because* we were sinners and didn't deserve it! Through one man (Adam) we were cursed with sin, but through one man (Jesus Christ) the curse was reversed and we were given a second chance.[200] When sin increases, God's goodness and mercy toward us increase even more.[201] Although it's tempting to feel like our lives are useless battles spent fighting the same old enemy, we know it isn't that way. God gives us strength to continue to fight— and to win. Remember that temptation is *not* sin. We may always struggle with a certain temptation, but we do not always have to sin. This does not have to be a losing battle.

When I was going through a difficult time, I began to rationalize in this way: "God is more pleased when I try and fail than when I don't try at all. My weakness is nothing new to God. He knows that even when I say sorry, I may still struggle. He wants to see that I will keep fighting to do the right thing." I truly believed this until I realized that, although this was partially true, it wasn't enough. This was like making a personal peace with the enemy. This wasn't victory.

At one time in my life, I struggled to forgive people when they continued to disappoint me in the same area. When I told Mom about my problem, she said she understood, but she reminded me to keep forgiving. Then she said, "When someone keeps disappointing you, you tend to expect that they will continue to disappoint you. But it is not fair to expect someone to fail. You have to keep praying for that person. This does not mean that you ignore

---

[199] Romans 5:8
[200] Romans 5:12-19
[201] Romans 5:20

125

the possibility that they might fail again—after all, you have to be realistic—but you shouldn't *expect* them to fail, or you are giving up on them."

This made a lot of sense to me and, when I put it into practice, I found that it helped my heart to stay in the right place, even when I was disappointed yet again. As I learned more about not expecting people to fail, I realized that I wasn't applying the lesson to myself. I was more gracious toward others for their sins than I was toward myself. While I extended forgiveness and kindness to others for their failings, I punished myself for mine. I let myself believe that everyone else had the ability to fight their faults, but that I didn't. Yet we all have the same Source of strength! The Lord never gives up on us; we have no right to give up on ourselves.

Even though we understand that we are sinful beings and that we always have the potential to fail in our struggles against sin, we should not *expect* that. That is giving up the fight before we have begun. Instead of expecting that sin will be too strong for us, we should expect that, as we try to do the right thing, God will strengthen us to achieve victory![202]

If you're anything like me, you might be thinking, "That's wonderful, but I can't *make* myself follow through on my good intentions. I can't *make* myself have self-control at that moment of temptation."

Before you start believing that you're a helpless victim to your own sin, ask yourself two questions:

"If a train were coming down the track at 200 miles per hour and I were standing in the middle of the track, how quickly would I move to get out of the way? What if I were crippled? Would I still make myself get off that track?"

"If a heavy object were about to fall onto a loved one and I caught it just in time, how long would I hold that object to protect that person I loved? Until I get tired? Or until my loved one is out of danger?"

This is the truth: Everyone knows how to move quickly when a train is coming and everyone knows how to hold onto that heavy object when a loved one's life is at stake. The problem is not that we are helpless victims of our sin. The problem is that we are not

---

[202] 1 Peter 5:10

willing to do *whatever it takes* to do God's commandments.

Ye have not yet resisted unto blood, striving against sin.[203]

One night I found myself struggling fiercely over an area in my life in which I knew I needed to turn control over to God. I wrestled for a long time trying to convince myself to do the right thing. Suddenly, I saw the truth.

"Wait a minute. If I can convince myself into doing the right thing, I can convince myself out of it."

Our own minds are two-edged swords; they can cut in one direction and they can cut in the other direction. If we rely on our own arguments to convince ourselves to do the right thing, we're looking for strength in the wrong place.

When I look in the Bible, I see a very different approach to righteousness. I see a righteousness that was so automatic that people did not have to convince themselves to do the right thing. They did not have to evaluate every situation to see how to apply righteousness in that particular situation. They just did the right thing without hesitation! When Joseph was tempted to commit adultery with Potiphar's wife, he didn't run down a checklist of the pros and cons. No, he ran away from the temptation!

How do we know how to respond righteously? First, we need to know the character of God, so that we are familiar with how He expects us to respond. Secondly, we must leave no time to second-guess our obedience to the Lord. If we find ourselves in a mental debate, we should ask ourselves, "Why am I even debating this? I need to obey!" Then we should do the right thing—immediately.

There is nothing complicated about this. It's hard, but it's not complicated. Make a habit of simply doing the right thing, automatically and with all your might.

Complete victory *is* possible. I discovered this when the Lord began to deliver me from a struggle that I thought was undefeatable. I had to fight for this victory—He didn't just hand it to me on a silver platter—but God honored my many prayers for deliverance and my choices to obey Him. This does not mean that I will not be tempted again, but it does mean that I can choose never

---

[203] Hebrews 12:4

to sin that way again. Every sin is a choice, and God gives us the power to choose righteousness. If you think an addicting sin is impossible to overcome, don't believe the lie. Jesus Christ is breaking chains every day. Accept nothing less than victory. Our God is not bound, and with his strength, neither are we.

Respond to Temptation with Praise

This concept is best explained through two excerpts. The first is something I wrote to a friend who needed encouragement during a spiritual struggle. The second is an excerpt from my diary from the same time. The information is a little fragmentary, but this is the picture that God allowed me to see. This is when the lesson was still raw and fresh in my mind, and maybe its very rawness and freshness will make the picture a little clearer in your mind too.

From the letter to my friend: I had been struggling with an issue for over a year and all my attempts to "fix" the problem had been useless. Every time I failed, I would pray that God would take away my weakness and that I would not have to be ashamed of my life before Him. But in all my praying for God to become my only Vision, and for Him to destroy in me whatever was not His, I missed the very thing I was asking for. I was focusing on God fixing my problems, on God taking away this weakness from me, on God making me clean. They were all good things to pray, but I was praying for things for me. I was focused on me.

It was a complete revelation not to pray, "Father, please take away this sin that is getting between you and me," but to pray, "Father, I thank You that You have made a way for me to know You despite my sin. Thank You that this sin is giving me the chance to praise You for cleansing me. It is not the sin and the hardships that I am thankful for, but I am thankful for the opportunity they give me to thank You for providing a way for me to one day meet You in Your kingdom without their stain on my life."

If you fail, don't get discouraged. Pick yourself up, thank Him that He gives you the chance to try again, and forget about the sin. He's forgiven it, He's forgotten it—why shouldn't you? It doesn't matter if you sin a hundred times in a day; as discouraging as that is, you are still going forward if you turn every failure into praise and every weakness into a chance for God to be strong in your life. I know it's hard to believe that anything good can come out of falling into the same pit time and time again. But there is still good in it so long as you keep climbing out. Don't pay a penance; don't punish yourself; don't feel guilty for a little longer because you deserve to feel guilty. You have a whole lifetime to fail God, but that just means you have a whole lifetime to praise Him for His goodness.

Don't resolve to abstain from sin. The resolution is useless. When I decided that I would give God glory and praise *whether I sinned or not* (and whether I felt like it or not), the power of sin in my life began to wither rapidly. Righteousness is not found in trying to be righteous but rather in a simple desire to glorify God.

From my diary: Mom shared with me that she is wary of such things as "desert times" and "dry times" in one's spiritual life. Such things are often based on feeling ("I just don't feel close to God") and they focus more on the self (what I'm feeling, how I'm doing in my Christian walk) than on God. Such a Christian walk seems more based on experience than on faith and more focused on what I get out of the relationship (fulfilling spiritual experiences or feelings) rather than on what I can do to serve God. That made a lot of sense to me, especially when we both concluded that the desert time for the Israelites was not an experience of void. There was the water from the rock, the manna from heaven, and many other wonders. Most importantly, God's presence did not dissipate in the desert time; He was always there in the pillar of fire or the pillar of smoke. A desert time is not a back-step in the relationship. It is just another stage, another chance to serve God in new circumstances. In effect, Christianity is not a road of highs and lows; it is a straight road that, by its very straightness, regulates the highs and lows. It is well in trial and in peace, so what real distinction is there between trial and peace? They are both chances to praise God.

I thought I would get closer to God by destroying my bondage to my particular sin. Yet in reality, I could only get closer to God by praising Him. The focus should not be my sin, but His goodness. While I was praying and seeking God and thanking Him for my blessings, I was unconsciously doing the very thing that will make my sin of no effect. How can the devil stay around to tempt me if every failure of mine turns into a song of praise to God? My sin is strong because it feeds off of the thought and time I give to it, even thought and time spent on strategizing about how to crush it. My sin will weaken if it is not fed, and if all my thought and time is directed instead to God and how good He is to me.

Rejoice evermore. Pray without ceasing. In every thing give thanks: for this is the will of God in Christ Jesus concerning you.[204]

---

[204] 1 Thessalonians 5:16-18

Realistic Love

ঞ 13 ০৪

Recognizing True Love

Marriage is an exclusive, life-long relationship. Attacks against purity are attacks against the exclusivity of marriage. What attacks might damage the second criteria of marriage—its permanence—even before we reach the altar?

The answer: False views about the marriage relationship and about ourselves. These false views fall into three categories:

1. Mistaking false love for real love.
2. Nurturing false or unrealistic expectations for our husbands and for our relationship.
3. Giving in to the fears and pressures that we face now as singles.

Today's media and culture feed us a lot of lies. The only way we can protect ourselves and our future marriages is to recognize the lies and cling to the Truth.

True Love v. False Love

My pastor once presented a sermon series on how to spot counterfeit truths that people were trying to pass off as Biblical truths. He compared the situation to learning about counterfeit paper bills. We could try to learn the marks of a counterfeit bill, but there will be new counterfeit bills all the time and they will have different marks, some of which we've never seen before. Trying to memorize and identify counterfeit marks is a long and never-ending process. There is a much better, easier, and more effective method to identify counterfeit money: Just learn what *real* money ought to look like. If we become intimately familiar with the real thing, we'll automatically recognize the fake thing.

Every relationship is based on love, either the presence or absence of it. That's why I wrote so much about love at the beginning of this book. Once we know what the Bible says about love, we will recognize false love immediately. We've been conditioned by our society to long for false love and to overlook true love. Movies, books, and songs reinforce an incorrect view of love. We must guard against false love, because a lot is at stake.

Just a quick review of love before we jump into this section:

1. Love is other-centered.
2. We must love God.
3. We must love others.
4. We must love our enemies.
5. Love is not a feeling; love is an attitude and an action.
6. Love requires sacrifice.

Keep these six main things in mind as we contrast the actions and mindset of false love with the actions and mindset of true love.

1. True love is action; false love is feeling.

A lot of people mix up attraction with love. When their heart goes pitter-patter and their breath comes short, they think, "I'm in love!" In reality, they are not in love. They are feeling attraction, passion, fondness, or some other feeling, but they are not experiencing love. Attraction is a feeling; love is acting in a way that shows concern for another person's good, whether or not we even like that person. Love demands more than fine feelings; it demands commitment and sacrifice.

Don't get me wrong; there's nothing wrong with attraction, although we have to be careful where we let it lead us. Attraction and love can even accompany each other, but let's not confuse the two. It's like violins and bass; they are both part of an orchestra and have a similar sound, but they're not the same thing. The violins (attraction) often go off on fanciful excursions in the air, dancing and running. They are lively and beautiful and stirring. The basses (love) are hardly noticed in a full orchestra, yet without them, we miss the deep heartbeat and resonance of the musical piece. We can have an orchestra without violins, but we can't have an orchestra without the bass section.

A lot of people marry while they're still strongly attracted to each other. For a time, all seems to be going well and then they eventually start to feel a little less attraction, a little less excitement. People start to panic. "I'm falling out of love!" No, they're not falling out of love. They're just going through a phase in which their emotions and feelings aren't as excited as they once were.

Many people have been conditioned to believe that "love" (i.e. a feeling of attraction) is the only basis for a good relationship, so when the "love" drains out of their relationship, they rationalize that they no longer have a valid relationship. They are free to go looking for "love" again. The relationship ends tragically, sacrificed to the idol of "love."

Among the couples of my acquaintance who have been married for decades, I've seen a different trend. Their emotions go up and down. Sometimes they feel fond of each other and sometimes they rub each other the wrong way. Their God-given love for each other—that commitment to seek their spouse's ultimate good—is the one thing that holds them together. Through perseverance, love has rewarded them with relationships that have only grown stronger and more beautiful with the years. The love came first and the feelings followed.

The reason why people prefer false love to true love is because false love makes no demands. False love offers immediate romantic fulfillment and requires only passion—no sacrifices, no commitment, no demands. However, its benefits eventually fade. True love hurts more, demands much more from us, requires responsibility and commitment, and appears to have fewer benefits, even though it really has more benefits! If we want lasting love, we need to be willing to put in the work that it takes. Not many people are willing to do that—and that is why true love is rare.

2. True love commits to act out love; false love waits to be "in love" before acting.

When I asked my parents whether they were in love when they got married, they looked at each other, blinked a few times, and replied, "No, I don't think so. Not in the way you're thinking of it."

While I did a complete double-take, they continued, "Well, we liked each other—a lot—and we knew that we loved the Lord. We also knew that, with the Lord's help, we could make it work. We were willing to commit to each other. Being 'in love' was irrelevant to us at the time. Even so, we have gotten even fonder of each other over the years!"

That shocked my sense of romance. My parents weren't in love when they married? What kind of heresy was that?!

134

I'm not advocating jumping into a mediocre marriage. As my parents say, marriage is hard enough without marrying someone to whom you feel little attraction. However, the state of "being in love" is not some sort of marriage guarantee. It does not "hallow" a marriage or make it more meaningful. Yes, love should be the basis for our relationships, but are we talking about true love, which is an attitude and an action according to God's design, or are we talking about the things commonly mistaken for love: affection, attraction, feelings, or emotions?

Often, people use "being in love" to test whether or not they should get married: "Well, are we in love? Then let's get married!" People assume that this feeling is the same as a commitment to being faithful and loving, so "being in love" becomes the basis for their relationship, when really it should be the result of a committed relationship. The commitment should come first, then the passion. After all, why waste passion on a relationship that is not committed?

If we ran our relationships with God this way, no one would be Christian. If I were to wait until I get passion for God before I committed my life to Him, then I would have no relationship with God because the passion simply doesn't come until I have given myself away to Him. I do not always feel like following God, but I do not (and should not) base my relationship on my feelings. Our emotions go up and down from day to day. Using passions as a meter to test the healthiness of a relationship is one of the biggest lies of our culture. The test of true love is whether we will look at the lack of feeling and say, "It doesn't matter how I feel. It matters whether I continue doing my duty." Some people would say that sounds so crude. It's a crudity that has saved marriages and resulted in beautiful relationships.

If we rely on our emotions, then when those emotions fail us, we feel like victims: "The love drained out of my relationship somehow!" But if we rely on the definition of true love—duty, sacrifice, service, and forgiveness—we can see clearly that we are not victims of love's whims. Love does not plant itself and pluck itself up. We ourselves are the gardeners of love and we either plant it or we pluck it up. Love is a choice; what do we choose?

135

3. True love sees potential; false love expects fireworks.

The problem with trusting the state of "being in love" is that people turn up their noses at the thought of marrying for any other reason than "love." If "love" is the only thing upon which we base marriage, then the intention to marry "only for love" can backfire. We might pass up a relationship with someone whom we would have actually grown to love very much if we'd given the relationship a chance to grow. People whom I first considered unattractive or uninteresting have ended up becoming more attractive and interesting to me as I got to know them better. If my parents had decided they would only marry for passionate "love," I wouldn't even exist, because their "disgust at first sight" love story would have never had a chance to blossom.

Many women have bypassed the quiet growth of love in favor of the fireworks, and therefore bypassed a good and godly man. Why do they do this? Because they lack patience. False love wants instant gratification; true love is willing to wait and to watch. A foolish woman expects love to shout through a megaphone; a wise woman keeps still enough to hear love even if it whispers.

4. True love places righteousness before the relationship; false love places the relationship before righteousness.

"Love" is used as an excuse for many evils. There is a defiance to "being in love," a belief in which it doesn't matter what sort of crimes are committed, so long as those things were done for the sake of "love." If people endure all sorts of punishment and persecution because of their obedience to the criminal demands of "love," they feel like martyrs. Ninety-nine percent of our movies and media reinforce that "being in love" is some kind of get-out-of-jail-free card when it comes to unethical or immoral behavior.

False love looks to "love" to call the shots, and it places the relationship above all other considerations. True love looks to God to call the shots and places Him above the relationship. When my father asked for my mother's hand in marriage, he strongly believed that the Bible taught that a father's blessing is crucial to the marriage. My father and mother were both adults living outside of their parents' homes, so Mom was not even under her father's roof anymore. Still, my father was firm. He told my mother that if her father did not like the match, then they could not marry. Their entire relationship rode on her father's blessing. Thankfully, her father agreed to the match. I have always admired my father's spirit in this story. He was in his thirties, he really wanted to get married, he had found a wonderful woman, but he was prepared to give up what might have been his last chance to marry, in order to keep a clean conscience before God. *That* is precisely the difference between true love and false love.

Our longing for "love" might blind us to both opportunities and dangers. That is why, when it comes to serious relationships, we can't just "follow our hearts." The Bible says that our hearts are deceitful and desperately wicked.[205] Rather than followed, our hearts should be led by God's Truth.

5. True love evaluates the spiritual attractiveness of others; false love evaluates only the physical attractiveness of others.

People often complain about the "sexual objectification" of women. Models who are famous for their bodies condition men to think of women in a sexual way. We women are no more holy than men; if we don't keep our minds under Godly control, we can end up just like that.

I've heard girls say things like, "Oh my goodness, look at that guy! He is *so* hot! *So* cute!" If a girl thinks a guy is "hot" because of his looks, she is devaluing him because she is not taking into account all the other things that makes him a special person—his relationship with Christ, his personality, his inner spirit, his talents, his experiences, his beliefs. We shouldn't squeal "Oh, he's so cute!" in the same way that we'd squeal over a puppy or a pair of shoes that we liked; we should value him as a unique individual and, especially, as a Godly man. Flippant comments about a guy's sexiness or good looks show that we do not treat men with dignity or see them through Christ-like eyes.

Most importantly, a guy's worth is based on more than "hotness" or personal appeal. It is based on his relationship with God. When the prophet Samuel went to pick a replacement for

---

[205] Jeremiah 17:9

King Saul, who had displeased God, Samuel looked for all the wrong characteristics. God had told Samuel that one of Jesse's sons would be the new king, so when Samuel saw Jesse's oldest son, Eliab, who looked strong and tall and handsome, he thought, "This has *got* to be the king!" But God said: "Look not on his countenance, nor on the height of his stature; because I have refused him: for the Lord seeth not as man seeth; for man looketh on the outward appearance, but the Lord looketh on the heart."[206] God chose Jesse's youngest son, David, a young man who was not very big or impressive but who loved God with all his heart.

Looking into a man's heart is not something we can do instantly the way God can, but when we try to know a guy as a friend and a brother in Christ (not even as a potential "candidate"), we will get deeper and deeper glimpses into his heart. I would hope that we would look beyond the Eliabs to appreciate the Davids. If we are looking for a guy who is "hot" in terms of being Christ-like, then we are truly valuing a guy in the right way.

6. True love centers on a relationship; false love centers on an action.

A girl once told me that her first kiss had been very special to her. I knew that she had been kissed many times by many new boyfriends. I didn't doubt that her first kiss was very special—how could a first kiss be anything but special?—but I felt that her experience missed something important: The kiss itself had been more important than the person with whom she had shared that kiss. That special moment had been shared with someone that she'll never think of again, except to remember, "Oh yeah. He was the first guy I ever kissed. He's not part of my life now, but I'll never forget that special kiss!"

That's what false love offers. It promises to fulfill our physical or emotional desires, but does not offer us a *relationship*. When false love is the motivator, we don't care for the specific relationship as much as we care about a thing, an act, a feeling, a memory. When it comes to your first kiss, shouldn't there be more to it than just a

---

[206] 1 Samuel 16:7

random pair of lips? Shouldn't that kiss come with something more than just passion? How about a whole person who loves you and who has committed his life to you and to whom you have also committed your life? In God's design, the relationship is not about physical intimacy, but the physical intimacy is about the relationship.

7. True love centers on the person; false love centers on achieving a desired state of life.

Many women plan their weddings long before the event actually takes place. They know the décor of their reception, the style of their wedding dress, and the details of their dream honeymoon. The only thing that's missing? A husband. We want to be married, but we spend more time thinking about the marriage than the person. That seems backwards to me. Marriage is not about a condition of life; it's about the other spouse.

If you ask a true Christian what Christianity means to her, she won't say, "Being a Christian means I'm saved." She would say, "Being a Christian means I have a relationship with Jesus Christ!" Being saved is wonderful, but she has matured and now realizes that loving and knowing Jesus Christ is the best part of being a Christian. She loves the *person* in her life more than she loves the *condition* of her life.

Marriage is a good desire and, since we don't know the identity of our future husbands, it's a good idea not to have specific expectations about our husbands. But once we're married, we have to remember to find a special joy in our *particular* men, not just in the fact that we're married. Marriage is specific to each couple. Many unhappy women have been married, but a happy woman loves the man—not the marriage. A bride has not simply joined the ranks of married people; she has united with one special man.

8. True love commits; false love leaves a way out.

Suppose we hear about two people who sacrifice for each other, serve each other, and do everything with each other. They even live together, but they aren't married. Is this really love? Perhaps there is some love, but the core of love is missing. What is the core of love? Commitment. Without the commitment that comes with marriage, the commitment that clearly states, "I will have an exclusive relationship with you and I will be faithful for life," these two people have not put the seal of true love on their relationship. They have left the back door open "just in case."

True love has no back door, no contingency plan, no pre-arrangement for "what happens if this relationship doesn't work out." True love demands full-hearted commitment on God's terms. True love commits and keeps that commitment. Although every healthy relationship requires commitment, marriage requires a commitment unlike any other commitment. Even Christians today walk into marriage believing that their good intentions and their "I dos" equal commitment. Only one thing equals commitment: A clear understanding before God that, barring death, this relationship is *permanent*. Period.

Of course this is easier said than done, but I know people who have practiced this kind of commitment. I know marriages that commitment has saved. If we hope to get married, we need to fully grasp the importance of commitment and determine to start practicing now in our family relationships. If we cannot love our own flesh and blood, people who will be a part of us no matter how estranged we may become, how can we commit to anyone else?

9. True love is serious about relationships; false love is casual about relationships.

The one thing that a relationship should never be is casual, no matter what kind of relationship it is. If a young woman were to tell me that she wants a boyfriend but doesn't want (or isn't ready for) a serious relationship, all my warning bells would go off. I would ask her, "What is your motivation for having a relationship? Are you looking for what you can get—or what you can give?" Even in basic friendship, I have a commitment and a responsibility to look out for my friends' good, to encourage them in righteousness, to speak the truth in love to them, and to protect their physical and emotional health as I would protect my own. I have no right to treat the relationship lightly.

This is especially true in a romantic relationship. When a guy and a girl want a special relationship with no commitment and no clear future for that relationship, they need to look ahead at the possible implications of their actions. "Wait, if we act like we have a special, exclusive relationship, but we have no definite ideas about where our relationship is going, are we just in a relationship so we can say that we 'have somebody'? If we're not serious about each other (i.e. considering each other for marriage), why can't we simply be good friends?"

No relationship—whether with a family member, a spouse, a friend, and especially a romantic interest—is insignificant. We need to consider every relationship carefully. Is it a relationship worth having? And if it is, are we "winging it" or are we behaving with commitment and responsibility?

Recognizing Love

To sum up: True love requires acts of service and an attitude of patience, looks for potential, glorifies righteousness and spiritual attractiveness, centers on self-sacrificially serving the other person, and offers sober commitment. If it is about how we can serve God and serve another person, that is love. If it is about how we can get some kind of satisfaction from another person, then it is false love. False love says, "I love you," while saying "I need you and I want you." True love says, "I love you," while saying, "I will serve you and I will do what is best for you."

Thou shalt love thy neighbor as thyself.[207]

---

[207] Matthew 22:39

‱ 14 ‱

Some Dangers of Romance Stories

Romance might be defined this way: *A romance story focuses on the development of a relationship between a man and a woman who are attracted to each other and who wish to or eventually begin a romantic relationship.* A story may contain elements of romance even if it is not labeled a romance. Many romance novels now disguise themselves as historical fiction, science fiction, fantasy, or modern fiction. We can distinguish whether a book is actually a romance at heart by asking ourselves the following questions:

- Is the main character seeking a romantic relationship throughout the action of the story?
- Does the story focus primarily upon the actions of two characters who are romantically attracted to each other?
- Are we disappointed if something disturbs the relationship between two people in the story?
- Do we spend the whole story waiting for two characters to "get together" or get married?
- Does the book often mention the words *love* or *marriage*?

Many works can be identified as having romantic elements. Jane Austen novels are romances. Some Shakespeare plays (such as *Romeo and Juliet* or *A Midsummer Night's Dream*) are romances. Amish romances are (obviously) romances. Even Song of Solomon from the Bible is a romance.

It is important to realize that not all books with romantic elements are bad; the afore-mentioned Song of Solomon is an example of an appropriate romance. However, many romantic stories that seem innocent can scar our purity or can lead to unrealistic expectations, even without our knowledge. That is why we need to be discerning and we need to identify whether or not a book is worth our time to read.

The Six Dangers of Romance

There are six main dangers to the genre of romance.

1. We create the action ourselves.

What makes a tempting book more dangerous than, say, a tempting movie? Both are foolish to view, in my opinion, but written materials have a unique danger because they involve us in the action. When we watch a movie, we passively soak in the action; all the actions, characters, visuals, and sounds are already supplied for us, so we don't have to do a thing to create the action. However, when we read a book, we use the description of the action to form pictures and sounds in our minds. Of course, the author has given us the recipe for how to create the action, but we are the ultimate creator. We become part of the action. When *our* imaginations become the vehicle for creating a story and when *our* minds work to bring the story to life in our minds, how much harder is it to delete that scene from our minds? How much more responsible are we for any bad pictures that form in our minds?

2. Romances focus on the pursuit of "love."

Another danger is the tendency to focus on the wrong things. Romances tend to glorify the relationship between a man and a woman and to make "true love" the focus of all pursuits. These stories perpetuate the idea that somehow people are more complete if they are successful in attracting the attention of someone else. We always feel as if something is "missing" if the main character has not yet attracted a partner. Great emphasis is placed on emotional needs: finding "someone who will understand," filling the void of loss, securing a happy future, overcoming fear of close relationships. These stories give us the feeling that "if only they get together by the end," everything will turn out all right. This focus is not consistent with the Bible's teaching. The Bible emphasizes over and over that the only true fulfillment comes from an intimate relationship with Christ, not with another person.

3. Romances encourage unrealistic expectations.

Whether or not we know it, books that center on romantic relationships often lead us to expect certain things out of a "truly good relationship" (stability, sympathy, companionship, satisfying intimacy, and so on). There's a hint of "happily ever after" to the story. We expect that a few minor disagreements may crop up every now and then, but nothing serious will enter the relationship. This mindset reinforces our expectations for certain things—things that no human being can reasonably give to us—and when we don't get those things, we feel cheated.

Our future husbands will not be like the men in books. They won't always know the right thing to say, they won't always be romantic, they won't always recognize an opportunity to be sympathetic or sensitive, they won't always lead in the way that we want. They will have irritating idiosyncrasies and frustrating faults. They will be as much men of reality as those heroes are works of fiction. If we look at fictional relationships as a pattern for real-life relationships, we could absorb unrealistic expectations that will prevent us from being able to truly bond with our future husbands.

5. Romances often skip marriage.

Romances give the false idea that marriage is supposed to be some kind of perpetual romance, a permanent continuance of all the passion that courtship ignited. This effect is achieved by rarely dealing with life after marriage. In fact, a great deal (or all) of the book is spent leading up to the inevitable marriage at the end. The satisfying nuptial scene at the end leaves the readers with a feeling of "happily ever after."

The genre, it seems, has picked up on an embarrassing truth— that people consider "romance" to happen mostly before the wedding, not afterward. The story of how people meet and fall in love is infinitely more interesting than how they keep their marriage together over the rest of their lifetimes. Even after the heroine is successfully married off, there is a desire to get back to that idyllic pre-marriage excitement. Therefore, the author conveniently reconciles the situation by doing away with the husband, offering an opportunity for a second young man to console the grieving widow and eventually fall in love with her. Then, of course, the author skips the years of childbearing and childrearing; who wants to hear about marital quarrels, endless dirty diapers, and the drudgery of daily life? The author then focuses on the daughter of the happily-married couple, the daughter who will, of course, begin her own journey to romance.

When I watched my friends begin to pair off, I noticed a disturbing trend. Most people were very interested in each other's romances only up until the time when two people got safely engaged. When a relationship became a "done deal," there was no more tension or speculation and the romance-seekers transferred their attention to the people who were still forming relationships. Of course, the rockier the relationship, the more people wanted to hear about it. I realized that this was exactly the type of excitement that romance novels offered. A straightforward courtship and engagement never sells as well as a tangled and strained relationship, a love triangle, and numerous obstacles. A generally decent, steady lover never excites passions as well as the charming daredevil, the man with the mysterious past, the downtrodden sufferer, or the forbidden lover. The stories of the daily trials of keeping a marriage together never sell as well as the stories where we wonder which of the two eligible bachelors our heroine will pick. Through this constant reinforcement of the excitement of courtship and the continual promises that the marriage will be just as rosy, we are taught that courtship is the most exciting and fulfilling time of our relationships. So we train for the courtship and ignore the marriage.

6. Romances tend to "demote" God.

When you read a story with romantic elements, does the couple seem more concerned about keeping a healthy relationship with God than with keeping a healthy relationship with each other? I know many Christian romances attempt to focus on God, but often He's just a side character. Sometimes, He's even demoted from a side character to an afterthought. ("Oh yeah, let's ask God to bless our relationship.") Other times, He's dropped in favor of "basically Christian values." For instance, I read an article about the author of romance novels that were filled with graphic scenes, but she protested that her books were moral because the characters always got married within the first few chapters, so most of the scenes were between husband and wife. I don't know about you, but I don't need to know the details of someone's intimate relationship—

whether they are married or not! "Basic moral values" don't cut it when you're talking about the relationship that is the earthly expression of Christ's relationship with us.

People think that a relationship is "Godly" if the couple asks God to bless the relationship, if they pray together, or if they read the Bible together. Those are all important things, but they don't prove that a relationship is centered around the Lord. A relationship that is truly centered around the Lord involves not just Christian activities, but complete submission to the Lord. It requires two people who are willing to sacrifice everything—yes, even their desire to be with each other—in order to see God better glorified in their lives. The Lord comes first; the relationship follows afterward. Unfortunately, a lot of romance novels have plot lines that center around questions like, "Can God bring them together?" instead of questions like, "Can they submit to the Lord even when His plans may differ from their desires?" We can't squeeze the Lord and Christian values into our relationships. We must shape all our relationships around the Lord.

Christian Romance

I have to be honest: I have not been impressed with most of the Christian romance novels that I've read so far. Their view of love is similar to the world's view of love and God seems like an afterthought or a garnish. Here are a few examples from novels by well-known Christian authors.

Example One: A young woman commits to marry only within the faith (as she should). When she meets a handsome young nonbeliever, she tells him that she can never marry a non-Christian, but admits that she loves him and will never marry another man. This is a very foolish choice! The Lord says clearly that we are not to be unequally yoked;[208] that is, that Christians should not have close relationships with non-Christians. The woman was right to say "No" to a marriage between herself and the non-believer, but why did she then give her heart to him? A Christian woman should *not* give her heart to a man who has not given *his* heart to God. She

---

[208] 2 Corinthians 6:14

146

should save her heart for the man who can love her with a Christ-like love. She should not flirt with the idea of loving a man who can offer her nothing more than worldly passion.

Example Two: A non-Christian man exhibits immoral behavior toward a young woman. I suspect that the author intended this scene to portray the young man's godless lifestyle, to contrast it with his life after conversion. The motive was worthy, but the method of execution was dangerous. Instead of delicately passing over the details of the young man's impure life, the author included the intimate and sensual details of the passionate kiss that the main character shares with his love interest. An author can write about an action without including details that make the action seem appealing and without sparking tempting thoughts in readers. In other words, an author can represent sin without glorifying sin. The Bible includes stories of many sins but it never presents the sin in a way that tempts. Yes, sin is appealing, but need we be so realistic that we tempt people to mentally flirt with sin? This is *not* the work of someone who truly respects the purity of Christian readers.

Example Three: The heroine has valid concerns about entering a relationship with a young man, who continues to pursue her. At one point, he is injured and is temporarily incapable of understanding and reacting to his imminent danger. In order to "wake him up" to reality, the heroine can think of no other recourse than to kiss him. As a result, he follows her to safety. The woman has foolishly initiated physical contact in a non-committed relationship. Although she continues to show reluctance to enter a relationship, couldn't her kiss be interpreted as a sign that she is re-thinking her values or willing to pursue a closer relationship? Having kissed the man once, won't she be more open to doing so again? In real life, if we once take a step toward compromise, it is easier to take that next step, and the next. One degree of deviation can become an enormous difference over time.

Example Four: A man pursues a relationship with a young woman inappropriately. In one scene, drunken and depressed, he grabs her and roughly kisses her. In response, she tries to speak gently to him. This is the precise moment when we should *shut someone down!* When a man acts inappropriately toward a woman, it is *not* the time for the woman to be gentle, or to concern herself with

147

his emotions. If she does not leave the situation, she runs a great risk of allowing her sensitivity to compromise her purity.

Example Five: A young man becomes convinced that Christianity is true, but he is afraid that his love interest will think that his acceptance is made in the hopes of winning her love, rather than because he is convicted of the truth. Essentially, he refuses to give his life to Christ because he is afraid that she will misunderstand his motives for doing so. Of course, the book happily resolves this situation; the man believes that the woman has died in a tragic circumstance, but she miraculously survives, finds that he has converted, and they get married. This is the worst lesson by far. Why would anyone risk his eternal soul for fear of losing the respect and love of a human being? Why would he put himself in danger of God's judgment because he is afraid that his motives for accepting Christ may be misunderstood? If that is his fear, his motives truly *are* wrong!

There are many more common and concerning threads in romance stories, such as secretly meeting and carrying on a relationship without parental knowledge or consent, emotionally or physically entangling one's self before committing to a relationship, or emotionally stringing along various suitors because of an inability to decide which one is best. All of these make for entertaining stories, but exhibit very destructive patterns if followed in real life.

But wait! Aren't messy relationships true to life? Can't a story show realistic relational mistakes and difficulties? My answer: Sure. But if it does so, it had better show realistic consequences too. So far, I haven't seen much of that in romantic fiction.

Sugar-coated Lies?

I didn't always feel this way about books with romantic elements. My research started when I read a magazine article in which a wife confessed that the romance novels she had read as a young woman led her to expect more from her marriage relationship than was realistic or right. Romance novels damaged her marriage before she ever reached the altar. I did not want to be that woman, so I thought hard about what she had written.

Some people call romance novels "women's pornography." When I first heard that idea, it shocked me and I thought that people were overreacting. However, the more I look into the issue, the more I realize that these books have the potential to do just as much damage to a marriage as pornography. They can ignite expectations that lead to dissatisfaction; the perfect dream world might become more appealing than a good reality. They can also reinforce unwise, vulnerable mindsets that have the potential to become ticking time bombs in our marriages. I don't want my marriage—or yours—to be the next victim. You might not agree with my position on romance novels, but please give the matter a *serious* look. Your future marriage could be at stake.

℘ 15 ℴ

Realistic Relationships

When I was in my mid-teens, I really wanted a Belgian Sheepdog. For two years, I researched everything I could about Belgians. I called breeders. I reviewed styles and pedigrees and genetic diseases. I looked into dog shows and breeding. I thought I had it all figured out. One day, it became clear that this was not the right time in my life to have a dog. I was bitterly disappointed, angry, and sad.

When I look back on that time now, I realize that if God had let me have my way, my life would have been extremely complicated by a dog. College and work soon consumed so much of my life that I would have neglected my dog. Thankfully, my family later got a dog so I could enjoy canine companionship without all the personal responsibility. It took years for all of this to become clear to me, but once I understood it, I realized that God really *does* know best.

Many women have daydreamed about the perfect courtship and marriage, but many have found that neither courtship nor marriage matched up to their expectations. Many have been disappointed that the real guy didn't end up being like their dream guy and their real marriage didn't end up being like their dream marriage. Yet if we had never daydreamed in the first place, we would not have been so disappointed. The real thing might be very beautiful and very exciting in its own way, but we don't always recognize it because we're too busy comparing it with the thing that we expected.

With that in mind, here are some ways in which we ladies might build up expectations that could later disappoint us and harm our marriages.

Expectation #1: Marriage is an escape hatch.

Suppose a young woman really hates it when her father seems unsympathetic to her feelings and he brushes her off when she wants to talk about things that she feels are important. She struggles with resentment, mentally reminding herself that she will never marry a man who won't listen to her. Years later, she marries a man who is an excellent listener and who is happy to spend time talking about the things she feels are important. After some time has gone by, however, she is really bothered by her husband's habit of coming home and watching television even when it is obvious that she needs help with things around the house. She remembers that her father, for all his faults, had been great at helping out her mother. She tells her feelings to her husband, but he makes excuses and there is little change in his behavior. The young woman had thought that marriage would be an escape from a particular frustration. Now she realizes that she has actually exchanged one frustration for a different frustration. This time, she can't get married to escape her current frustration; she already *is* married, for life!

We may be tempted to think that marriage will bring the glorious change we always wanted. I caught myself one day as I thought about something that made me feel uncomfortable and inadequate. I wished that I could feel more confident in my abilities and skills. I thought, *Well, someday I won't feel this incompetent; I'll just know what I'm doing.* Something (or Someone) made me stop and examine this thought more closely. I found out that "someday" meant "when I'm married." I had thought that when I got married, I would feel more confident, more competent, and more comfortable with the daily pressures of life.

Where did I get *that* idea from?

Many single women assume that marriage will suddenly cause some dramatic, wonderful change in their lives. They expect to feel more mature, more in control of things, and more skilled than ever before. What a shock when they get married and feel like they've always felt!

Marriage, by itself, will not make the changes that we want to see. We have to make those changes ourselves, to the best of our ability, with God's help and with the Bible to guide us. Don't wait for marriage to make you the person you should be; work to become that person now. That way, whether married or single, we have the mindset we need to face *all* situations and to make the best of them.

151

Expectation #2: Marriage will fulfill all our desires.

Many women have entered marriage believing that their days of loneliness, sexual desire, and spiritual dryness are over. When they *do* face loneliness, unfulfilled sexual desires, and the same old spiritual battles, they think there must be something wrong with their marriage. There isn't anything wrong with their marriage, but there is something wrong with their expectations.

Marriage will never fulfill all of our desires. One of the worst things we can do is daydream about what it will be like to be married. Our fantasies ultimately will not come close to the reality. The reality might be a good and sweet thing, but if we expect something different, we will fail to notice and appreciate that good and sweet thing. When we daydream, we make up little husbands and situations for ourselves, but those daydream-husbands are designed to make us feel good and they always react the right way in any given situation. They do not make demands on us, require us to sacrifice, have irritating habits, or have the flaws or roughness of real-life people in real-life situations. In short, daydream-husbands are just extensions of our desires, our wants for ourselves, and are therefore just another way for us to view marriage as "all about me!" instead of all about the other person, as it should be.

Emotional Needs

Sometimes we believe that getting married means that we will have a forever friend who will be attentive, caring, compassionate, and thoughtful. There are two major flaws in this way of thinking. First, we expect a human being to provide a level of companionship and closeness that only Jesus Christ can give. After all, He is the *only* one who will never disappoint us, never let us down, never misunderstand us, and never do something that would be bad for us.

If our husbands expected us to be their ultimate companions and to fulfill all of their emotional needs, we would never be able to fulfill all of those desires. So why do we think husbands can do that for us? It isn't fair to God or our husbands to expect a human to do something only God can do and it isn't fair to ourselves to expect a kind of husband that we can never have. These expectations are unfair to everybody.

Our husbands will not always understand us. They will not always be available at the times when we want them. They will not always give us the emotional support we want. They will not always be the friends we want them to be. They might want to be all those things, but they can never live up to our expectations, because they are human beings. Also, as much as we might want to be all those things for our husbands, we can never live up to their expectations either.

Furthermore, do we really want our husbands to be the "perfect" companion? What about those times when we think that we need loving, tender, emotional support, but we actually need tough love? If our husbands were gentle and patient and understanding all the time, could it be possible that this would make us very self-centered and bossy? What about those times when it's not our husbands' job to support us emotionally but our job to support them? Our desires for a perfect companion can be very selfish. As my mother once said, "You must give, never ever expecting anything in return."

Physical Needs

There's a temptation to think that when we get married and have a Biblical outlet for our physical needs, we will no longer struggle with any type of sexual temptation. It doesn't work that way. If it did, why do so many people commit adultery? Divorce? Separate? Look at pornography? Have unfulfilling marriages? Obviously there are many reasons for why relationships aren't perfect, but it's certainly true that the expectation for fully satisfying intimacy can cause people to feel discontented with their marriage relationships. A married woman once told me that she still has to clamp down on her thoughts sometimes. Another married woman, speaking about romance novel relationships, said, "You think we married women don't long for that type of relationship too? It's not just unmarried women who have those feelings!" There will be times in our future marriages when our husbands "aren't enough." We'll still have to squash discontented or tempting thoughts. Marriage can help to satisfy the need for physical intimacy, but marriage is not a perfect "safe haven" from all temptation.

Spiritual Needs

We all have spiritual needs, but it's not a man's job to fill them. It's God's. Of course, a husband should be a spiritual leader in his home, as the Bible indicates, but he is only a man. God may give him a door into your heart, but only God Himself can do the real work. A husband—just like any other man—will not always impress us with his spiritual life or his zeal for the Lord. Guess what? We won't always impress him with ours, either. If a human being supplied the answers to our spiritual needs, would we ever desire to seek the Lord on our own? Would we ever truly step out in faith? I believe it is dangerous to be our husbands' conscience or spiritual policeman. We need to be careful to distinguish between encouraging him in the Lord and forcing him to be "spiritual." When Michal scolded David for dancing without enough clothing on, she—not David—was judged.[209] She tried to be more spiritual than David and reaped bitter consequences. It is not our job to lead our men spiritually; it is our job to *support* them spiritually.

Expectation #3: Marriage will meet our ideals.

Looks

One day at my young adult Bible study, a visitor told his love story. He said that he had a specific picture in his mind of his future spouse—her hair, her height, her eye color, even her nationality. He met many women who fit all of his criteria but the most important one: a completely devoted relationship with the Lord. He was disappointed, but he couldn't compromise. One day, he met a girl as he was working at a mission. Everything about her was exactly opposite of his dream girl—everything but one thing. Her love for the Lord was genuine and infectious. The young man realized that he could not lose her and he soon asked her to marry him. As he concluded his story, he added, "You young people, you might have your own ideas, but you don't know what God has for you. His spouse for you might seem all wrong, but it will be the right person for you."

My own parents had a similar love story. They call it "disgust at

---

[209] 2 Samuel 6:16-23

first sight." Dad was in his thirties, a short ex-hippie with thick glasses and a receding hairline that was gradually eating away at his luxuriant, shoulder-length, curly dark hair. Mom thought: "Who is that weirdo?" Mom was a petite average-looking undergraduate from a completely different background. Dad thought: "Totally not my type." Despite their differences, they had three main things in common: their short stature, their love of hiking, and their committed faith in the Lord. Two years after they first met, they got married.

Sometimes my friends and I joke about what kind of husbands we would like to have. We compare our ideals of height, weight, physical features, and last names. However, we understand that we don't always know what is best for ourselves. Perhaps the Lord will give us husbands that are different than our ideals, but who are the right husbands for us.

We should remember too that we might not meet our future husbands' ideals. My husband will probably have to adjust his expectations for a wife as much as I'll have to adjust mine for a husband. If the Lord plans marriage for your future, expect that He will both rearrange your expectations and do above and beyond what you could ask or think.[210]

Personality

There's danger in expecting a future husband to look a certain way, but there's also danger in expecting him to act a certain way. For example, I once read a magazine article in which one woman wished her husband would bring her flowers, even though he was helpful with the baby. Her friend, whose husband always brought her flowers, wished that her own husband would help to change the baby's diaper. In the end, both women had to learn to be grateful for their own husbands' kindnesses.

As a newlywed, my mother hoped that sometime Dad would surprise her with a date and whisk her away to a cozy little diner. She soon learned that Dad just isn't that type. He loves to please his wife, but scheduling is not his talent. On the other hand, Dad has

---

[210] Ephesians 3:20

always been willing to cook meals, repair the house and vehicles, patch the plumbing, supervise the homeschooling, care for the kids, and be Mom's special handyman. Mom learned to be gracious about those things that were not Dad's specialty and to be grateful for those things that were.

We might have ideas of what we'd like our husbands to do, but we can't expect that they will fulfill those ideas. To be fair, they'll probably have lots of ideas of what they'd like us to do and, unfortunately, we won't live up to some of those expectations. We should practice acceptance and gratitude in our current family relationships, so that we can respond to our future husbands with kindness.

Situation

A friend of mine once quipped, "If you want to see your husband, don't marry him!" Before she married, she and her fiancé were able to find time for each other. After the wedding, as her husband worked third shift and she worked during the day, they seemed to have little time to connect. Marriage was not what she had envisioned. Thankfully, she was prepared for the difficulties, but her expectations still had to be adjusted.

The same friend admitted that when she was living as a single in her parents' home, she wished that her other family members would take more pride in an organized, tidy home. When she got married, she discovered that she did not always have the opportunity or the energy to keep her home clean. Her friends who visited were amazed. "Hey, hon, what happened? I always thought you were the neat-nick at your house!" My friend wondered: Did her mother once have good intentions too?

Within weeks after their wedding, my parents found out that I was on the way. All of Mom's dreams of being an available and able helper disappeared in a wave of nausea. Unbeknownst to my parents, my mom had gotten mononucleosis before her marriage. Once pregnant, she also got extreme morning sickness (which, unfortunately, lasted the whole day). Instead of coming home from her part-time job and cooking Dad yummy meals, she crawled into bed while he called out from the kitchen, "What do you want me to cook for you tonight, honey?" Often Mom was so nauseous that

Dad ate his culinary creations by himself. By the time Mom and Dad moved to another house, just prior to my birth, they hadn't even unpacked the boxes from their first move.

That was only the start of their marital misadventures. Six kids, many jobs, several obstacles, and a couple homes and states later, my mother has now accepted the one important rule of her marriage: "Hold onto my man and hang tight for the ride!"

Hold your hopes for your future marriage lightly. Learn to be flexible as a single, and your husband may one day bless the wonderful adaptability of his special woman.

Expectation #4: Marriage will stay the same over time.

At one wedding that I attended, the pastor said, "Now, husband, you need to understand that your wife will not always have her girlish figure. Wife, sorry to say, but your guy won't always have abs of steel. You'll both change." We all chuckled, but every married person in the crowd knew it was true!

There's a host of changes that can happen between "now" and "then" and we have to be prepared for that. I know wives that have had to deal with their husbands' illness or health condition, major changes in their husbands' income, and more. Husbands may also change in personality or beliefs too. They might become more conservative or more relaxed. They might become more active in ministry or they might need to minister in less vigorous ways. They might change their views on a certain Biblical doctrine. They might become more intense or more gentle. They might become more vocal in leadership or they might become leaders by example. One thing is certain: People change. We will change too. We can't expect that our relationships in marriage—any more than our relationships with anyone else—will remain the same over time.

Expectation #5: Bad things happen to other people.

One morning in July, I wrote:

This morning, at 6:40 a.m., the phone rang. It was "J" and she said that "A" is gone. He went during the night and she doesn't know how to tell the children that their daddy went to be with Jesus forever...

I went into my bedroom and cried and prayed... I understood now...that the perfect love story or the perfect marriage does not happen on earth. It was something that I had always known in my head, but not in my heart. "J" is living that reality right now... Even if it had been the perfect marriage, it was as fragile and transient as a spider's web.

How do you know if, once you have something, you will be able to keep it? How do you know that you can live with your beloved spouse until ripe old age? Everything could be snuffed out in a minute.

What if this young woman's story becomes your story? What if this is my story? Can we say, like Job in the Bible, "The Lord gives and the Lord takes away; blessed is the name of the Lord"?[211]

Many women enter marriage thinking that they have finally come through all the chaotic feelings and frustrations of singleness into a place of marital stability. Nothing could be further from the truth. Every marriage has its own problems, some of them within the relationship itself and some of them from outside sources that affect the relationship. Either way, things happen. Everyone thinks that tragedies happen to "other people." What if *you* are that "other person"? Are you prepared?

I personally know wives who have weathered all of the following: constant poverty-level income; serious injury to the family's primary breadwinner (husband) which resulted in job loss; homelessness; a nasty church split that resulted in the loss of many friends; irreversible infertility; repeated miscarriage or stillbirth; tragic loss of some or all of their children; abandonment and infidelity of the husband; prolonged and debilitating illness in either the husband or the wife (or both); a life-threatening disease, such as cancer, in either the husband or wife (or both); estrangement from grown children; permanent paralysis due to an accident; and more. Imagine yourself as the wife in each scenario. How would you respond to your circumstances?

I don't intend to depress you. I just want to show real life. We can't spend our lives fearful of the "what-ifs," but we have to be prepared for reality. What if you cannot bear children? What if your husband cannot father children? What if you lose a child? What if

---

[211] Job 1:21

God calls you to move far away from your home and family? What if you face extreme financial difficulties? What if your husband loses his job? What if you become homeless? What if you lose all your possessions due to a disaster? What if one of you gets ill? Becomes paralyzed? Contracts a long-term disease? Battles depression or an addiction? Endures an amputation? Dies? Are you ready and willing to face the broken dreams and the marital challenges that might accompany any one of these scenarios?

Only one thing is certain in this life, and that is the Lord Jesus Christ. We might have to deal with problems that we thought we would never face. The only way to prepare our hearts is to trust the Lord with our whole life and with the lives of our loved ones, and then to live out that trust day by day, knowing that the Lord works all things together for good.[212] Sometimes we can't see the good that God is bringing out of pain, frustration, sorrow, and disappointment, but He gives a promise in Ecclesiastes that has been a tremendous comfort to me: *He hath made every thing beautiful in his time.*[213]

I've heard it said that pain in the midst of beauty can be compared to broken glass. God picks up the pieces of shattered glass and puts them together, and makes a stained-glass window through which His light can shine even more beautifully than before. He is glorified through our pain, just as we were made righteous through Christ's pain on the cross. No matter what challenges our marriages might have to overcome or what losses we might face, we know that we have a loving God who knows what it is to suffer. We know that when we trust completely in Him, He will give us the strength we need to face any difficulty. Only He knows how to guide us through the field of broken dreams to the place of perfect peace.

Radical Women

Richard Wurmbrand was a Jewish Romanian minister who knew what it meant to suffer for Christ, but Richard was not the only one with daring faith. His wife Sabina and son Mihai also

---

[212] Romans 8:28
[213] Ecclesiastes 3:11a

denied themselves for Christ. In his book, *Tortured for Christ*, Richard describes how Communism took over Romania. The church ministers, bishops, and pastors publicly declared that communism and Christianity were basically the same, and they pledged loyalty to the Communist government. Hearing these statements, Sabina could not take it any more. She told her husband to speak and to restore God's stolen glory. He warned her that his boldness would equal her widowhood. She replied that she did not wish to be married to a coward.

Richard stood up, spoke, and spent the next 14 years in a Communist prison, enduring brutal and humiliating tortures. Meanwhile, his wife Sabina also suffered. She had to work at slave labor, eat grass to stay alive, endure torture and obscenity from women overseers, and accept the mockery of guards who made a cruel game of throwing her into the river and fishing her out again. She had lost everything—but not quite. After two years, she was allowed to see her 11-year-old son, who was earning his own living and whose faith had been shaken by suffering. He barely recognized her, but she immediately shouted for her son to believe in Jesus Christ, before the guards furiously wrenched her away. Mihai, weeping, realized that Christ must be true, since He could be loved despite such suffering. Mihai gave his life completely to the Lord, simply because of his mother's example of enduring faith.

Sabina's body was broken, but the Holy Spirit in her was unquenchable. We women want to hold on to our men and keep them safe. Sabina put her man directly in the firing line because she cared more about Christ's reputation than about her husband's safety. Even to an unmarried women like myself, this kind of devotion to the Lord is mind-shattering. If God were to give me a husband, could I risk losing him for the sake of my Lord? Would God's glory mean more to me than the person I love most?

We may think that God will never ask such a hard thing of us, but we do not know what may happen. Torture and separation were not in Sabina's mind on her wedding day, but she became a woman with one thought: Christ, first and foremost. Knowing this, she did not hesitate when the moment came to sacrifice; she had prepared her heart to give up everything for her Lord.

Sabina is not some special breed of Christian. She is what it *means* to be a Christian. Every true Christian woman is—and must be—a Sabina. In fact, the Sabina Wurmbrands of this world are called the spiritual daughters of another woman who lived thousands of years ago: Sarah, the wife of Abraham.[214]

Sarah was a woman who knew how to suffer. Based on a word of the Lord to her husband, she uprooted her life in Ur and followed her husband into a nomadic lifestyle in an unknown land. As far as we know, she never saw her family again. Furthermore, she could not bear children. For 90 years, she watched slave girls and sheep bear their own children. Where was the son that God had promised her and Abraham? For decades, she asked herself that question. Taking matters into her own hands and encouraging her husband to make her slave-girl Hagar into a surrogate mother only made her heart-ache worse. As soon as Hagar became pregnant by Abraham, she began to despise Sarah.

We often point out Sarah's flaws—her lack of faith in the promise and her temper toward Hagar—but I see her as a very human woman with a deep, open wound. After all that she and her husband had been through, it was too much to hope in a still-unfulfilled promise made decades ago, and too much for a slave girl to flaunt pregnancy in her face. When Sarah laughed at the Lord's promise that she would have a son within the year, I wonder if it was the laugh of a woman who would rather accept her pain than to continue to live with unfulfilled hope.

But God's goodness was not limited by Sarah's doubts. She conceived, carried, and bore a son. Despite her joy, the fulfillment of her greatest dream cost great pain; I suspect that, at 90 years old, pregnancy and natural birth were profoundly painful experiences. Still, I can only imagine her tears of gratitude and wonder when she finally held the son that had been promised twenty-four years earlier.

The Bible holds up Sarah as the primary example of a godly wife,[215] yet I can think of few women who would be willing to do what Sarah did. If our husbands told us to radically change our lives based on a word that they had heard from God, would we

---

[214] 1 Peter 3:5-6
[215] 1 Peter 3:1-6

trust them and honor their leadership? If our husbands led in a direction that required us never to see our families again, would we go with them? If we faced infertility, would our God and our husbands still be enough? Would we be patient enough to wait two and a half decades for the fulfillment of our greatest desire? Are we willing to have the faith of Sarah?

We are called to be women who are willing to turn our backs on everything we think we need to be happy, in order to find our happiness in the Lord. God may not require certain sacrifices of us, but we need to be willing to make them if He does. There is nothing half-way about a relationship with God. It's all or nothing. The question is: Are we willing to give everything?

Developing
a
Relationship

ঙ্গ 16 ৫

Appropriate Relationships

Now we come to the topic that many young ladies love to discuss: how to develop appropriate and God-honoring relationships with guys, especially with guys who might be "possibilities." On the purity end, how do we stay pure while developing a deeper relationship with a guy? On the expectations end, how do we prepare for fulfilling marriages while still being flexible enough to recognize a man who is a realistic (although imperfect) possibility? Should we even look for or consider possible "candidates" at all, or should we just wait for God to surprise us with a love story? How do we recognize "the one"? What can we do to prepare for a marriage that is not just mediocre, but excellent?

First, let's begin with a discussion about crushes. I've seen two main reactions from young ladies who ask my advice about crushes. The first is: "I want to tell you all about him, because he is the best thing that ever happened to me!" The second is: "Help me get over this quick! I'm panicking because I like this guy and I'm afraid that I shouldn't!" Honestly, both obsession and panic are risky and foolish responses to crushes. Let me explain why.

Crushes: Obsession

A young woman may not realize when she's obsessed, but she will betray herself. When she talks about "her special someone" constantly with her friends and sends long e-mails to people about him, that's obsession. When she constantly imagines conversations with him or imagines marrying him, that's obsession. When she arranges her schedule to make sure that she'll meet him, that's obsession. When she changes her plans based on how well they fit in with *his* plans, that's obsession. When she carefully chooses her outfit and hairstyle before she goes to a place where she knows she'll see him, that's obsession.

I have seen many young ladies with broken hearts because they allowed themselves to become emotionally attached to young men.

These girls may not have been impure physically, but they allowed a young man to have a claim on their affections without him showing the real responsibility and commitment that a romantic relationship requires.

If you allow yourself to feel emotionally attached to any young man who strikes your fancy, you make your emotions cheap. How much is your affection worth when it can be influenced so quickly and easily? I have seen young women giggle, blush, stammer, and melt when an attractive young man so much as looks at them. They make up elaborate schemes in order to meet the guy or let him "accidentally" learn their phone number. A couple of weeks later, the object of their attention is an entirely different young man. I wonder what kind of habits they are building when they teach themselves to constantly evaluate likely "candidates" and to feel emotional "highs" when he casts a glance in their direction. If we do not teach ourselves how to contain our emotions now, what will prevent us from having feelings for other men even when we are married? As singles, we are in training for marriage.

There's nothing wrong with enjoying the company of a certain friend, but when it comes to wanting more than a normal friendship, there's danger that "the wanting of more" will interfere with the friendship. It's awfully hard to keep up a good friendship when you're always looking over your shoulder to make sure that you look "just so" in front of him. You're so wrapped up in trying to attract his favor that you can't just be yourself. Everything you do or say is prompted by the motivation to make him like you, not the motivation to be a good friend to him. You might get frustrated with him because he thinks it's still a normal friendship and you want a more special type of friendship. Now a perfectly good friendship is going sour because he's not living up to your private expectations!

It is *not* wrong to like a guy, but it's shallow to be easily captivated by a man. Yes, I admit that I've been attracted to various guys. At the same time, I am careful to recognize that I have no "claim" on them and that I must still be discreet around them. I try to keep myself from daydreaming about them and I try to have just a Godly friendship, not a desire for "something more." Don't sell your emotions cheaply; reserve them for the man who is willing to make a commitment to you.

Commitment. Yes, everything comes back to commitment. It is a foolish thing to become very attracted to a person who (1) hasn't expressed any particular interest in you or (2) isn't ready to pursue a serious relationship with you (i.e. marriage). Many girls tell me that they are "being careful" with their emotions or are "willing to wait" for a man who is not yet ready. Truthfully, you cannot expect that an attraction to a guy, his attraction to you, or even your mutual attraction to each other will result in marriage. Neither person has a "claim" on the other until there is a commitment to marriage—in other words, until you are officially engaged.

What He Does, What She Interprets

It doesn't necessarily mean a man is considering you for a serious relationship when...

1. He does something nice for you.

One time, on a family hike with some good friends of ours, I happened to hike at the same speed as one of the young men from the other family. At a particularly rocky section, the young man hopped up and then offered his hand to help me up. For half a second, my inner romantic asserted herself.

"Oh my goodness! He's helping me up! How gallant! How kind! Maybe he likes me!"

The next second, my rational self took over.

"You silly, he helped up your sister too! Or didn't you notice? He's probably just heard you huffing and puffing behind him for the last half hour and felt like he ought to be gentlemanly and give you a hand."

Guess what? My rational self was right. It turned out that he was just being friendly and helpful, like any good guy ought to be, because I later discovered that he was seriously interested in a different young woman.

When a guy opens the door for you, offers to carry something for you, sits and listens to your woes, or does any other nice thing for you, it probably just means that he's trying to be a gentleman. Guys like to be heroes to women in general, but they can't marry every damsel in distress that they help!

166

2. He likes to talk with you and listens to you.

Many young men on various occasions have asked for my opinion. A guy friend might have a sticky ethical or philosophical question burning in his mind, or might want to pick my brain about the peculiarities of the Biblical culture, or might enjoy discussing the nitty-gritty of writing with me. All of these young men have shown that they respect me and value my opinion.

Sometimes I have felt a flutter of excitement.

"He's paying attention to me! He's talking with me! He even said that he can't talk with anyone else about this stuff because no one else is interested! He said I'm one of the most intelligent and godly girls he knows! (Gasp of realization) He must *like* me!"

Then I find that he is seriously pursuing another young woman. Wait! If he liked me so much, why did he want to marry *her*?

Guess what? In a guy's mind, paying attention to a girl, enjoying her company, even saying that he likes her, is not the same as wanting to pursue a serious relationship with her. The definition of *like* can be totally different for guys and girls. To a guy, *like* may mean, "She's fun to hang out with" or "She's a good friend." To a girl, *like* often means, "He wants a deeper relationship." When girls confuse their definition of *like* with their guy friends' definition of *like*, a lot of heartache can result.

3. He shows his appreciation of you.

When a guy thanks you for the nice things you do for him, for his family, or for others, it means that he appreciates you. Period. For example, a young woman might encourage a young man to pursue his career in music. One night, after attending one of his concerts, she might meet him in the hustle and bustle.

"Great job!" she says. He grins back.

"Hey, thanks for coming to watch me," he says. "It was great knowing that you were rooting for me."

Suddenly, the young woman is hearing wedding bells and seeing visions of white veils and candles. But all he did was say thanks! He's probably thinking, "That was nice of her to encourage me," but she's assuming that he likes her (girl definition of *like*).

When a guy says "thanks," most of the time it just means thanks. We girls always want to read into their words and their actions to discover a secret motive. Girls have told me how he "looked at them" and they *knew* that he loved them. Might I suggest that the guy simply happened to look in the girl's direction and decided "I'll be friendly and smile"? Ninety-nine percent of the time, when a girl interprets a guy's look as "soulful" and "meaningful," the guy has a completely normal motivation behind his action.

4. He says that he wants a special relationship with you.

This is the hard one to say, but it has got to be said. When a guy says, "I love you" or even says, "I'm really interested in you," it does not mean that the relationship is going to lead to a wedding. I have seen this happen over and over, with both Christians and non-Christians.

Sometimes the guy is just plain playing with the girl's emotions. Guys know that a girl will melt if the right things are said. There are hundreds of lines that a guy might use to touch a girl's emotions and to get her to lower her defenses with him. Thousands and thousands of women have told the same story: "He said he loved me. Then he wanted me to prove my love. I wanted to keep him, so I agreed to sleep with him. Then I discovered that he only wanted me for my body and soon he left me."

Not every guy who gives a girl "a line" is looking to get her in bed with him (although that's more common than you would think!), but he often does want *something* from her. Perhaps he just wants the status of "having a girl." A young woman can't assume that, just because a guy (even a supposedly Christian guy) says he loves her, he means that he wants to marry her. A wise young woman will think: "How has he acted toward me up until now? Has he proven himself to be a good and godly friend, first and foremost? Does he respect my space and my personal boundaries? Does he care more about the Lord than about anything or anybody else? Do I see the fruit of the Spirit in his life?" These are the sort of questions to ask yourself if you want to know the difference between a trap and a genuine prospect.

Furthermore, sometimes a guy begins with good intentions but changes his mind. He might tell the girl, "I really like you and I would like to pursue a deeper relationship with you." He may be a really nice Christian guy who has been a good friend, and he may show every intention of following through with his pursuit of the young woman's heart. He may spend all his free time with the young woman, he may shower her with gifts, he may constantly affirm his love to her. Some people call this stage "an engagement to get engaged." Many young people have believed that they were one step away from engagement and, suddenly, the other person decided that this relationship wasn't the one for them. The rejected people have been devastated because, in their hearts, they were engaged already. Their trust has been shattered; they are afraid to ever again enter a serious relationship.

As I watched all this heartbreak, I made the decision that I would never, never invest my emotions in a man until he had made a formal, verbal commitment—not just signs of affection or words of love or even "I hope to one day marry you." I need a commitment that says, "I have irrevocably committed to marrying you." In simple terms, if a guy wants to "secure" me, he needs to get engaged to me. Sure, in a developing relationship, it will be hard (and perhaps foolish) to keep all emotion out of friendship. I acknowledge that I will feel affection for him before an engagement is made. However, I will guard against future expectations for that relationship until I have his commitment to marry me. No one has the right to claim my exclusive attention or affection until he has committed to me for life.

One final note: We need to be very careful with our expectations. Our friends may slyly suggest that a certain guy is "the one" and, even though we may deny any romantic interest, we may secretly take that idea and run with it. Even our dreams may plant suggestions in our vulnerable minds; many young women I know (including myself) have had dreams in which certain eligible bachelors have shown romantic intentions toward them—even if the young woman has never particularly thought about that guy in that way! If you think it is dangerous to allow sexual fantasies into our minds, it is equally dangerous to allow romantic fantasies into our minds. Save your heart and emotions for the man who has proven that he is worthy of them, and who has made an official lifetime commitment to you.

Crushes: Panic

While it is very risky to be deeply attracted to a guy who has made no real commitment to you, it is equally foolish to panic because you like someone. In all honesty, there is nothing wrong with respecting, admiring, or even liking a guy. In short, being attracted to someone is *not* a sin. Attraction should be controlled in a godly way, but I can't find any place where the Bible says that it is sinful. The only sin lies in carrying our imaginations, thoughts, and actions in an ungodly direction.

God created women to desire to have husbands; it's right there in Genesis: *Thy desire shall be to thy husband.*[216] Attraction to a young man is natural, and is meant to develop into a beautiful passion in marriage. Your attraction toward someone doesn't have to be eliminated; it simply must be controlled until a commitment has been made.

Don't panic when you have a "crush" on someone. Simply ask yourself several questions: Am I still focusing on God? Is this guy worth being attracted to? Is he godly? Is either one of us ready for marriage? If not, should I really be thinking about him at this point? If so, shouldn't I tell my parents so that they can help to guide me in a good direction?

Remind yourself of several things:

- God must be first in my heart.
- I must guard my thoughts concerning this young man, to avoid building unrealistic expectations.
- I must continue to behave in a way that is pure and modest, whether I am around him or not.
- I should resist the temptation to alter my plans, personality, or lifestyle in order to please or impress him. Just as I would not want him to mislead me about his normal habits, I do not want to mislead him about mine.
- I will trust this relationship to God's guidance.

On the one hand, it is wise to make sure that we don't give our hearts away to men who do not become our husbands. Women who have had multiple relationships bring baggage from their

---

[216] Genesis 3:16

170

previous relationships into their marriage relationship. On the other hand, some people have rightly pointed out that misusing the idea of emotional purity can result in emotional coldness.

While it's dangerous to give your emotions away easily, the opposite extreme can be equally dangerous. Sometimes young ladies and their parents become so concerned about "saving it all" for marriage that they believe that any emotion before marriage is evil. For some young ladies, this means that they destroy any attraction to a guy prior to the engagement or the wedding day. Some women keep themselves so emotionally distant from prospective suitors that they consider marriage to people in whom they have no real interest.

This, in my opinion, is an overreaction that can lead to unsatisfying marriages. Jacob loved Rachel before he married her.[217] Michal loved David before he married her.[218] Christ loves His betrothed Bride, even though the final union has not yet taken place.[219] It is not wrong to feel affection for someone before the vows have been said. If we don't allow ourselves to feel any attraction to someone even before engagement, how do we know we want to get engaged to that person? And if we're repulsed by someone, is commitment to that person really a good idea?

Emotional Balance

There is a balance. God made us emotional beings and He does not call emotion a sin. He simply expects us to control our emotions in a godly way. Too much emotion can lead us into temptation, which in turn can lead us into sin. Evaluating a relationship solely on its ability to stimulate our emotions is foolish; emotions change all the time!

On the other hand, too little emotion before marriage can cause unnecessary and avoidable dissatisfaction within the marriage. The Song of Solomon shows that passion within marriage is very good and desirable. God didn't give us emotions for nothing! Once a commitment to marry has been made, it is both appropriate and

---

[217] Genesis 29:18
[218] 1 Samuel 18:20
[219] Ephesians 5:25-27

wise to gradually release the emotions. By the wedding day, we should be ready and excited to live out the passion of our own Song of Songs.

There are many ways to approach this issue practically and to attempt to maintain a proper emotional balance. More than likely, you and your family will make a mistake on one side or the other, or err on both extremes at different times. Don't be discouraged: aiming at the mark and missing it is better than just taking a wild shot. I believe that if you honestly try to maintain a good and Biblical balance, God will reward you with wisdom.[220]

---

[220] James 1:5

ᔥ 17 ᔥ

Considering a Match Wisely

It is important not to build expectations for the type of men we hope to marry. Obviously, we don't always know what (or who) is best for us and sometimes God's best for us is surprising, but it *is* best. On the other hand, we shouldn't assume that the first guy who shows up is God's hand-picked husband for us or that we are somehow more spiritual if we choose husbands that we don't care for. How do we know God's will when it comes to deciding if a man is right for a husband?

Knowing God's Will

Seeking God's will is a good thing. Does He always tell us exactly what to do? It is evident in the Bible that sometimes He does. We know that He may indicate certain paths very clearly.

Sometimes, however, God's voice is not clear. One night I was on my knees trying to decide between two job choices. One of them was more stable and offered more room for advancement. The other one was more risky, offered no room for advancement, but did promise to be an adventure. I was afraid to choose wrongly and I wanted God to make up my mind for me. I wanted Him to point clearly to one or the other and say, "Accept that one." I had only five minutes to make up my mind before I had to call someone and give a final answer. In those five minutes, God didn't speak to me.

I reviewed my options and finally chose the one that appealed most to me. I have often thought back on that choice and I have been extremely grateful that I chose the way that I did. Perhaps God was leading me and I didn't know it, or maybe He really did step back and let me make my own decision. Either way, the important thing was that once I had made my decision, I was committed and I trusted the Lord with the outcome.

That's the way that it often works with marriage and with other big decisions. I don't believe that the Lord usually tells us exactly what to do in specific situations. He gives us guidelines in His

Word and expects us to obey them, but sometimes He lets us choose those things that most please us within Biblical guidelines.

Let me put it this way. Suppose a child is about to eat breakfast, so she asks her parent, "What should I eat for breakfast?"

Her parent replies, "Eat cereal."

Her parent doesn't care what type of cereal she eats, whether Cheerios or Raisin Bran or Fruit Loops. The child is given the freedom to choose the type that pleases her most, within the boundaries that her parent has given her.

I think it is often the same way with God. The Bible gives us certain guidelines about the type of person we are supposed to marry—we must marry within the faith, look for someone with evidence of the Spirit in his life, look for someone who understands Biblical marriage and its purpose, and so on and so forth. When it comes to specifics, there is often no obvious answer. We are allowed to choose the man who, within those guidelines, most pleases us.

In some marriage stories, I can see God's hand very clearly. We know that He helped Abraham's servant find a divinely-appointed wife (Rebekah) for Abraham's son Isaac.[221] There are some people, even today, whose love stories are obviously and miraculously God-orchestrated.

Although I believe God does arrange *some* relationships, it's a trap to believe that we have no responsibility in the process. For example, even Isaac and Rebekah's marriage was divinely arranged, Rebekah was still given the choice of whether or not to marry Isaac.[222] After she agreed and became Isaac's wife, the Bible records significant marital problems between she and her husband. After battling infertility for decades, they finally had children, who became a source of strife and competition between them. Nevertheless, they did not divorce or cease to work together as a couple. The marriage that God had ordained still required responsibility, personal choices, and commitment—and they kept that commitment until death.

In contrast, I've seen cases where the relationship went sour and

---

[221] Genesis chapter 24
[222] Genesis 24:58

the frustrated spouses blamed God: "You picked this spouse for me! But You picked the wrong one!" This echoes Adam's guilt-shifting attitude: "This woman whom *You* gave to me..." [223] Obviously, it was the person's attitude—not God's choice—that was wrong, but we need to be careful how we view God's involvement and our own responsibility. Even if God arranged a marriage, we are still responsible. Although God will give us strength to face the difficulties of marriage, we will make choices about how we deal with situations and we will receive the consequences of those choices.

There's a flip-side to the "divinely-arranged marriage." Some marriage stories seem to result simply from a willingness to follow God, like the parent/cereal analogy. The daughters of Zelophehad were given this commandment: "Let them marry to whom they think best; only to the family of the tribe of their father shall they marry." [224] My mother feels that she was in a situation like this; she knew several young men who were godly, available choices, but she liked Dad the best.

I think we need to be careful of putting God in a box and saying, "He always plays this or that part in marriage." He is involved, but His involvement is different for different couples. The issue still comes down to my parents' words of wisdom: "Marriage is about trust, not so much trust in your spouse, but trust in the Lord." Once the choice is made, trust the Lord with the outcome and then follow through on your decision with all of your strength. There is no turning back.

What About Online Matchmaking?

The teens pass by...the twenties are slipping away...the thirties approach...and there are still no prospects. Is it okay to go looking for a guy, even on the internet?

This is a tricky subject, but it is one that is becoming more and more relevant as people meet on online matchmaking sites. In fact, I know at least two Christian young women who got married this

---

[223] Genesis 3:12
[224] Numbers 36:6

way. There's a lot of mixed reactions when you hear of a young woman getting married to a man she met online.

"Woah! Is that, like, safe? How do you know what kind of guy you're getting?"

"Isn't that kind of getting ahead of God? If there are no prospects, maybe He doesn't want you married now."

"Wow, that sounds unusual but...does it actually work? I mean, could it work for me?"

I honestly don't have all the answers to those questions and I suspect that the answers might vary according to the people and the situation. However, I'll point out some of the things that I notice about the trend.

1. When a young woman uses a matchmaking service, there is a possibility that she is going beyond her parental parameters.

In other words, there is a tendency for a young woman to look for a young man on her own. Biblically, it is important for parents and families to be involved in a developing relationship. Fathers should be especially involved. I know of a young woman who used the service with her parents' blessing and supervision, and I feel that her situation presents a safer and more Biblically responsible approach to online matchmaking than making matches on her own.

2. A young woman who uses a matchmaking service advertises her availability.

People laugh about the old-fashioned idea of a "mail-order bride," but technology is bringing us closer to that idea. Of course, it's not too different than Rebekah going to marry Isaac, a man she'd never seen before. On the other hand, there are a *few* differences.

Let's face it: Both guy and gal are advertising their availability, and they're both reviewing each other's profiles and specifications to see how it all measures up to their preferences. I'm not saying anything about the rightness or wrongness of it—as far as I can see, it's hard to either defend or condemn online matchmaking from a Biblical standpoint—but there's a lot of expectation. This puts the young man and the young woman in a tough spot because they've already signaled that they are looking (maybe desperately) for a potential mate. Therefore, their relationship starts out with romantic interest, rather than developing romantic interest as a friendship matures.

Admittedly, this can happen even in non-online situations, with similar ramifications. For example, a young woman I know entered a relationship with a young man whom she didn't know well at all. Further communication showed that he intended to take the relationship in a serious direction, and an unofficial courtship developed. Both young people had to get to know each other with the added distraction of romantic attraction. It was difficult to behave naturally and comfortably around each other, because both the young man and the young woman felt the pressure of the expectations for the relationship. This hindered the growth of the friendship and, in the end, it proved to be one of the reasons that the relationship broke off.

With online matchmaking, the difficulty is even greater, because the relationship has the potential to get very serious very quickly and to give a false idea that "the perfect match" has been found. That can put the young people in a very compromising and tempting situation.

3. Some people feel that turning to online matchmaking is getting ahead of God.

The reasoning goes like this: "If God wanted you married, wouldn't He have sent someone by now? If you try to do things yourself, aren't you taking a chance that you're missing out on something better that God has been preparing for you, if you're only willing to wait?"

I can't answer those questions, because I wonder the same thing myself. I also wonder if the answer might be different for some women than for others. Perhaps, for some people, online matchmaking *is* God's way of bringing a young man into a young woman's life. Who am I to say?

On the other hand, if marriage is in a woman's future, God is not limited. He's been bringing people together for thousands of years; He doesn't need social media to help Him out. The woman who waits has no lesser chance of getting married than the woman who makes herself available through online matchmaking.

177

4. How do you know what kind of man you're going to get?

Given the limited face-to-face contact that these kinds of relationships may have, there is a greater likelihood that certain important factors might not surface until *after* the couple is married. That's one of the reasons why I'm so nutty about keeping your parents in the loop; they can recognize trouble that a younger person might overlook.

We young ladies are very optimistic and young. It is quite possible for us to overlook something important. Especially if one or more candidates haven't worked out, we begin to wonder: "How many opportunities can I lose before there's none left? Is this guy my last chance?" That kind of pressure can be very damaging, because a young woman might ignore or might not see something important about the guy because she wants so desperately to get married. Is it really worth it?

Let's put this close to home: If you were going to buy an expensive car, something that you'd spend the next decade paying off, would you buy it online, having never seen or driven it, just taking the seller's word for it? If you were planning on buying a house in which you would live for the rest of your life, would you buy a house online, relying only on the pictures and the seller's description? With marriage, we're talking about an exclusive, life-long commitment in which you'll be sharing your life, your body, your future, and your dreams.

My main concern with online matchmaking is this: What a man writes by e-mail or letter, or chooses to say over the phone, can be very different from the way in which he expresses himself in daily situations toward people with whom he is familiar and whom he is not trying to impress. A man's behavior as a guest may even be very different than his behavior in his own home. Long-distance relationships make direct observation of a young man's normal environmental context very difficult, and therefore increase the risk tremendously.

Some parents, recognizing the limitations of online matchmaking, have done their own "background checks" on potential sons-in-law, by asking the young man's family, friends, and co-workers to give information about the young man. A young man should have the honesty and the good reputation to pass such a test. Still, given the limitations and disadvantages of online matchmaking, I think it is harder to know what you're getting into than it would be compared to knowing someone *before* the relationship takes a romantic direction.

Single and Looking

There are other ways to advertise "single and looking" than by using a matchmaking service; sometimes we try to be our own matchmakers.

For example, a video on YouTube featured a young Christian man, who spoke about modesty, about women honoring the Lord with their bodies, and about their responsibility to please the Lord with their dress habits. Just as I expected, half of the comments to the video included some anger from women who felt that he was being too harsh: "What's wrong with dressing sexy every now and then? Especially if I already have a boyfriend?" The other half of the comments made my jaw drop.

"I would marry you if I knew you."

"Where are the guys like you?"

"Are you single? I'm in love with you!"

"I wish there were men like you in my area. Any chance you'll head my way?"

"If I had a man like you, I would be complete."

Here was a young man trying to treat women like dignified human beings, not objects. Here was a young man trying to show women that they don't need a man to complete them and therefore do not have to dress to impress men. The response of the young women? To advertise themselves to him and to show that they were eager to receive his attention. They would not tempt him with their bodies, but they would entice him with their words.

It saddened me greatly to see these young women market themselves to the latest bachelor. But I knew that there are other ways for young women to advertise themselves. For example, I've several young women whose blogs subtly advertise their availability in their titles, their profiles, and their content, subtly signaling, "I am a lovely Christian young woman who is dedicated to purity and who is waiting for her husband to arrive!"

Remember the passage about love? Love does not vaunt itself[225] or draw attention to itself. Love simply serves others, quietly. Advertisement is pride, and pride makes no woman beautiful. Only humility makes a woman attractive. A godly woman does not draw attention to herself, but to her Lord.

But he that glorieth, let him glory in the Lord.[226]

We are complete only in Christ. No man will ever complete us. We do not need to make broad hints to gain attention, as if we are desperate to find our missing half. We have no missing half. If we truly take God at His Word, we have no need to throw ourselves at our Christian brothers in hopes that one of them will take the hint and whip out an engagement ring. Don't just hand out your heart; treat it like the precious, unique gift that it is. Young men are attracted to the mystery of a woman who keeps her dignity, who watches him from a distance, who leaves more to be discovered. A young man will not value a heart that is too easily given, but he will prize the heart that has been reserved for a special purpose.

It's not about playing "hard to get," which is just another way to flirt and advertise. It's about acknowledging that your heart is God's. Jesus Christ paid a high price for your heart; therefore, do not treat it lightly or give it out cheaply.

Ye are bought with a price; be not ye the servants of men.[227]

We enslave ourselves to men when we believe that we need one to make us whole. We enslave ourselves to men when we believe that we need male approval and attention to make us happy. We enslave ourselves to men when we actively try to attract them. Let Jesus make us whole. Look for the approval and attention of God. If He is our only companion in life, then a life spent pouring out our love to Him is not wasted. It is the fullest life possible. If marriage is in our future, we will see that Christian young men will be attracted to us without us even having to try, because these men have seen the beauty of God's love in us. If we honor God in our bodies and spirits, God will honor us.

Humble yourselves in the sight of the Lord, and he shall lift you up.[228]

---

[225] 1 Corinthians 13:4
[226] 2 Corinthians 10:17
[227] 1 Corinthians 7:23
[228] James 4:10

ఔ 18 ಇ

Qualities of a Potential Husband

Welcome to everybody's favorite section: How to know if a man is worth considering for a husband. Remember that most of these things involve studying the Bible, not just "searching your heart." The Bible is the ultimate authority—not your heart—so be prepared to go digging into God's Word!

I do not intend to discuss "choosing a husband" in the sense of presenting a shopping list to jumpstart a woman's hunt for the perfect man. That is neither a wise nor a Biblical way for a young woman to approach the issue of marriage. My intention is only to discuss the Biblical qualities that a godly and responsible man should possess prior to marriage, and to provide some suggestions which a young woman and her family should prayerfully consider when evaluating a possible match.

He Must Know and Love Christ

This is the most essential criterion for a husband. There is nothing unclear about God's will here.

Be ye not unequally yoked together with unbelievers: for what fellowship hath righteousness with unrighteousness? and what communion hath light with darkness? And what concord hath Christ with Belial? or what part hath he that believeth with an infidel? And what agreement hath the temple of God with idols? for ye are the temple of the living God; as God hath said, I will dwell in them, and walk in them; and I will be their God, and they shall be my people. Wherefore come out from among them, and be ye separate, saith the Lord, and touch not the unclean thing; and I will receive you.[229]

God's will is clear: Believers must marry only other believers. We are meant to be a separate people, special and holy to God. This does not mean that we cannot be friends with unbelievers (as the Bible explains elsewhere) but it does mean that we cannot enter into

---

[229] 2 Corinthians 6:14-17

a marriage relationship with them. The Bible does talk about special cases in which one of the spouses becomes a believer after marriage and remains married to an unbelieving spouse, but that is not the same as a believer deliberately agreeing to marry a nonbeliever.

The Christian woman who knowingly marries a nonbelieving husband runs the high risk of having her heart tempted away from the Lord. In fact, she has already been tempted away from the Lord because she allowed her heart to be claimed by a man that the Lord specifically told her not to marry. Having made that choice once, she is more vulnerable to making that choice again. Her love for her husband has already led her away from the Lord, to the point where her faith is secondary to her romantic relationship.

When a Christian woman chooses a non-Christian man, he can never truly love her the way she ought to be loved. As we know, a person who cannot love a perfect God cannot love an imperfect spouse. A person who has not given his or her heart to God does not know how to fully give his or her heart to a spouse. It is not because they do not want to; it is because they simply can't.

In the Christian's heart, Christ is the most important thing. In the non-Christian's heart, Christ is not. Two Christians who marry each other are drawn even closer together because their "most important thing" is the same. A Christian and a non-Christian who marry cannot be drawn together because their "most important thing" is different.

Furthermore, if we really love someone, we want to know that we will be able to meet that person even after death. When it comes to Christian spouses, that is possible. Even though the death of a spouse is agonizing, the Christian spouse knows that they will meet together again in the presence of the One they love the best. When a non-Christian spouse dies, the Christian spouse feels the unbearable heartbreak of knowing that they will never be able to meet again.

This concept goes even deeper. Eric and Leslie Ludy, authors of numerous books about relationships, have a love story that proves the importance of God's central role in the relationship. Eric and Leslie knew that their relationship was right when Leslie's father explained that he knew the relationship was of God because Leslie had grown closer to God through her relationship with Eric.

If a man is not actively drawing you toward God, then he is actively drawing you away from God. If you compromise on this issue, you will compromise on other issues. A non-Christian man is not worth it, no matter how "different" he may seem. The only truly different man is the man who is willing to live, suffer, and even die for Christ. If you choose a man with a "halfway faith," what does your choice says about *your* faith?

My parents' wedding rings are braided, made of three strands of gold intertwined with each other. Why? A braid symbolizes the nature of their marriage, for marriage does not involve just two people. It involves *three* people: the man, the woman, and the Lord. This illustrates the Biblical proverb: *A threefold cord is not quickly broken.*[230]

No relationship in Christianity is about just two people. It is about what God creates between two people out of their unity in Him. He is the common ground. Never accept less than a man who belongs first and foremost to the Lord, and only secondly to you. Your relationship cannot be about you both, as if the relationship is an end in itself. First and foremost, your relationship must be about the Lord. As Jesus said, *Whoever loses his life for my sake will find it.*[231] Love Christ more than you love each other and you will love each other more.

Agree on Your Biblical Roles

Earlier in this book, I wrote about the roles of men and women, husbands and wives. Whether you agree with me or not, it is your job to look into the Bible and study everything that it says about men, women, husbands, wives, relationships, fathers, and mothers. The Bible is the only truly reliable source of advice about relationships, so both spouses should be knowledgeable about how the marriage relationship should be structured Biblically. I believe that men were created to be the leaders of the home and that women were created to be their helpers.[232] You should investigate this concept for yourself.

---

[230] Ecclesiastes 4:12
[231] Luke 9:24
[232] For an explanation of this assertion, please refer back to the chapter entitled "Authority in Relationships."

Remember, this is not about deciding what *you* think the relationship should be like. This is about studying what the *Bible* says your relationship should be like. It's not about having personal beliefs. It's about having beliefs based on the Word of God. You're an intelligent Christian; you should be able to give solid, Biblical reasons for your beliefs.

It is necessary for the man to know what the Bible says about roles. It's not okay for a guy to say, "I don't know" or "Whatever you want, dear." That shows laziness and irresponsibility. He's trying to leave it all up to you to put the structure in your relationship. A man needs to study God's Word on his own and take responsibility for his relationship with God and for how that will affect his other relationships. Spouses need to study and learn about each other, yet a man who does not put the effort into studying God's ways will not put the effort into studying his wife.

Having said that, it's okay if he generally knows what he believes but is still learning. That shows that he's honest enough to admit that he does not have all the answers and that he's man enough to seek the truth. After all, isn't that what knowing the Lord is all about? If you both agree on the basics of what your roles ought to be—who is the leader, who is the supporter, and how you should interact in the decision-making process—then there is no reason why you cannot explore more about God's ways together.

Agree About Children

We know from Genesis that children are and should be a natural result of a God-honoring marriage. After all, God commands Adam and Eve to be "fruitful and multiply"[233] and Psalm 127 identifies children as rewards and blessings. Christians should consider the Bible's view of children before they even get married, because that will have a direct influence on their marriage. I can't tell you how many times I've heard of marriages becoming strained because one spouse wants more or fewer children. Ask these questions:

- According to the Bible, what should your attitude toward children be?

---

[233] Genesis 1:28

- Based on what you know about the Biblical attitude toward children, how should that influence your thoughts about the number of children you have?
- Is it ever Biblically permissible to use any type of birth control (if so, what type) or practice any type of family planning or child spacing? What about waiting to have children?
- According to the Bible, how should children be disciplined?
- According to the Bible, how should children be taught about God's ways and expectations?
- What type of education do you plan for your children?
- What happens if you face infertility? Would you have fertility treatments (if so, what types) and/or would you adopt?
- Do you ever plan to adopt regardless of whether there are biological children?

These are not just small issues. Both the man and the woman should be knowledgeable about the Bible's teaching on children and they also should be able to agree on the important child-related issues about which the Bible is not completely clear.

Agree on Important Specific Doctrinal Beliefs

Christians have argued for centuries over free will and election, whether speaking in tongues is or is not a valid spiritual gift in the modern age, whether there is universal reconciliation or eternal damnation, whether the rapture will be pre- or post-tribulation, and a host of other issues. Although Christians should be able to agree that we love Jesus Christ with all our hearts, we can't ignore the fact that some issues have the potential to be very divisive, and it would be foolish to overlook those issues when considering a spouse.

For example, some people believe that the Lord mercifully intervenes to bestow salvation and that the human part in salvation is completely passive (election). Other people believe that the Lord offers salvation and lets people respond to the offer, and that the human part in salvation is at least partially active (free will). My best friend happens to be one of the former, I happen to lean more toward the latter. We are very good friends and we care more about our love for the Lord than about our disagreements. However, we have both come to the conclusion that although we are very good friends, my friend could never marry a man who believed similarly to me about those issues and I could never marry a man who believed similarly to my friend about those issues. Why? Because these beliefs influence what churches we attend, how we present the gospel to others, and how we view our own relationships with God. We can overlook those issues in a friendship, but in a marriage, those issues can cause significant disagreement.

The big question is this: How do we know which doctrinal issues are most important for us? Well, that depends on each case. For example, suppose that you believe that children should grow in the knowledge of the Lord and make a commitment to God once they reach an age where they can fully understand that commitment. Suppose you are considering marriage to a man who believes that children of believing parents are under a sort of "covenant" and that, through the teaching of their Christian parents, they grow up as believers unless they prove rebellious. You might rationalize this situation one of two ways. The first option is to feel that the difference is incompatible. The second option is to feel that, although your beliefs are different, you both agree on the important thing—that parents should bring up their children in the "nurture and admonition of the Lord."

The potential differences are endless. Once you get married, you will still have differences. Even if you were fortunate enough to marry someone with whom you agree on everything, it is likely that one or both of you will change your mind after further study of the Bible. Ultimately, in this process, let the Bible be your guide, consider the possibilities, talk with your parents (or, secondarily, a trusted mentor or friend), and be honest with yourself about your level of tolerance for a certain difference.

Consider Your Preferences

A friend who breeds dogs asked me: "What if a guy is courting me and he seems to be 'perfect' for me, but then I find out that he is allergic to or just simply doesn't like dogs? I'm having a hard time imagining a life without dogs. Do I say no to him, even though I agree with him about everything else? Or do I say yes and give up the dogs?"

I had been trying to ignore the same fear. It seemed foolish to say "no" to a guy because I wanted to keep pets. It seemed equally foolish to say "yes" to a guy and spend the rest of my life feeling envious of people with pets. It also seemed foolish to expect that I would be able to change his mind and allow an exception for me.

My conversation with my friend got into deep waters. Would God ever send a "perfect" husband with one horrible flaw? Wouldn't it be cruel of Him to make us choose between the hope of getting married and the love we have for animals, a love that defines our personalities? Is there a Biblical answer to the problem?

We both felt that God would take our preferences into account in planning out our future lives, but we also both felt that God doesn't necessarily do everything we want Him to do. Sometimes He faces us with choices that aren't necessarily between an obvious good or an obvious evil; sometimes He gives us choices that are simply choices, with advantages and disadvantages accompanying each option. My friend and I agonized over the dilemma and never came to a full decision. In the end, we both had to say, "We'll cross that bridge if we ever come to it."

In some ways, the man you marry determines the sort of person that you become. If you marry a man who likes indoor pets, cozy home décor, and activities like tennis and sailing, you will have a different life than if you marry a man who likes homesteading, long hikes, camping, and deer hunting. If you marry a man who is quiet and leads by example, you will have certain benefits and certain frustrations that are different than those that go along with a man who speaks his mind and leads with passion.

It is worth thinking about the kind of person you envision living with for the rest of your life. For example, I know a woman who became good friends with a man whose favorite activity was tennis. She liked him but couldn't envision herself playing tennis for the rest of her life. She wanted to hike and explore. So she chose a man who liked hiking and exploring. There was nothing wrong with the first man, but his lifestyle simply wasn't her preference.

Regardless of what sort of man you marry, you will have to give up some things. For instance, the woman who liked hiking also liked skiing, but her husband was not able to afford the cost of regular skiing, so she had to give up skiing regularly when she married him. Instead, she and her husband continued to hike together. In essence, she gave up one desire in order to have another desire.

It is not selfish to have preferences. Some similarity is necessary. However, make a distinction between the essentials that God requires and the preferences that you desire.

Find a Friend

"You can take any random guy off the street and make him a lover," my mom once said. "But when it comes to a husband, you want more than a lover. You want a friend."

On my wedding day, I hope to say that I am marrying my best friend. I want to say, "I did not say 'yes' to you because you were oh-so-romantic and because you made my heart go pitter-patter. I said 'yes' because you have proven yourself to be a faithful friend, and if I must live the rest of my life with someone, I want to live it with my best friend."

Many people have found that they had a growing and exciting relationship before they were married but afterward, things seemed to go downhill. I think one of the reasons for this is that, once they became "lovers," they forgot to be friends. Friends continue learning about each other and finding things to agree or to disagree about amiably. Friends tell each other the truth and confess to each other. Friends point each other to the Lord and put each other first. Friends don't take their relationship for granted, and they keep the relationship always pressing forward.

There is room in a friendship to include others. Some couples become so obsessed with each other that they are completely unaware of anything else. Their worlds revolve around each other. They call each other every day, perhaps several times a day. They make promises of love and always talk about how much they love each other. In their little world, everybody and everything else is totally excluded, yet we have to watch their embarrassing public displays of affection.

A friendship, even when occupying an exclusive sphere such as marriage, is warmer, friendlier, and kinder to those on the "outside." There is less public demonstration of affection; you'll notice that most happily married couples have much less obvious physical contact that most lovers. They do not feel compelled to prove their love to each other; they simply live their love every day. They are attached by a common goal and—to some extent—they have space in their relationship for others who share that common destination. Thankfully, marriage offers a chance to have both a lover and a friend, but we should never forget that the things that strengthen a friendship also strengthen a marriage.

One of my friends spoke frankly: "When my friends got married, suddenly they seemed to be in their own little world and nobody else mattered. This abandonment frustrated me and I decided that I would never do that to my friends. When I got married, my husband and I maintained our friendships with others." Consequently, she and her husband continually opened their home to others, making no distinction between their single and married friends. They have blessed me in countless ways and, as a single, I value their friendship to me.

The Commitment

This is the truth: No matter what decision you make, you can't look back. Once you're married, *you're married*. You don't have the luxury of re-evaluating your decision. You can only trust God with your decision and then pursue your course of action with all your heart. It's like the decision I made about which work opportunity to accept. As I was agonizing over the choice, my mother gave me some wise advice that set the pattern for the rest of my life: "Pray, evaluate your options, make a choice, and once you've made a choice, give it two hundred percent. For better or for worse, that's what you chose and you need follow through on your choice."

Lot's wife made the decision to flee with her husband from the city that God had doomed to destruction. The angels who rescued Lot's family warned them, "Don't look back." Yet, after making that choice, Lot's wife looked back at her old life and she immediately turned into a pillar of salt.[234] In the New Testament, Jesus speaks these words, "No one who puts his hand to the plow and looks

---

[234] Genesis 19:26

189

QUALITIES OF A POTENTIAL HUSBAND

back is fit for the Kingdom of God."[235]

When you have made a marriage decision, you must follow through. If I pass up the man who doesn't like animals, I can't spend the rest of my life bemoaning the fact that I couldn't marry him. I said no; why look back? Maybe he was my only suitor and I can't get him back. That would hurt—a lot—but I would still have to live with the fact that, at the time that I made my choice, I knew what I was choosing. I can't be crippled by regret; that's a waste of the precious life God gave to me.

Oppositely, if I agree to marry the man who doesn't like animals, I can't spend the rest of my life trying to make him change his mind and grumbling when he doesn't. Nobody forced me to marry him. I knew what I was agreeing to. Now I have to live with it. Losing animals was the price I agreed to pay when I said, "Yes."

It would be stupid for me to marry a man who hates animals, with the expectation that I will be able to convert him to my viewpoint. I might succeed, I might not, but it's awfully conceited to think that I, in a few years, can change a preference or a habit that he has spent a lifetime building up.

Maybe God will never give me that dilemma. Personally, I hope He doesn't! But if I do have to make that choice, I know that I can't afford to second-guess myself once I've made a decision. The results are in God's hands; it's my job to make sure I follow through with patience and trust.

Finally, it's a really stupid idea to marry someone expecting that you'll be able to get him to change an ungodly pattern in his life. I knew a young woman who married a man who struggled with addiction to pornography. He promised that he was changing, but once they were married, there was no real progress. His addiction cost them their marriage. Never, never, never make the mistake of thinking that you are going to be some man's savior or of expecting a man to change "once you are married." If the man has not let God change him, what makes you think that he will let *you* change him? If the man has not put the work into changing before he is married (simply out of love for Christ and not just to impress you), what makes you think he will put the work into changing after he is

---

[235] Luke 9:62

married? True change requires more than good intentions; it requires heart-surgery by God Himself. Remember: You marry the man that he *is*, not the man that he may become.

Compatibility

Despite the need to make sure that there's a certain level of compatibility in a marriage relationship, I believe that our modern idea of compatibility is unbiblical.

High on the list of reasons for divorce is the issue of incompatibility. "We're incompatible," the spouses say, and no one asks any more questions. But the Bible says nothing about compatibility. In fact, it doesn't say anything about how your spouse should meet certain preferences. It talks about respect, honor, love, obedience, and sacrifice. It tells a man that if he finds a wife, he finds a good thing;[236] it tells him to rejoice with the wife of his youth and to find his satisfaction in her (as opposed to finding satisfaction through adultery).[237] Yet Scripture never talks about compatibility.

Rebekah made the decision to marry Isaac without having even seen him and while knowing that he was probably quite a bit older than she was. It was not a complete leap in the dark, since she knew he was a cousin. (In those days, marriage in the extended family was encouraged, because you had an idea of what sort of situation you were marrying into.) She knew that he was from a God-fearing family and that he was well off and quite capable of caring for her (as evident from the jewelry and gifts given to her). Women in those days didn't think, "Well, is he fat or slim? Does he like dogs or not?" Instead, they thought, "Well, does he have the basics: similar religious beliefs and the capability to provide?" Appearance and personality preferences didn't usually enter the picture. When Rebekah made the choice to marry Isaac, her expectations for compatibility were low in today's standards, but she made the marriage work. In fact, her whole culture made it work. Men and women simply got married with the commitment to learn about each other, treat each other responsibly, and learn to love each

---

[236] Proverbs 18:22
[237] Proverbs 5:19

191

other. Strangely enough, with all this neglect of compatibility, the divorce rate was lower in that society than it is in ours.

If you need more examples of women who married husbands without the luxury of considering their "compatibility" with that man, check out the books of Ruth and Esther. Ruth married Boaz out of a duty to provide heirs for her husband's family line. Boaz was probably much older than Ruth, but he was also very rich and very kind. It made sense to marry him. Esther never even had a choice about who she married; she was grabbed by the king's men, beautified for two years, and then taken into the king's chamber one night. Apparently she pleased him, since he made her his queen. There are other women in the Bible who married or were given in marriage, and they didn't spend time agonizing over whether they were compatible with a particular "candidate." They considered the basics and agreed to the marriage, committing to be good wives to the men they married.

Admittedly, this worked mostly because both parties knew what to expect. In that culture, the husband expected to be the leader and the wife expected to support his leadership. There was never a question about how many children or about birth control or about child training methods. They had as many children as they could and they used very basic and time-honored training methods. In today's society, the reason for the complicated "screening" process is because our culture has a diversity of views; even Christians have significant differences. Still, compatibility is a big lie. Nobody is compatible, even people who seem "perfect" for each other. If spouses were completely compatible with each other, they would never learn unconditional love, which requires loving someone who doesn't meet your conditions.

In the end, it's not about compatibility. It's about commitment. I've seen marriages in which the two spouses are completely different and I wonder, "How did they ever get together? Don't they just rub each other the wrong way all the time?" But they make marriage work. They don't just look for a compatible relationship; they *make* a compatible relationship through their commitment.

ജ 19 ൙

Candidate Checklist

Suppose that you and your family are keeping an eye on a certain young man. What qualities should you look for? I know that we've gone through some in-depth discussion on this topic so far, but this is the advice in a nutshell, plus a few things that are worth your consideration.

What is his walk with God like?

Anyone can talk the talk, but can he walk the walk? Is he serious about reading his Bible? Is he preparing for Biblical leadership of his family? Does he govern himself in a godly manner, soberly and with self-control?[238] Is he firm about his convictions, yet humble enough to consider a Biblical argument from another viewpoint? Do you see the fear of the Lord in him? Do you see the love of the Lord in him in the way that he interacts with and serves others? Is he careful to keep himself pure, both in body and in mind?

There is a difference between a spiritual man and a godly man. Spiritual men make a show of wanting to follow God. They punish themselves for their sins, they are the first to suggest studying the Bible or praying together, and they are always willing to give spiritual advice. They pray about everything before they make a decision, then they announce what God told them to do. Rather than fixing a problem using an obvious, common-sense approach, they make a show of asking God for His help. These same men, however, may constantly argue with authority, struggle with diligence, spend their money unwisely, treat women without dignity and respect, grow angry quickly if questioned, hold grudges, fail to show basic thoughtfulness, or expect constant attention. Disturbingly, some spiritual men take advantage of nice

---

[238] Titus 2:6

Christian young women, whom they hope will have no baggage to bring into marriage and who will make sweet, submissive wives.

Know the fruit. If a man claims to be a Christian, expect that his spiritual state will be reflected in his relationships and habits. Invite the opinions of your family and friends to make sure that you aren't missing something which they see as a red flag. Ask yourself: What is the fruit of your relationship with this man? Does he draw you closer to himself, or closer to God?

How does he treat his parents, particularly his mother?
In the same way that you are preparing for marriage by the way you treat your father, the man is preparing for marriage by the way he treats his mother. If he's polite, caring, and helpful of his mother, chances are that he'll be the same toward a wife. If he's not showing godly fruit in this area, he's probably not been thinking ahead. You don't want a guy who's ungentlemanly or unprepared.

How does he treat his siblings, particularly his sisters?
If he's impatient with younger siblings, that's a bad sign. A father needs to be patient and understanding. I know men who think their little siblings or their children are frustrating and annoying. They only appreciate children that are old enough to speak rationally with them and that aren't messy, foolish, or annoying. Personally, I'll never marry a man of that type, because those men are thinking selfishly about their relationships with children, instead of serving and teaching the little ones with Christ-like gentleness.

Furthermore, if the guy has sisters, what do they think of him? The same way you're practicing wifely skills on your brother, he'll be practicing husbandly skills on his sisters. How does he treat them? Do they feel that he's aloof and distant? Domineering and impatient? Warm and inclusive? It's worth knowing what kind of reputation this guy has with his own family members. You'll be sharing in that reputation if you marry him.

How does he respond to family?
When a guy likes a girl, there is a tendency for him to want her all to himself. He might give a passing nod to the rest of her family,

but he's tempted to monopolize the girl's time and her attention. A truly mature young man will respect and include her family. After all, these are the people who raised her and who shaped her life. They know her best.

When a young man gets serious about me, I don't want him to treat my family like accessories to my life. My family *is* my life. He must respect their influence and their part in my life and he must understand that, although a marriage relationship will take priority for me, he will never replace my parents and siblings. I expect him to give me similar access to his family. These are the people who influenced him, for good or ill, and it is my responsibility to know them. They tell me something about him.

This concept holds true even when a family is really messed up. For example, you will learn something about a guy who treats his parents with as much respect as he can, even when they are not respectable. He will learn something about you from the way you treat your family too. No matter how our culture looks at family, God views family as very, very important, especially when a marriage is being considered.

Is he preparing for his future responsibly?

A young man should be getting ready to have his own family, and he should exhibit the skills necessary for providing for a family. He should have a direction for his life, with an openness to God's leading.

This does not necessarily mean that he needs to have all his ducks laid out in a row. I know several men who chose to marry before attaining full financial stability. Of course, getting married in those circumstances causes a lot of difficulty. These men had to support rapidly growing families on limited incomes, which was very stressful. A lot of potential troubles—marital, financial, emotional, and even spiritual—can come from that type of situation. This does not mean that such hardship automatically squashes happiness. Despite the difficulty, God's provision and goodness has been demonstrated many times in the families of these men.

That said, those who wait for ideal situations wait forever. A wise woman looks for potential. Is the man just wandering through life, waiting for the light bulb to go off in his head and give him the perfect direction to his life, or is he really trying to prepare responsibly for the future? Do his choices show a desire to be hardworking, responsible, and God-honoring?

This is more than just a financial issue; this is a character issue. You need to know that a man would take his responsibility as a husband and as a provider very seriously. My mother pointed out to me that I couldn't marry a man solely because of his potential; what if he never truly lives up to it? It would be ridiculous to marry him with the hope that he will someday be the man that I see in him.

What do your parents think of him?

Your inexperience is a disadvantage. You've never been married before; you don't know all the issues of which you need to be aware. Your parents' experience is a huge advantage to you. You don't have to make mistakes, because you can ask your parents and learn from their mistakes and successes. Your parents may see problems with a potential "candidate" that you had never considered. Or they might notice a young man that you're overlooking, who may be a great match for you. Many young women have leaped into marriages against their parents' wishes, because they were "so in love," and found out later that their parents had some valid concerns. I know that sometimes there is strain between young women and their parents. It's still worth it to know what they think, because he will be part of their lives if you marry him.

How does he deal with stress?

Marriage itself will be one of the major stressors in a young man's life. His income will become more important than ever. His desire to please his wife and to provide for his family will consume him. What does he do when he is stressed out? What are the comforts to which he turns? How does he interact with others when he is under pressure? This is not a matter to pass over lightly. This is a matter for deep consideration, because you need to know what to expect from a man when inevitable hardships occur.

What is his work ethic?

A woman I know once remarked, "I knew that my husband was the man for me because of his work ethic. The same attitude that he put into his work was the same attitude that he would put into our marriage. His work ethic has had a tremendous impact on our marriage."

When you consider a man, ask yourself: How does he work at home? Does he motivate himself to begin projects? Does he clean up his project materials or leave them scattered all over the house? Does he take responsibility for things like clearing away his dishes from the table, or does he leave that for others? Does he routinely offer to help others?

How does he work in the workplace? Does he show up for work on time? Does he live peaceably with his coworkers and boss, as much as possible?[239] Does he try to work diligently, efficiently, and thoroughly?

This seemingly small issue has the potential to greatly influence a marriage. A man's work ethic reveals his character. The attitude he shows toward his work will translate into other areas of his life.

Is he responsible with his resources?

How does he spend his time? Does he immediately gravitate toward video games, television, and the computer when he is home? Does he spend time on worthy projects? Does he use his time responsibly, but rarely includes service to others?

How does he spend his money? Does he tend to buy items that he rarely uses? Does he balance his own accounts and maintain a budget when he can? Does he spend his money on expensive items when cheaper items would be acceptable substitutes? Does he generously or grudgingly give to those in need?

What kind of friends does he have?

On my first day of high school sports, my coach saw that I was alone and, before he introduced me to one of the young teenage girls on my new team, he gave this piece of advice: "You are judged

---

[239] Romans 12:18

by the friends you keep." My experience in high school sports proved the truth of those words, because my choice of friends either built my character or tore it down. If you want to know a man, take a look at his choice of friends.

Does he reach out to nonbelievers, while still being careful about their influence on him? Or does he reach out to them without discernment and caution, spending too much time with them? Does he gravitate toward only the good-looking or higher-class people? Is he peer-oriented, or does he interact well with people of many ages and backgrounds? Do his friends encourage him in the Lord and show mature faith? Do his friends tend to be foolish and goofy, or do they show sober-mindedness with appropriate humor? Do his female friends trust that he is honorable, appropriate, and courteous? Do his guy buddies know him to be responsible, thoughtful, and godly? Does he favor spending time with his friends over spending time with his family, or does he balance his social life with his family life?

How does he take care of his body?

When a friend and I discussed this issue one day, I asked, "Are we just being petty? I mean, what if God gives me a fat husband? Couldn't a guy be godly but unhealthy?"

My friend replied, "God knows a man's heart and I can't judge, but honestly, I see a man's body care as a character issue. God calls our bodies the temple of the Lord, and a man who does not at least try to make his temple as healthy as possible shows an improper mindset."

My friend and I were careful to make a distinction between healthy and "hot." We acknowledged that a man could be fit without being a gorgeous hunk, and that a man might struggle with valid health issues. Our main concern was that a man's attitude toward his body indicated his level of forethought, self-control, and motivation. Does he show moderation and wisdom in his eating habits? Does he maintain a healthy level of activity, to the best of his ability? Does he have a plan for a lifetime of health?

The crux of the issue lies not in a man's state of health, but in his attitude toward his health. Some men use their natural health and vigor as an excuse to be reckless or overly competitive, an attitude that they will probably translate into their treatment of their wives. Other men try hard to show responsibility in the care of their naturally weak bodies, which indicates the level of care that they are likely to show toward their wives. Remember, the Bible equates a man's care of his own body with his care of his wife.[240]

If nonbelievers were to form an opinion of God based on a man's attitude toward his health, what would they think? It is important for a man to present his body to God as a living sacrifice, holy and acceptable—not merely in a sexual sense but also in a physical sense.[241] A man who knows how to master his body understands the basis for also mastering his spirit.[242]

And every man that striveth for the mastery is temperate in all things. Now they do it to obtain a corruptible crown; but we an incorruptible.[243]

---

[240] Ephesians 5:25-30
[241] Romans 12:1
[242] 1 Corinthians 9:24-27
[243] 1 Corinthians 9:25

≈ 20 ≈

Personal Checklist

We've talked a lot about how to recognize a desirable, godly man, but marriage isn't a one-way street. After all, we're talking about *two* people. So let's talk about us—your side and my side of the equation in regard to possible future marriage.

Are you prepared for Jesus' return?

Don't try to answer it all at once, because this question is loaded. Just keep it in the back of your mind as we continue this discussion, because this is where the crux of the issue lies. You don't know whether or not you'll ever meet an earthly bridegroom, but you do know that you will one day meet your Heavenly Bridegroom, either after your death or when Christ comes back, as He promised.

When I was in my mid-teens, I had a dream about Jesus' return. It was a beautiful, mind-shattering, terrifying dream. I realized that God is bigger and more powerful than I ever expected. I also recognized that He is more pure than I realized. His presence can bear no sin. In my dream, I was like an amoeba before a human being; He was so far above me in every way that I despaired of ever measuring up to His greatness and glory. His beauty was so powerful, His love so fierce, His purity so bright that I knew I was nothing in His presence. I knew that I should be happy to meet Him, but instead, I was afraid that He would see my sin and my worthlessness. It has been many years since I had that dream and God has finally brought me to a place in my relationship with Him where I long for His return. I used to cringe at the very thought of His return; now I can't wait to run into my Bridegroom's arms.

When we think about the possibility of marriage, how much do we think about the certainty of Christ's return? When we prepare for earthly marriage, how much do we prepare for our Heavenly marriage? When He returns, will we be like the ten foolish virgins in the parable, whose lamps had run out of oil during the wait for the bridegroom? Or will we be like the ten wise virgins, who bought enough oil to last them through the waiting period and who were therefore allowed to join the wedding party?[244] Are we ready—right now—to meet our Heavenly Bridegroom?

Are you prepared to be the best wife possible?

One day, as I finished a prayer that God would bring me a husband, He prodded my heart with an unexpected question.

"And...?"

"And what?" I responded. "Is there some important criterion for my husband that I've missed?"

"Yes. You missed his other half."

"His other half?" Pause. "Oh. You mean me."

Suddenly I recognized my selfishness. I wanted God to pick the perfect husband for me, because I wanted to make sure that I got, if not the best, at least the closest thing I could get to best. But what about my husband? Was he going to get the best I had to offer?

So I prayed something that I had never prayed before.

"Dear Lord, help me to become a good wife, to know what to practice to become a better and godlier woman, and to prepare for the man that You will bring into my life. I don't know what his preferences are, but help me to be ready for those preferences. Prepare me to be a loving, supportive, and submissive wife. Help me grow into the kind of person who can bless him daily."

I decided that whenever I presented God with my preferences for a husband, I would also consider my future husband's desires, needs, and preferences. Only God knew what kind of man he would be. Even though I didn't know him yet, God could still shape me into a complementary partner for this special man.

When preparing for marriage, it is good to consider ourselves— not our wants, but our defects, our problems, our immaturities, our faults, our sins. We are already in good practice for this. As Christians, we are already learning how to surrender our will to the will of our Heavenly Bridegroom. Now we must translate this into a selfless attitude toward an earthly bridegroom.

---

[244] Matthew 25:1-13

What does your speech say about you?

Suppose an interested young man listens to your speech to find out more about you. After all, if he marries you, he's going to have to live with you and your mouth for the rest of his life. What will he learn from what you say? Will he find that you're a gossip? That you are often negative or angry? That your language is...ahem...unladylike? That you're nice and everything, but you just don't stop talking?

Or will he find that you are patient, forgiving, and kind? Will he find that you speak respectfully about other people, even when you have differences with them? Will he find that you know the value of silence? Will he find that your speech is thoughtful and wise? Will he learn that you keep important confidences safe?

As a jewel of gold in a swine's snout, so is a fair woman which is without discretion.[245]

For of the abundance of the heart his mouth speaketh.[246]

Your speech reveals your thoughts. If a thought is too embarrassing or shameful to share with other people, then don't think it, because it will come out in your speech. This verse is literally true; I've seen it happen in my life and in other peoples' lives. My own mouth betrayed me. Yours will betray you too, even if you're careful. If you want to be discreet and wise in your speech, learn to be discreet and wise in your thoughts.

What does your clothing say about you?

Suppose an interested young man evaluates your clothing and behavior to learn more about you. Will he see in you a woman who will be careful to reserve her body for her future husband, and not to make herself "eye-candy" for other men? Will he see in you a woman who respects her God-given femininity and beauty enough to keep it special for her God and her husband? Will he see in you a woman who is as guarded about her body as she is about her speech? Will he see that your attitude and your clothing reflect your relationship with Christ?

Your attitude says a lot about who you are and Who you

---

[245] Proverbs 11:22
[246] Luke 6:45b

represent. You could wear a full-body potato sack with holes for your eyes and *still* be immodest. It's the attitude that determines whether or not you are modest. Ask yourself, "If I love Christ and I want to show an attitude that is pure, modest, and humble, how would I dress? How would I act?"

What does your use of time say about you?

Suppose an interested young man set up cameras in your home, your workplace, and your church to learn more about how you use your time. What will he find out about you?

In your Candidate Checklist, we learned that it was a good idea to find out whether the young man is preparing responsibly for his future. How about you? Do you have a direction? If you are unsure what direction God is taking you at this time, are you filling your time with good activities? Do you find yourself bored most of the time, or do you find something to do, even if it's something you don't like? Do you spend most of your time for yourself or for others? If necessary, it can even be helpful to keep a log to evaluate your time management (I use this technique sometimes). Once you know your weaknesses, you can take steps to correct them.

How much time do we spend on recreational activities like social networking, gaming, scrapbooking, and playing? I'm not saying any of these activities are wrong. They aren't. Fun provides both a good outlet for stress and a healthy balance to work.[247] That said, the amount of time you spend on these things says something about you and has an impact on your life.

Your future husband will want to know that he can count on you to spend your time wisely. He will want to know that you are motivated, responsible, and diligent. He will want to know that you have a habit of being an efficient, capable manager, who is not excessive in her activities or sloppy about her work. He will want to know that you take time out of your busy day to reach out to other people and to be a godly, encouraging presence in their lives.

Time is not a renewable resource and you can't grab back time or add more. God has numbered the days of your life and He

---

[247] Ecclesiastes 3:1-13

knows exactly how much time you have left.[248] You don't. Your time here on earth is limited and, as a Christian, your purpose is to glorify God with whatever time you have left. Spend it wisely.

Lord, make me to know mine end, and the measure of my days, what it is: that I may know how frail I am.[249]

What do your relationships say about you?

Suppose an interested young man interviews your family, your friends, your co-workers, and your enemies about you. What do you think they will say? Especially, what will those closest to you tell him?

My family—especially my sisters—would probably give him an earful about me. They would probably have a lot of nice things to say (at least, I hope so!), but they would also admit that I have some weaknesses. Those areas are not destined to impress a possible suitor! Sometimes I take the bull by the horns and ask a random family member how I'm doing. They're very honest and usually my improvement in a certain area is not as great as I had hoped. But these areas are worth reviewing, because if they really bug my family, they may bug my husband. Some of the things my family members dislike about me seem unimportant, but I consider changes to my life because I want to show them that I respect their input and their feelings. It's a life-long process, but it is my joy to see my relationships blossom!

Ask your family and friends how they would describe you to a guy who wants to know more about you. Ask them to be brutally honest. Look for patterns in what people say about you, because that can help you identify areas of weakness. It takes a lot of guts to look at yourself through the eyes of other people, because the appearance is usually not as flattering as you hoped. However, when you work at your relationships and ask the Lord to help you fix your weaknesses, you become a woman who is more desirable and more precious all the time.

---

[248] Job 14:5
[249] Psalm 39:4

≫ 21 ≪

How to Pray For a Husband

You'd think it would be obvious, but if we want the Lord to answer a prayer, we have to pray that prayer first. Once, I was frustrated because I wasn't married and I couldn't understand why God didn't give me even a teensy bit of hope that I would get married *eventually*. Then it struck me that I hadn't even prayed about it. I had prayed more about my struggles with temptation than I had prayed about my desire! I realized that this was because I felt selfish to pray for something I wanted, but the Bible says that God cares about our desires!

Have we asked God to give us that thing we desire? It's not wrong to ask, because Jesus told us to ask! We must understand that God doesn't always give the answer we want. He gives the answer that is best. Whether or not His answer is the one we hope for, He still wants to know the desires of our hearts. We must dare to tell the Lord our whole heart.

How should we ask? I see six main patterns in the Bible: an understanding of God's giving heart, persistence, heartfelt sincerity, respect, gratitude, and right motivation.

God Gives Good Gifts

Ask, and it shall be given you; seek, and ye shall find; knock, and it shall be opened unto you: For every one that asketh receiveth; and he that seeketh findeth; and to him that knocketh it shall be opened. Or what man is there of you, whom if his son ask bread, will he give him a stone? Or if he ask a fish, will he give him a serpent? If ye then, being evil, know how to give good gifts unto your children, how much more shall your Father which is in heaven give good things to them that ask him?[250]

Suppose you are a mother and your child tells you, "The one thing I want most in the whole world is a puppy." You know it would please her, it would teach her responsibility, it would give

---

[250] Matthew 7:7-11

her companionship, and it would show how much you love her. Wouldn't you go out of your way to help that child get a puppy, not just any puppy, but the very best available?

Now suppose that your child is allergic to dogs. You wouldn't just say, "Sorry, kid. No can do." Of course not! You would search tirelessly for a substitute that would thrill her heart, something even better than a puppy.

This is similar to the way that God grants our desires. He loves to bless us and if, in His wisdom, He sees that our desire is a good thing, He is willing to grant that desire. If, in His wisdom, He sees that it would be a bad thing for us, He substitutes it with another, equally wonderful thing. If even sinful people can give good gifts, our Heavenly Father knows how to give even better gifts! Trust that He loves to bless us.

Pray with Persistence

And he spake a parable unto them to this end, that men ought always to pray, and not to faint; Saying, There was in a city a judge, which feared not God, neither regarded man: And there was a widow in that city; and she came unto him, saying, Avenge me of mine adversary. And he would not for a while: but afterward he said within himself, Though I fear not God, nor regard man. Yet because this widow troubleth me, I will avenge her, lest by her continual coming she weary me. And the Lord said, Hear what the unjust judge saith. And shall not God avenge his own elect, which cry day and night unto him, though he bear long with them? I tell you that he will avenge them speedily. Nevertheless when the Son of man cometh, shall he find faith on the earth?[251]

If we truly desire something, we will bring it before the Lord constantly. I know it sounds like nagging, but from this passage it is clear that God listens when we pray with persistence. The widow would not give up and we should not either. If we want an answer, we must continue to ask, not until we get tired of asking, but until we get an answer. God wants to know that we will seek Him with all our hearts.

---

[251] Luke 18:1-8

Pray with Heartfelt Sincerity

Hannah could not have children and this broke her heart. Every year, she went to the temple during the Jewish feasts and wept, prayed, and fasted. The Bible says that she was in "bitterness of soul" and that she "wept and prayed in anguish."[252] She begged God to remember her. She vowed that if God would give her a son, she would dedicate him to the Lord. God heard her prayer and gave her a son—Samuel, the last and possibly the greatest judge in Israel. If we ask with the heartfelt sincerity that Hannah showed, God will listen and give an answer.

The Bible is full of instances when people seem to make outrageous demands on God—Restore this person's life,[253] Give me children,[254] Make the sun stand still,[255] Give me superhuman ability to destroy my enemies[256]—and God answered them. If we only pray reasonable prayers, we will never see miracles! God tells us to pray with faith.

When a person in the Bible makes a request of God, notice that he does so boldly. He does not say, "O Lord, I pray that You will do this. Only if You want to, of course. I really want you to answer my prayer, but don't feel obligated to do so." What sort of response can God give to a prayer with so little conviction? If we ask for something from God, let us lay down all our cards. Let us ask Him with boldness and sincerity, believing that He can answer our prayer.

Pray with Respect

Go to now, ye that say, To day or to morrow we will go into such a city, and continue there a year, and buy and sell, and get gain: Whereas ye know not what shall be on the morrow. For what is your life? It is even a vapour, that appeareth for a little time, and then vanisheth away. For that ye ought to say, If the Lord will, we shall live, and do this, or that.[257]

No one demands things from a king. Those who make requests

---

[252] 1 Samuel 1:10
[253] 1 Kings 17:21
[254] 1 Samuel 1:11
[255] Joshua 10:12
[256] Judges 16:28
[257] James 4:13-15

of a king know that he has the authority to say either yes or no. God owes us nothing. When we ask with perseverance and with sincerity, we must understand that God is ultimately in control of our destinies. We may ask with boldness: "Lord, this is the desire of my heart. I ask that You grant it." We may never ask with disrespect: "Lord, I demand that You grant my desire!" A young woman of God remembers that she may be bold in her requests, but she must be ready to accept the answer, whatever it may be. Ultimately, she must say, "Thy will be done."

I once asked my father, "When I ask things of God, how do I know the difference between boldness and arrogance?"

My father replied, "How do you know the difference between boldness and arrogance when you ask things of *me*?"

Pray with Gratitude

Be careful for nothing; but in every thing by prayer and supplication with thanksgiving let your requests be made known unto God. And the peace of God, which passeth all understanding, shall keep your hearts and minds through Christ Jesus.[258]

A friend and I once talked about our prayer life. She said that she prayed often. I asked her if she ever thanked God. She looked startled and asked what I meant. "Well, think about it," I said. "If someone always said, 'Please give me this, please do that for me,' wouldn't you feel like they just wanted stuff from you? But if someone says, 'Thank you for all the wonderful things you do for me,' then you know they love you for who you are, not for what they can get from you. It's the same way with God. We should thank Him all the time!"

A local pastor did a sermon series on the Lord's Prayer, in which he pointed out that the prayer begins with praise: "Our Father, who art in heaven, hallowed be Thy name. Thy kingdom come, Thy will be done, on earth as it is in Heaven..." It also ends with praise: "For Thine is the kingdom and the power and the glory forever." This is a good model. Every time we ask for something, we should also thank God for all the prayers He has already answered and all the blessings He has already given.

---

[258] Philippians 4:6-7

Pray with Right Motives

Ye lust, and have not: ye kill, and desire to have, and cannot obtain: ye fight and war, yet ye have not, because ye ask not. Ye ask, and receive not, because ye ask amiss, that ye may consume it upon your lusts.[259]

Why are we asking? Do we ask because we want something that will satisfy our desires? Or do we ask because we want something that will please and glorify God? Don't get me wrong; it's *not* selfish to ask for something you want. Trying to over-spiritualize our desires is hypocrisy, because God understands that a desire is a desire. Hannah prayed for a child, and her request was based on her desire. But what did she do with the child she desired? She gave him back to God.

And she vowed a vow, and said, O Lord of hosts, if thou wilt indeed look on the affliction of thine handmaid, and remember me, and not forget thine handmaid, but wilt give unto thine handmaid a man child, then I will give him unto the Lord all the days of his life, and there shall no razor come upon his head.[260]

When we ask for something, we need to be willing to give it back to God. Everything—and everyone—we have is on loan from God. Here's a way to test your motives: If God gives you a husband for a time and then takes him away, will you still love God? Will you still accept the life He has given to you? Are you willing to give your desire back to God?

Pray For Your Future Husband

Unless God makes it clear that you will be a single woman for life, there is nothing wrong with praying for your future husband. I initially worried that praying for my future husband would make me more discontented, but I find that it makes me more content to wait, because I know that he is worth waiting for. It reminds me that if I marry, then my future husband is actually alive somewhere, doing something at this very moment. That thought makes me more determined to be a good wife for him someday.

Many parents pray for their children's spouses, long before

---

[259] James 4:2-3
[260] 1 Samuel 1:11

those spouses arrive. In wedding after wedding, I've heard parents praise God for answering decades of prayers for their children. If our parents can pray for our future spouses, why shouldn't we?

Pray for your future husband. Pray that he will love the Lord more than anything. If he cannot love the Lord, he cannot truly love anyone, even you. Pray that the Lord will lead him and strengthen him spiritually, preparing him to be a good husband and father. Pray that he will do well in his job or career. Pray that the Lord will protect his health.

Pray also for your father. Until you marry, your father is your Biblical authority. Pray across any geographical or emotional distance between you and your father. Pray for his relationship with God, his job, his health, his mind, and his relationships. If you are in good practice to pray for the current man of your life, however imperfect he may be, you will be a fit prayer-warrior for the new man of your life when you marry.

Pray for yourself too, that you will be ready to serve your husband, and that God will mold you to his specific needs. Pray that you will be the best woman for this one-of-a-kind man.

Single
&
Content

ℬ 22 ℛ

The Truth About Singleness

Although God created marriage, the Bible is clear that marriage is not for everyone. Even those who *do* marry experience a period of singleness first. Since most people end up marrying, the market is awash with books, movies, sermons, speeches, and studies about marriage. However, very little is said about singleness. Sure, people talk about singleness *in preparation for marriage*, but few people address the issue of singleness as either a life stage or a lifetime commitment.

Godly, contented singleness is just as great a gift as an excellent marriage. So why are so many single women unhappy? It all comes down to the lies that we believe about singleness: pressures we feel from society, fears and expectations that we have for ourselves, and ignorance about the true benefits of singleness. My hope is to plant in you seeds of hope, purpose, and contentment that will make you a single woman who is every bit as happy and fulfilled as a bride.

Truth #1: Marriage is not for everybody.

God has not made us all equal in terms of marriage. This is apparent following a discussion in the Bible about divorce. The disciples began to feel disillusioned about marriage ("Good grief, is it really worth it?") and Jesus answered them.[261]

His disciples say unto him, If the case of the man be so with his wife, it is not good to marry. But he said unto them, All men cannot receive this saying, save they to whom it is given. For there are some eunuchs, which were so born from their mother's womb: and there are some eunuchs, which were made eunuchs of men: and there be eunuchs, which have made themselves eunuchs for the kingdom of heaven's sake. He that is able to receive it, let him receive it.

Some of us will marry and serve God as a pair. Some of us will marry and produce godly children. And some of us will produce

---

[261] Matthew 19:10-12

the precious fruit of godly singleness. Whatever lifestyle God has given to each of us, He equips us for that life. The one whom He has chosen to keep single will not always have an extreme burning desire to be married; she will be given the ability to live out singleness with gladness and purpose. This does not mean that she will be temptation-free. It simply means that the Lord will give her the ability to live purely. It is the same ability that He gives to each of us who desire to do His will, except that the ability is meant to last for a lifetime of singleness, not simply for a season of singleness.

To give you an example, a friend once told me about a missionary woman who was called to the mission field from an early age and who loved the Lord with all her heart. When the Lord revealed to her that He planned for her to remain single all her life, she desperately wanted God to change His mind. She wanted to get married! Because she loved the Lord so much, He was able to bring her to a place where she trusted His will for her completely. Whereas she had first revolted against the thought of lifetime singleness, she now revolted against the thought of marriage. Such a complete transformation can only be done through the Lord, and it requires full commitment and trust in Him.

If this story scares you and makes you worry that God will ask the same sacrifice of you, you're not alone. It scares me too! However, if we love and trust the Lord, it also offers encouragement. We know that God will not leave us to face singleness alone, whether it is singleness for a season or for a lifetime. Are we willing to trust Him with our singleness?

Truth #2: Marriage both gives and takes.

I believe that young women should savor their singleness. To savor something means to enjoy it fully, to drink it in, to make the beauty of it last as long as possible. We should savor our singleness the way we would savor our favorite dessert, a beautiful sunset, a fun-filled day, or a quiet moment. Our singleness is worth it. If we spend our time wishing we were married, we're not fully appreciating the fact that we are single. That's a sad thing, because singleness offers many benefits that disappear once we are married.

My newly-married friend mentioned that she missed the

opportunities to bond with her sisters at the end of each day. I thought about her words and about my cousin's reminder, "These are the best years of your life." There are times when all I can see of singleness is the difficulty of fighting discontentment and of longing for a husband. Then I remember that marriage will separate me from many freedoms and opportunities that I now enjoy.

Managing a household is not easy. Paperwork is endless, finances continually demand attention, and the needs of the husband and any children must come before one's own needs. Getting together with friends or having lunch with someone may not be as easy as it used to be. A lot of old hobbies and pursuits may fall by the wayside. Ask yourself, and be honest: What do you love now? How might marriage impact those pursuits or opportunities? Are you ready to make that change if it is required?

We take many blessings for granted. Once we marry, the blessings of singleness will fade. Marriage has its own blessings, but how will you be fully grateful for the blessings that marriage has to offer if you've made a habit of overlooking the blessings that singleness has to offer?

Truth #3: God comes first, whether we marry or stay single.

Some people say that our life on earth is practice for our life in Heaven. The first and greatest commandment is to love the Lord our God with all our hearts, soul, mind, and strength.[262] That is what we are supposed to do now, on earth, and that will not change when we get to Heaven. Some things *will* change when we get to Heaven. For instance, in our eternal lives, there will be no marriage.

Jesus answered and said unto them, Ye do err, not knowing the scriptures, nor the power of God. For in the resurrection they neither marry, nor are given in marriage, but are as the angels of God in heaven.[263]

Although marriage is a shadow and a sign of the marriage of Jesus Christ and the Church, it is not something that gets us in practice for what we will be doing in eternity. It will fade away when Christ returns. There will not be any need for more children, or for the satisfaction of physical desires, or for companionship, or

---

[262] Mark 12:30
[263] Matthew 22:29-30

for a symbol of something better to come. We will have the real thing—a complete and whole relationship with Christ—and He will satisfy *all* desires.

For thy Maker is thine husband; the LORD of hosts is his name...[264]

Just as marriage is special because it points to our Heavenly marriage, singleness is also special because it prepares us for that eternity. We are not distracted by a relationship that is a shadow of our Heavenly marriage; we can begin preparing for the Heavenly marriage right away. This does not mean that marriage keeps us from preparing; it just means that singleness allows us to prepare with less distraction.

Have you ever read the verse: "Delight yourself in the Lord and He will give you the desires of your heart"?[265] What does it mean? Well, here are some thoughts:

There's a tendency to believe that if we behave in a godly way, He'll give us what we want. My answer: God is not Santa Claus. He doesn't tally up our good deeds, good intentions, and good desires to determine whether or not we've earned our treats. When we delight ourselves in the Lord, *He* becomes the desires of our hearts. As we draw closer to God, our wants and desires become all about Him. We desire Him more than we desire anything else—yes, even more than we desire a husband. When God becomes the desire of our hearts, it is easy to obtain "the desires of our hearts," because He is constantly giving us more of Himself, so we are constantly having our desire fulfilled.

God desires to bless us with the things we want and He also wants to become the sole and greatest object of our desires. It's a danger to be selfish ("I want God to give me stuff!") and it's a danger to overspiritualize ("It's wrong to want anything but God!"). Whether God gives us only Himself or whether He brings us our earthly desire, the command is the same: Delight yourself in the Lord! When we truly delight in Him, relish His presence, and desire a relationship with Him, I believe He both rearranges and fulfills our desires in a wonderful and mysterious way.

---

[264] Isaiah 54:5a
[265] Psalm 37:4

215

ᴕ 23 ᴘ

The War Against Singleness

Godly singleness is under severe attack. Satan hates godly singleness just as much as he hates godly marriage. Why? The answer takes us all the way back to Genesis. Eve had everything she needed to be happy: a loving God, a devoted husband, and a home in paradise. Then the serpent (Satan) presented her with his great lie. "You need something more in order to be happy. Just eat this forbidden fruit and *then* you'll be truly complete." Eve believed the lie and women ever since have grasped for forbidden fruit in hopes of discovering a truly satisfying life.

If Satan can convince a woman that her singleness is a curse— that she needs a man in order to be happy—then he has accomplished his goal. When a woman, through God's strength, decides that she needs no one but the Lord to make her happy, the battle has just turned against Satan. Singleness with contentment is a crushing blow against the kingdom of darkness and it is worthy of all the songs of the angels.

Pressures from Society

When I was growing up, it seemed that every movie and book included a love story on some level. Now that I'm grown up—it's worse than ever. At the time of this writing, I am 24 years old. Believe me, there's not many people of my age in my area who have not paired up in some way (dating, courting, engaged, or married). People have been nudging me since I was a teenager. "Why don't you have a boyfriend? Have you even gone out with anyone yet? How will you know what you like if you don't try it out a bit first?"

When they learn that, no, I have not gone out with anyone, no, I do not have an interested bachelor, and no, I will not try things out first, they begin to worry about me. Society teaches that our worth is related to our success in attracting romantic interest. Even if we are successful in every other way, we are considered incomplete if we have failed to attract someone. Surely, if a young woman is talented, reasonably good-looking, and pleasant, she should have attracted a man by now! People wonder: Is she socially impaired, controlled by domineering parents, trapped in a "nothing" area, or passing up all the worthy opportunities because of her impossibly high ideals?

People approach the subject of singleness in many ways.

The Matchmaker: People are very uncomfortable when a young adult has "nobody." The older a single woman gets, the more people notice her for her lack of suitors. Even the people who love her best grow concerned and many feel that they need to help out. One time my sister helped an elderly woman, who promptly exclaimed, "You're so sweet, dear! Have I got the grandson for you!" My friend was nonplussed when someone in her church introduced to her "the perfect guy," who was just as embarrassed as she was. Thereafter, the whole church seemed to wait breathlessly for the young people to make the match happen.

Your reactions to any of these situations might vary from amusement to panic.

"Yeah, guys. (Laugh) Thanks for the concern, but no thanks! No way that's going to work out!"

"Um...uh...thanks. I guess."

"Eek! What am I going to do? I don't know anything about this guy, but this woman seems to think it's a done deal!"

"Uh oh. It wouldn't have been a problem if he'd been somebody I totally would never consider...but as it turns out, I like him, and now it's hard to think about him as just a brother in Christ!"

The Warner: Then there are the people who try to combat the poison of society's lie by going to the other extreme. They may tell us, "Don't think about marriage yet; you have a whole life ahead of you!" For some of us, marriage is all we've thought about since we've played Mommy with our baby dolls. Often, these comments come from women who are already married, and there's a rebellious little voice inside us that whines, "Yeah, but you're married. Easy for *you* to say 'Don't think about marrying yet.'" However insensitive these comments may seem, there might be a story behind the advice. Adults, especially our parents, might say things like this because they are trying to warn us against mistakes that they made in the past. They might be afraid that desperation will cause us to make bad choices.

Of course, there will be those times when someone says this just because they think we are too young. I have known mature young women who were quite ready for the responsibility of marriage. Others told them that they were "too young" to marry. Some of these people had themselves married at 19 and had a happy marriage. I do not understand this contradiction, but I can well sympathize with my teenage married friend who exploded one day, "If one more person tells me that I'm too young to be married, I'm going to throw something!"

The Sympathizer: A younger friend once said to me, "I don't know how you do it! If I were your age and still single, I'd be going crazy!"

At the time, I was feeling pretty upbeat about life, so I said something breezy about how busyness helps me to stay focused and content. A few months later, while I was struggling with intense frustration, I remembered the conversation and privately snapped to myself, "What do you mean? I *am* going crazy!"

My sister once said: "It would be nice if people would admit every once in a while that it's hard." Admitting that trying to do things God's way despite all the pressure is *not* the same as saying, "Oh, it must be so hard to be single!" The difficulty lies not in being single but in going against our human natures and our culture's lies in order to follow God. I'd gladly welcome anyone who agrees that a Christ-like life is hard!

Of course, I also realize the irony of it. Nobody says, "Oh, it must be so hard to be married!" Or "Oh, it must be so hard to be in college!" Or "Oh, it must be so hard to work a job!" Everyone expects us to just deal with the pressure as a part of life. So why is singleness the exception?

Truthfully, singleness affects different people different ways. Some of us are completely content being single; we love the freedom to follow the Lord and to enjoy the benefits of singleness. If people assume that we are discontent, we are puzzled that such a

218

wonderful time of life should be considered a bummer. Others of us consistently struggle with being single. Although we appreciate acknowledgment that singleness can be hard, when attention is drawn to the difficulty, it just reinforces the frustration. A third group of us are not consistent at all; sometimes we are grateful to the Lord for our precious time of singleness and other times we can't wait to get married. Assumption about how we're feeling at any particular time can be frustrating because people usually assume wrongly. When we're happy, people assume we're frustrated. When we're frustrated, people assume we're happy. Assumptions can be dangerous; young women are not all the same!

The Comforter: "Don't worry. Someone will come along for you. Just you wait and see." Many people mean well when they say such things, but this can feed wrong expectations. We should ask ourselves: "What if I'm the girl whom God sends to some distant country to serve Him as a missionary? What if I'm the girl who will be permanently debilitated by an accident? What if I'm the girl who will be killed soon by cancer? What if I'm the girl who waits...and waits...but never experiences the fulfillment of her dreams for marriage?" There is no assurance that someone will come along for a particular girl. There is only hope.

The Truth-teller: I cannot change society for you. I cannot guarantee that your interactions with the matchmaker, the warner, the sympathizer, and the comforter will be encouraging. But I can warn you never to perpetuate the mistakes that others make.

Please, do not match-make your friends. Do not arrange "coincidental" meetings between a possible couple. Do not tease others about their lack of romantic possibilities or about the possibility of a certain somebody liking them. Do not joke about who they might like. Don't show automatic enthusiasm when your friend feels affection for some guy she knows; how do *you* know if that is a good match? Could you be encouraging her to tempt herself? I have seen so many young women do these things to each other. Their meddling often does far more harm than good. For those of you who still don't understand this, read *Emma* by Jane Austen. It's very entertaining and it's also a clear picture of the dangers of match-making others. Relationships are serious business. Marriage relationships are *extremely* serious business. When you touch someone else's relationship, you touch something very sacred. Do not treat it lightly.

Please, do not tell others *not* to think about marriage yet. If marriage is in a young woman's future, she *should* think about it, even when she is very young. A young woman needs a good foundation long before she enters a permanent, committed relationship. If a young woman truly wishes to get married, direct her to God's Word to learn more about singleness, marriage, and relationships. Ask her about the motivations behind her desire. Encourage her to prepare responsibly. Remind her that her singleness is a gift to be used wisely.

Please, do not sympathize with a young woman's discontentment. Acknowledge her feelings, admit your own struggles, agree that godliness is a hard road, but never leave her wallowing in gloominess. Encourage her to value her singleness. Strengthen her for the struggle against temptation, sin, and discouragement. Do not do so in an artificially optimistic way, or she will feel that you are simply trying to put a patch on a deep wound. Take the time to listen, but then remind her that her worth is based on her relationship with the Lord, not on her success in attracting a husband.

Please, do not comfort with platitudes. The reality is that *if the Lord wills*, it will happen. A woman once told my mother that there was no certainty that my mother would marry, but added that the odds were heavily in her favor. After all, numerous studies and statistics testify that Christian young women usually get married. This woman was a good friend to my mother, by encouraging her, not with glib assurances, but with truth.

Be a good friend. Be cautious. Be sensitive. Tell the truth. And make sure that the vicious cycle stops with you.

Our Fears and Pressures from Ourselves

Everywhere, we see reinforcement of the belief that a woman's self-worth is determined by her success in attracting a guy. The girls with boyfriends seem to be popular even with other girls, because girls love to talk about each other's romances. Girls who don't have any guy interested in them might wonder why they are "overlooked." They might wonder, *Is there something wrong with me?*

If you are one of those young women, you need to know: YOU ARE NOT ALONE.

We women have many fears, fears about how our marriage prospects are affected by our situations or by our personalities and looks, and fears that we will be left behind. The following list includes some of the fears and frustrations that a young woman might face.

Fear of Limited Opportunities to Meet Godly Young Men

- Nobody I know is eligible or available.
- My location is a "dead zone" for marriage prospects.

If you've ever felt this way, let me tell you a story. There once was a girl named Rebekah. A man came out of nowhere one day to bring Rebekah a proposal of marriage from a long-lost relative. God had guided this messenger from hundreds of miles away (in those days, hundreds of miles was a long distance!) just to ask Rebekah to be the wife of his master's son Isaac. Location was completely irrelevant to God; He knew exactly who to find for Isaac.[266]

People have told me that, if I want to get married, I should move, because my rural area offers no prospects. Although I am sometimes tempted to believe this, I know that it is not true. Since when has location or eligible population limited God? Furthermore, I don't need a large selection of eligible bachelors in order to increase my chances of marriage. I just need *one*.

Are godly young men an endangered species? You bet! I've visited many blogs where young women wonder where all the godly men must be hiding. Surprisingly, I've also visited many websites where young men wonder where all the godly women must be hiding! I don't know why it's so hard for the two groups to find each other, but we know that matches are being made all the time. The only reason we're frustrated is because we feel like it's happening to everyone but us!

Sometimes we feel like Elijah: "God, I'm the only one left!" But God says, "Not so. I have reserved a number to Myself who are

---

[266] See Genesis chapter 24

faithful."[267] There is no "dead zone," no lack of prospects with God. If He can raise up children of Abraham from stones[268] and turn dry bones into living people,[269] He can bring opportunities for marriage to those who trust in Him. The question is: Do we trust Him?

Fear That Something is Wrong with Us

- Nobody notices me! (Everyone notices her!)
- I look too young to be eligible.
- I'm not attractive.
- I'm too attractive; I don't know who genuinely likes me for myself.
- I'm too opinionated.
- I seem to attract only the people I don't like.
- He already has so many friends; why would he notice me?

Believe it or not, I've experienced all of these fears (except the one about being too attractive). In response, here's a challenging thought: God gives us our appearance, our health, our personality—everything that makes us unique women. If we worry that those things stand between us and marriage, are we hinting that God made a mistake?

Look at the married women you know. Are all of them beautiful? Do all of them have attractive personalities? Look at the single people you know. Are all of them ugly? Do all of them have dull personalities? No! Don't evaluate yourself in those terms. Evaluate yourself in God's terms, because that's what a godly young man will be using to evaluate you.

God gives a kind of beauty and a type of personality that is attractive to those who are filled with His Spirit. In Ezekiel chapter 16, God compares Jerusalem to a woman. He tells how He found her abandoned at birth, raised her as His own, and betrothed her to Himself. He says this about her beauty: *And thy renown went forth among the heathen for thy beauty: for it was perfect through my comeliness, which I had put upon thee, saith the Lord God.*[270]

---

[267] 1 Kings 19:14, 18
[268] Matthew 3:9
[269] Ezekiel 37:1-14
[270] Ezekiel 16:14

God made her beauty perfect and special. She was not beautiful naturally; after all, she had been cast away! God delights in taking the ugly, weak, imperfect things of this world and making them beautiful.

When Moses spoke to God on Mount Sinai, his contact with God's Spirit made the skin of his face shine with glory.[271] Likewise, the Spirit of God lives inside of us and I truly believe that He shines through our faces to the world and recognizes other people in whom He also dwells.

When I was fourteen, I prayed for God to bring me a young woman to be my special friend. Some time later, I attended a homeschool event and I noticed a girl from across the room. There was nothing unusual about her (except perhaps that she was a little tall for her age) but I knew at once that I *had* to meet her. I could not explain why; I just knew it. Unbeknownst to me, she had been lonely too, and she also felt that inner nudge to speak to me. As if on a signal, we gravitated toward each other and talked so much that we missed out on all the refreshments. But we didn't mind! We had just made a friendship, a friendship that has grown closer and more beautiful with each passing year. I believe that we met each other because the Holy Spirit within us attracted us to each other. If God can do that with two young women, He can do that with a man and a woman who have been praying for His guidance toward marriage.

If we are truly living for the Lord, we will be noticed. We are like a light in darkness, a light that cannot be hidden. We are like a totally different race of human beings. True Christians have an uncanny way of attracting attention, even when they are not seeking it or don't particularly want it. We don't have to do *anything* to attract attention.

There is nothing more attractive to a true man of God than to see a woman who loves the Lord with all her heart. A true man of God will give an unattractive woman a second look if he recognizes the Holy Spirit in her life. But this principal works oppositely as well. If we are true women of God, are we judging men on their appearance? Do we gravitate toward the handsome ones, the

---

[271] Exodus 34:29-35

THE WAR AGAINST SINGLENESS

athletic ones, the popular ones, the ones with winning personalities? Or are we willing to appreciate the quieter, less attractive, less naturally talented, less successful ones and to love them because of their love for God? Will we be good friends to young men simply because they are brothers in Christ and not because we hope they'll notice us? Are we willing to give Christian young men the same kindness that we hope they will give us?

The Fear of Being Left Behind

- I don't want to be (or get) the "leftovers."
- All my friends are getting married!
- I want to be married by (or before) such-and-such an age.
- I'm afraid my younger siblings will marry before I do.
- What if I never get married?

Because of the emphasis on forming romantic relationships, society teaches us to fear loneliness above all else. Why else would people spend millions of dollars on social networking, beauty products, cell phones, and other things that impact our social status? Young women are especially caught up in this lie. If there is one thing we fear greatly, we fear loneliness. We fear drifting past some magical age of eligibility. We fear being the last one picked. We fear that our younger friends and siblings will leave us behind. Most of all, we fear never marrying at all.

Listen, I have struggled greatly with these fears myself. As of this writing, almost all of my friends are either in a relationship or already married and having babies. Most of them are younger than I. Every Christmas brings a flood of wedding pictures from old friends. Even my younger sister is engaged to be married. Friends and relatives have hinted for years that I should think about a relationship, if not marriage. "It's about time, girl!"

I won't pretend that my expectations or fears apply to everybody, but I do know this: We can't compare ourselves to other people. God does not have the same journey for everyone. He treats us like individuals. If we are not married yet, God is not choosing favorites or ignoring prayers. He is directing our lives with purpose and with love. Is He, perhaps, waiting to see if we will learn to love the path He has given to us, even if we cannot see where it leads?

Standing Alone

Whether or not we ever get married, it is necessary to come to that place when we face the thought of being alone. It is necessary to look loneliness in the eye and ask ourselves, "Can I be content to stand alone with God?" We must be willing to take that step into loneliness, where no one might follow.

Every true Christian must face this decision. God will take us to a place where we risk being alone with Him—no promises, no assurances, just the knowledge that we must be ready to turn our backs on the hope of all other relationships. It is as if each of us is Peter in the boat. Jesus is standing on the stormy water, telling us that we need to step out of the boat and walk to Him—alone, without the others in the boat, just us and Him on the stormy waves, just His hand between us and a watery grave. Can we make that step onto the water?

God once faced me with this question: "Will you love Me, even if I never give you a husband?" What a battle I had! It took me months to give Him an answer, because I didn't want to give Him the answer I knew He expected. Finally, I answered (very reluctantly), "Yes, Lord, I will love You no matter what!" It didn't feel heroic or spiritual. It hurt. In fact, I've had to revisit that decision when I find myself drifting back into a consuming desire for a human relationship. I know that God desires to give me good things, even perhaps a husband, but He wants my whole life. He wants me to be willing to be alone with Him. He asks the same thing of every Christian woman who desires a husband.

When we *do* take that step into loneliness, accompanied by no one but the Lord Himself, we discover a life of fulfillment that we could never dream. I can't explain it; I just know from experience that it is a life filled with peace and joy. Every day is an adventure. Stress melts away, because we aren't trying to control our lives; we're trusting God. When we find complete contentment in our Heavenly Bridegroom, we find contentment in the rest of our life as well. In the end, we are alone—yet not alone.

๛ 24 ଓ

Living in Contentment

If we are content, temptation and frustration have no power over us. It is hard for temptation to make us say, "I can't be happy until I have something more," if we already say with our whole hearts, "I am happy with what I have now." Contentment and thankfulness are two of the best securities we have in combating the lies about singleness.

What Is Contentment?

Contentment is a rare treasure in this world; any time you flip on the TV you are assaulted with ads that play on one of mankind's most prominent sins—greed. Crimes and wars stem from a desire to have more than one already has. But the virtue of contentment is hard to find.

True contentment can never be found outside of a relationship with Jesus Christ. He is the One who satisfies that longing for more, more, more! He also expects us to be vigilant against the seeds of discontentment. To help us fight these "weeds" of greed, He provides us with several virtues that help us to cultivate contentment in our lives.

The first of these virtues is humility. Humility aids the growth of contentment by teaching us that we do not automatically deserve anything. Greed says that we should have what we want now; humility says that we should think of our duties and the needs of others first. When we are satisfied to serve Christ and others with humility, we strengthen our ability to be content. I struggled personally with this—it was hard for me to envision that helping Mom out all day or supervising my brother's schooling would bring me personal satisfaction. God showed me that I needed to be ready to put aside my pride and self-centeredness and to find fulfillment in the "little" services I did each day. This process was humbling, but it brought me to a place where I could serve my family with contentment.

The second virtue is thankfulness. Greed makes our gratitude hollow by telling us that "What I've got is okay, but what I really need is more!" Thankfulness teaches us to view our current possessions as "enough." An ungrateful person is always discontent; a thankful person can be satisfied with even the smallest of gifts. A thankful person is a double blessing because her attitude encourages others to demonstrate a willingness to serve. If a mother praises her daughter for a job well done, the daughter finds delight in pleasing others. If the daughter shows appreciation for her mother's services to the family, the mother is strengthened to continue her important family role. God is teaching me to say "thank you" quickly and sincerely. Even when the circumstances aren't ideal, there is always something to be thankful for.

The third virtue is control of impure or discontented thoughts. The Bible tells us to "bring every thought to the obedience of Christ."[272] We are also reminded to think upon whatever is true, honest, just, pure, lovely, of good report, virtuous, and praiseworthy.[273] The enemy likes to sneak discontented thoughts into our minds. It is the mark of a true Christian to clamp down on those disobedient thoughts and discard them immediately. The mind is the hardest area to control, and I have found that it takes constant vigilance to guard against discontented thoughts. Night can be especially troublesome. When our bodies are tired, our minds can sometimes let down that protective shield. We need to be careful to keep our spiritual armor on all the time.

In conclusion, let me mention one thing: It is not wrong to desire something or to make a request of God; He loves to fulfill our desires (if they are good)! Also, although God's law warns us not to indulge in self-pity (that's discontentment), He does understand and accept true, heart-felt grief. For instance, Job in the Bible lost everything that was most important to him and we don't see that God scolded him for grieving and for not being content. Contentment, like all other virtues, has its own time and its own place.[274] However, in Job's case, we see that even in the midst of his hardship, he did not allow his faith to be shaken. God blessed Job's

---

[272] 2 Corinthians 10:5
[273] Philippians 4:8
[274] Ecclesiastes chapter 3

faithfulness by restoring—even adding to—his possessions and family. The happy end to the story should be an encouragement to all of us, that when we seek God, He will reward us at the end of our struggles by bestowing upon us the blessing of true contentment.

To recap: Contentment is the humility to realize that we aren't owed anything, the thankfulness for the things we already have, and the self-control to keep our thoughts on Christ. Simple? Yes. Easy to put into practice? No. Unfortunately. Keep reading for some practical ways to cultivate contentment.

Stay Busy

Although there is a spiritual side to contentment that involves surrender, there is a practical side. It is really hard to stay content when we are bored or when we're simply waiting for Prince Charming to show up. We don't know how long we will be single. It could be a year or two. It could be decades. It could be a lifetime. No matter how long singleness may last, it is Christ-like to be as productive as possible. Contentment is easier when we are busy with fulfilling work.

Of course, we are good at making ourselves unhappy and discontented. When I realized that being busy was a good way to be content, I figured that the kind of guy I hoped to attract would appreciate a diligent woman. So I threw myself into college and into work and into developing my writing skills. I felt pretty good about myself until I realized that I had found another reason to be discontent. Since I was doing so well at being a productive and industrious young woman, of course, I must be more eligible than ever! Any young man who appreciated a hard-working young woman must surely notice me! But they didn't notice me, no matter how hard I worked, so it was all for nothing!

God showed me that the point of staying productive was not so that I could increase my attractiveness to a prospective suitor. It was simply so that I would use my time wisely for God's glory.

I was peeved. Why did it *always* have to come down to God's glory? Why couldn't there be some kind of perk in it for *me*?

In the end, everything in the world will come down to God's glory. When Jesus comes back, it won't matter who got married and who didn't. What *will* matter is whether we've done things God's way. There is a reward for that, a special one, but we can't get it if we keep trying to get our goodies now.

As much as staying busy is an imperfect strategy, it teaches us what love and obedience looks like in action. This could be useful in training us for marriage, or it could be useful in training us for our eternal life with Jesus. In either case, it's the right thing to do.

Learning Surrender

Finding contentment involves giving something up. In a sense, it involves giving yourself up. It means saying, "Thy will be done." At that moment when discontentment comes knocking, we must have a clear understanding of who is supposed to win in the end— us or God. Here's the dilemma: If we choose that we win and get what we want, we lose, because we miss the better thing that God has for us. (He always has something better.) If we choose that God wins, we lose, because we have to give up what we wanted. In other words, we always lose, but one kind of loss is better than the other. Jesus Christ had this to say about losing to God:

And he that taketh not his cross, and followeth after me, is not worthy of me. He that findeth his life shall lose it: and he that loseth his life for my sake shall find it.[275]

Jesus Himself had to lose to God. In the Garden of Gethsemane, just before Judas betrayed Him, Jesus knew that He was going to endure a terrible death. He was so distressed that He sweat blood. Jesus prayed three times that His Father would find a way to save us without requiring His death. Yet even as He made this request, He added this: "Not my will, but Thine."[276] He left the final choice up to God and He was ready to obey—even to death.

This process of losing to God is something that we often call *surrender*. Surrender is not a once-in-a-lifetime thing, but rather a continual process. Jesus told a parable about the importance of counting the cost before you commit yourself.[277] You need to know that living a Christian life requires laying down your weapons,

---

[275] Matthew 10:38-39
[276] Luke 22:42
[277] Luke 14:26-33

229

lying flat on the ground, and crying, "I surrender!"

If any man come to me, and hate not his father, and mother, and wife, and children, and brethren, and sisters, yea, and his own life also, he cannot be my disciple. And whosoever doth not bear his cross, and come after me, cannot be my disciple.[278]

Our love for God should be so powerful that our love for other people and other things looks like hate in comparison. It will cost us something to surrender. Are we prepared for that cost? Are we willing to give up everything so that we can be His disciples?

My Surrender

At one time in my life, I struggled with the idea of surrender. I realized that surrendering meant giving up my desire to be married and leaving it all in God's hands. It meant that He could choose whether or not I would even get married. I didn't want Him to choose singleness, so I didn't want to surrender. I wrote:

I know that if the Lord cannot satisfy me, nothing can. Until I am satisfied with Christ, I will continue to be discontented. Until I trust Him enough to do what's best for me, I won't have the life I ought to have. I won't have the communion with my Father that I so desperately crave.

I am scared to really surrender to Him. That might mean giving up my desire to be married and have children. I cannot imagine why I would have such strong desires if they are never meant to be fulfilled, unless I am supposed to learn trust through the denial of my desires. If that is so, I would rather learn trust some other way. But if I do things my own way, what will such a marriage—or anything else in my life—be worth? And if I do things His way, I'm stepping out blindly and relinquishing all control over my life and desires. He might give me an unbelievably beautiful marriage. He might choose to keep me single.

Yet how could I face any Christian brother or sister—especially a man I might call husband—and say that I denied God full control in my life for the sake of the hope for human love?

And if I choose to surrender to God, how, specifically, would I do such a thing? Many Christians speak of surrender as a decision and a prayer. I could decide and I could pray, but how could I know it is for real? What,

---

[278] Luke 14:26-27

exactly, is surrender? Is it possible to surrender without knowing it? That does not seem right. On the other hand, I'm intensely wary of relying on an "experience of surrender" as proof of such a surrender.

I asked Mom what surrender is. Is it a decision? A process? Or what? She said it seems to be a decision that is continually remade. It is never a one-time deal because we keep sinning and trying to grab control back. Rather than trusting some decision or our puny power to keep it, she said it's best to tell God of our desire to surrender, and to admit that we can't. We might even have to ask for that desire to submit.

Some time after I had written this, while I still pondered, the Lord showed me the missing piece of the puzzle to surrender. I recorded my thoughts with these words:

I was afraid to surrender to God because He might choose to keep me single and I didn't want to agree to that. I was thinking and praying about that on one drive to work this past week and wishing I could come to a place where I could say sincerely that I would serve God in whatever way He wanted me to—single or married.

And then it hit me that I had been asking myself the wrong question. God spoke to my heart, in my own voice but with His words.

"You're asking the wrong question. It isn't 'Am I willing to serve God, whether married or single?' but simply 'Am I willing to serve God?'"

It was like a light bulb went off in my head. Suddenly I had no objections and no fears. I wanted to serve God! It's all I've ever wanted to do! Suddenly I could say with complete sincerity, "Yes, Lord, I am willing to serve You in whatever way You ask me to." For some reason, I was able to say that, even knowing full well that that included the matter of marriage and singleness. But now my service was not restricted to a choice of conditions—it included everything. Somehow it was easier to hand over everything than just that one area of my life. I wonder if there are more situations like this than I realize? How many times have I tried to be too specific in my spiritual life, when all I really need to do is grasp some simple root issue?

My experience with surrender taught me that surrender just means trust. It's that point when we look at God and say, "Okay, I trust You to do what is best for me." Sometimes we will trust a lot; sometimes we will trust a little. But when we always act out that trust, whether or not we feel trusting, we are living a life of surrender.

When we live a life of surrender, cushioned in that childlike trust of God, we are content. We know that He is in control, that He loves us, and that He understands our desires. He might not give us all that we want; after all, the point of surrender is not so that we get what we want but so that He gets the glory due to Him. If we want to be content, then we must say, "Not my will, but Thine." We will have to say it many, many times, but each time that we say it, God works another miracle in our lives. Even if it seems that we surrender about the same thing over and over, it is not a waste of time, because we are building Christ-like characters. Nothing is ever wasted if it is done out of a sincere desire to bring God the glory He deserves.

Content—and Still Praying

Can you be perfectly content as a single and still pray fervently for a husband? Yes. When Hannah (from the Bible) prayed for God to give her a son, her husband asked her, "Aren't I better than ten sons to you?"[279] This did not stop Hannah from praying for a son. When Eli the priest saw that Hannah was praying silently to herself, he saw her moving lips and thought she was drunk. When she explained the matter to him, he did not say, "You are obviously unspiritual. You need to be content with your childlessness." No, he told her, "May the Lord grant your desire."[280]

As I've mentioned before, we are allowed to pray boldly, only we must do so with a clear understanding that God is God. Some people seem very concerned when they learn that I am praying consistently for a husband, as if they believe I am unhappy as a single or unspiritual to want a husband when singleness is obviously a godly option. This surprises me, because I love my singleness and because marriage is a good thing to desire. It is possible to be perfectly content as a single and to strongly desire

[279] 1 Samuel 1:8
[280] 1 Samuel 1:17

marriage simultaneously. I don't know how it works; I only know it is a reality. Do not let yourself feel guilty for desiring a husband. It is a good desire. Also do not let that desire lead you to despise your singleness. Your singleness is a gift. You will know that you have reached this place of contentment when you experience peace no matter which of the two scenarios you envision for your future.

ಞ 25 ಚಿ

Worthwhile Singleness

Many women who long to marry invest very little in their lives after high school or college. They get a job just to feel like they are "doing something" until they get married. They do a ministry "just until they find Mr. Right." They make no long-term plans because they're afraid it might impact their ability to marry. Many young women choose not to further their education, not to involve themselves in some type of ministry, not to build a home business, not to expand their horizons—all because they are afraid that an interested young man may think, "Wow, she's just the sort of women for me. Oh, but she's in school now and won't be available for marriage for a few years. Forget that. I'm not waiting."

The truth is, a guy will value a woman who isn't wrapped up in the "someday my prince will come" mentality. A guy likes to know that she has an identity and a purpose outside of her relationship with him. Sure, if they marry, he wants to be "her man" and to be #1 in her life (after God, of course) but he also wants to know that she has proven herself to be a happy, healthy, and motivated individual as a single.

The same women who try to drift through life in "park" are the same women who add all sorts of things into their schedules in hopes of meeting likely "candidates." They pass up the chance to serve a pregnant mother on bed-rest in order to go to a young adult Christian conference where they might meet eligible godly guys. They resist pursuing further education or developing a business but instead spend their time involved in some activity that includes possible "candidates" whom they hope will notice the lovely young ladies who are so spiritually-minded. I've watched women rearrange their schedules, finagle "coincidental" meetings, and involve themselves in certain ministries or projects just so that they can make themselves look attractive to possible suitors. These women misuse their time, their gifts, and their opportunities in order to manipulate artificial possibilities for guys to notice them.

This time, these gifts, these opportunities—they will not be available forever. We single women are not in an intermediary stage, a middle place between childhood and marriage. We are not poised at the edge of "real life." Real life does not start "someday." Real life starts *now*. We're already living it! Our Prince has already come and He will come again. What will He find us doing? Waiting for "someday"? Or working *now*? The godly woman embraces her life, in whatever state she may be; she identifies goals and pursues them; she finds opportunities to serve; and she sets a solid foundation for her future, a future that will be productive and happy even if she never marries.

When considering a future of marriage or a future of singleness, we find ourselves faced by difficult questions: How do we prepare realistically for both possibilities? As I wrestled with this question, I finally came to this conclusion: I would prepare for marriage, but live as if my singleness will be permanent. How does this look in practice? Let me show you.

Develop Solid Relationships

Suppose that you will not have a marriage relationship and that the relationships you have now with family and friends are the only relationships you will have for the rest of your life. How would you treat your current relationships? Would you give up on them because none of them is the type of relationship that you wanted? Would you accept mediocre relationships or would you work hard to make them the best relationships possible? Remember, if we never marry, we will have to deal with these relationships for the rest of our lives. If we do marry, then the relationship skills that we have practiced with others will carry over into our marriage relationship.

To illustrate, one of my sisters had the opportunity to stay with relatives and attend a well-known music school after high school. She had my parents' blessing and a full four-year scholarship. Her relationship with our father at that time was shaky. She thought, "Once I put some distance between us, then our relationship will be better. We won't be around each other enough to rub each other the wrong way and I won't have to work at honoring him."

When she became convinced that it was not God's will for her to go to the music school, she realized that she no longer had the option of ignoring the rifts in her relationship, so she began the long task of repairing the relationship. This required a painful change in her own heart, but just a few years later, she looked back on that change of plans with gratitude. "It was a cop-out. I wanted distance to fix my relationship. I was running away from my responsibility to make a great relationship with my father. I learned that I can't escape forever. If I had gone to college, I would have missed out on the opportunity to re-connect with Dad and to discover that we *could* have a fantastic father-daughter relationship!"

I believe that we single women need to take advantage of our relationships with married people as well. When a friend of mine married, I was afraid that her marriage would separate us. When her mind was filled with her husband and her new life, what would we have to talk about? Even though she was younger than me, would marriage give her some secret source of wisdom or maturity that would send her spiritually "ahead" of me until I got married too? Yet the next time I saw her, I detected no change in her at all. She was still essentially the same person, with the same personality, tastes, likes, dislikes, quirks, and love for the Lord. My friend was still my friend.

We single women often cut ourselves off from very valuable relationships when we think that we cannot connect with married women because we don't understand married life. True, some married women are unapproachable because they're so wrapped up in their romance that they don't have room for anyone else. However, in many cases, *we're* the ones who are reluctant to keep up with the relationship, not the married women. If you got married tomorrow, you wouldn't want your single friends to abandon you or gradually grow distant just because you are married. Furthermore, you'll still feel intimidated by other married women. When you have kids, you'll feel intimidated by the people who have older kids, and then by the people with kids all moved out, and then by grandparents, and then by retirement... It's never-ending.

We always think women in different life situations are so different from us. In reality, they aren't. Women are women. Yes, different situations bring changes, but who we are at the bottom usually stays the same. We need to continue to try connecting with our married friends. We need that fellowship, and they do too.

Learn Life-long Skills

Suppose that you will be single for the rest of your life. What skills would you learn in order to become a happy, independent, accomplished individual? There is a multitude of skills that should be learned simply because they are useful skills to know: cooking, sewing, child care, simple repairs and maintenance for the house or automobiles, gardening, interior work, driving proficiently and safely, and more. For instance, when it comes to cooking, we can't rely on our parents to cook for us all the time; we can't expect that we can maintain a healthy body while living on frozen dinners, macaroni and cheese, and fast food; and we can't afford to eat out all the time. Similarly, when it comes to doing taxes or balancing a check book, we can't expect that our parents will always be able to do these things for us, or that we'll have the funds to pay an accountant to do the job.

I also feel that it is important for a young woman to learn some skills that we commonly associate with man's work. For example, my 17-year-old sister repaired a lawn mower, rather than leaving it for Dad to do. Her skill and thoughtfulness were a huge blessing to my father. One of my favorite stress-relievers is to chop wood. If pioneer women used axes, why can't we?

A wise and responsible young woman will take the initiative and learn how to do these things for herself. If she never marries, she will not be dependent on others to provide for her needs. If she does marry, she will be able to bless and serve her husband with her skills.

Further Your Education

Some work opportunities require special training, and college can be a great way for young women to prepare for the future. I say this with some reservation. I am concerned that going away to college, alone and unsupervised, can place a young woman in vulnerable and tempting circumstances. In the Bible, we simply don't see many examples of single young women unaccompanied by their fathers, husbands, or some kind of male guardian. Because of this, my parents made the decision to support us young ladies as we commuted to college from home or took online classes. They encouraged us to continue living at home even after college. Hard as that has been at times, no one in our family has ever regretted that decision.

Taking these reservations into consideration, college can be a great use of a young woman's time. She may learn more about her chosen field, make connections with others in that field, and become more desirable to prospective employers. I achieved my Bachelor of Arts degree in English entirely online, and my degree made me look more valuable when I advertised my services as a private writing tutor and when I accepted a local secretarial position. As a degree-holder, I was also allowed to administer standardized tests to those in the homeschooling community. People may debate the actual value of that "magic piece of paper," but the fact remains that many people still view a degree as a sign of quality and are more willing to give degree-holders a chance to prove themselves.

Some people do not pursue degrees, but do further their education. A friend of mine did not go to college but rather attended classes to learn sign language. To her surprise, the Lord opened up many opportunities for her to serve those of both the deaf and the hearing community. Her dedication to learning a new skill became a home business and ministry opportunity for her!

Some young women are afraid to pursue a degree because they fear it will signal that they are "unavailable." Honestly, guys don't think that way. When my father met my mother, she was still in the process of earning her degree. Dad didn't care; he proposed. Mom got married just before she graduated. Was it hard? Sure, but my parents knew that they would find a way to make things work. College is not a deterrent for an interested man!

A wise young woman prepares for the future. If she is willing to learn, God can open up amazing doors for her. If she marries, she can use that knowledge to help her family. If she does not marry, she can use that knowledge to further her career and to serve others.

Develop Marketable Skills

When I was about ten or eleven, my father made it clear that he expected all of his children to learn two marketable skills. "If you get married, you can use your skills to supplement your husband's income," Dad explained. "And if you don't get married or if your husband loses his job or dies, you will have a way to provide for yourself." Each of us kids began to practice skills that could be developed into a career or a business. We learned how to make and sell everything from cookies to felted items to earrings. When we became proficient in a certain skill, we shared our knowledge as teachers.

For example, when I'm not working at one of my other jobs, I write and tutor from home, while one of my sisters teaches piano. A friend of mine bought a breeding pair of German Shepherds and began her own kennel. Another friend of mine has used her marketing skills to help with her family's thriving rental business. A third friend makes jewelry to sell at various events. All of these young women have proven that their resourcefulness and skills can be used to generate income.

Having presented the usefulness of a job or home business, I feel responsible to add a warning. In the Bible, the apostle Paul instructs the older women to teach the younger women "to be sober, to love their husbands, to love their children, to be discreet, chaste, keepers at home, good, obedient to their own husbands, that the word of God be not blasphemed."[281] Many people forget that important little phrase "keepers at home." Society today tells a woman that she must have a career in order to be somebody, and insinuates that women who prefer to stay at home with their families are deliberately avoiding their potential. If a man were to say to his wife, "I will focus on my career; my family won't slow me down! If you want to come along for the ride, honey, that's fine with me," we would think he is very selfish. Yet many women today, eager to assert their independence, say the equivalent of this statement to their husbands. God values family-oriented women and, if you were to survey average men, they would also value such a woman for a wife.

[281] Titus 2:4-5

239

A wise young woman knows that it is never too early to learn marketable skills. If she never marries, she will have a way to support herself without burdening her parents or friends. If she does marry, she will have a way to supplement her husband's income and to provide him with the assurance that she can cope if things get tough.

Participate in a Ministry

The apostle Paul noted that the main difference between a married and an unmarried woman is this: The married woman focuses on pleasing her husband, but the unmarried woman focuses on pleasing the Lord.[282] A single young woman has many opportunities to minister to others, which are not available to women who are responsible for caring for their families.

When I was nineteen, my church bulletin advertised a training session at a local crisis pregnancy center. I had always felt a desire to minister to young women, particularly those who need counsel concerning relationships or pregnancy. With my parents' blessing, I volunteered for the training. After I became a client advocate, which is similar to a counselor, I spent one day a week at the center. I could afford this day because I did not have a family that relied upon me to make sure that the meals got on the table, the bills were paid, and the homeschooling was getting done. In contrast, my married friend who worked with me had to make changes when she became pregnant with her first child. She made the decision to reduce her ministry to women in crisis situations in order to focus on her ministry to her growing family.

We single young women have opportunities to serve which we may never again have. How are we taking advantage of our freedom as singles? During their singleness, friends of mine have ministered to pregnant women, elderly people, mentally and physically disabled children, younger women, their own families, and many others in various ways.

Ministry just means serving others in the name of Christ. You don't have to be involved in a nationally recognized ministry, go on a mission trip, or have your name on the church ministry list. I

---

[282] 1 Corinthians 7:34

choose to view my involvement with the crisis pregnancy center as equal to serving my family faithfully at home or visiting a sick elderly friend. Look around you, identify needs, and try to meet those needs. You may find yourself serving your own family first and then branching out into other venues, but all of it is ministry, if it is done with a cheerful heart and a willingness to glorify God through service to others. Don't worry about your inadequacy. When I volunteered at the crisis pregnancy center, my experiences were limited. For starters, all of my clients were sexually active and, obviously, I wasn't. Was this a disadvantage? Sometimes, it was. At other times, it gave authority to my discussions about abstinence. God showed me that my lack of experience did not disqualify me. Rather, my love and my desire to serve others and to glorify Him qualified me. God offers the same qualification to those who are willing to love others through service.

Many of us have longed to be a mother for all of our lives, and we can't wait for the day when we can welcome our own children into the world. But consider this verse:

Sing, O barren, thou that didst not bear; break forth into singing, and cry aloud, thou that didst not travail with child: for more are the children of the desolate than the children of the married wife, saith the Lord.[283]

What children does God mean in this passage? I believe He is speaking of the fruit of ministry and of service to Himself and to others. When we fully grasp the truth of this verse, we are prompted to pray, "If I must be lonely, let the children of my loneliness be much more than the children made of flesh and blood. May the fruit of my barrenness be more than the fruit of my body and let it all bring glory to You."

A wise young woman practices service. If she marries, she will be well-prepared to shift her selfless ministry focus from her "outside" ministry to her husband and children, and to pour out her energies into this new ministry opportunity. If she does not marry, she is equipped to follow a lifetime of purposeful ministry and to impact many people outside of the scope of her immediate family members. Either type of life, married or unmarried, is an incredible privilege for the godly woman.

---

[283] Isaiah 54:1

Care for Yourself

What? know ye not that your body is the temple of the Holy Ghost which is in you, which ye have of God, and ye are not your own? For ye are bought with a price: therefore glorify God in your body, and in your spirit, which are God's. [284]

If we were charged with caring for the temple of God, we would sweep it religiously, brush out the cobwebs, shine up the candlesticks, and keep that place spotless. In the same way, we should honor the living temple that God has given to us. It is the only body, and the only physical temple of the Holy Spirit, that we will ever have. Consider this: If people were to form an opinion of the Lord based on your appearance, what representation of God would they see?

Also, a wife should care for her body, because it is no longer her own; it now equally belongs to her husband.[285] Caring for her own body is as important as caring for his.

Please listen carefully to me. Many young women have reinterpreted "healthy" to mean "thin." Because of this, they have engaged in practices like self-starvation (anorexia) and bingeing and purging (bulimia). These are not healthy and show no more respect for God's temple than the opposite reaction of carelessness. In fact, these habits destroy a young woman's body, actually make weight maintenance more difficult, damage her internal organs and digestive tract, and often lead to depression, guilt, and shame. A healthy lifestyle requires balance: nutritious diet choices, moderate eating habits, consistent exercise, and sufficient sleep. Changes are made gradually, often over years.

For example, one of my sisters struggled with her weight in her teens. She was the slowest runner on the cross-country team, and repeated ankle injuries didn't help. She openly admits that, at that time in her life, she was lazy. As much as she wanted to be fit, she didn't want to put the work into moderating her lifestyle. However, she decided one year to get tough on herself. She ate only until she was satisfied, but not until she was full. She exercised for thirty minutes every day. Months went by and she seemed to make little

[284] 1 Corinthians 6:19-20
[285] 1 Corinthians 7:4

headway, but when she evaluated herself a year later, she could hardly believe her progress. She had lost fifteen pounds and she was the fastest runner in the family.

On the other hand, weight was never much of a problem for me, and in my senior year of high school, I was the fastest female hurdler on my track and field team. However, I found that at the end of many sports seasons and during the winter as I followed my own exercise program, I grew tired, irritable, and depressed. My wise father told me to cut back on the time and the intensity of my workouts until my emotions evened out. I felt that I was already perfectly moderate, but I obeyed. Within a few weeks, I felt like a new person. Exercise *can* be overdone, and I had to learn to moderate my habits to suit my body's needs.

We all have different bodies and different needs. Some of my friends live with difficult health issues, such as extreme dietary restrictions, but they do the best they can in their situations. As caretakers of unique temples of the Holy Spirit, we have the responsibility to make our temples the strongest and best temples possible.

However, this does not come without the right mindset. Are our healthy habits meant only to attract a prospective suitor, or are they meant to show respect for God's temple? A wise woman cares for herself because she knows that the same effort that she puts into caring for God's temple is the same effort she will put into caring for others, including her husband if she should marry. If she marries, she will be able to present her healthy body as a gift to her husband and she will have a greater chance of maintaining her health as she bears children. If she does not marry, she will have the energy and health to pursue whatever task God sets before her.

Worth More Than Rubies

Proverbs chapter 31 asks this question: "Who can find a virtuous woman? For her price is far above rubies." Although this passage is speaking about a wife, I believe that the same virtues that make an excellent wife also make an excellent woman—married or unmarried. What are these virtues that make this woman so valuable?

243

- **Skill**: *She seeketh wool, and flax, and worketh willingly with her hands.* This woman has the skill and the resourceful-ness to make something useful for the family out of the materials that are already available.

- **Forethought**: *She is like the merchant ships; she bringeth her food from afar.* In the old days, the merchant ships would take long voyages in order to bring food and spices and goods from far lands. People often had to wait weeks or months to see their orders arrive, so they had to look ahead when putting in requests. Likewise, this woman prepares ahead of time for the needs of her family.

- **Hard work**: *She riseth also while it is yet night and giveth meat to her household, and a portion to her maidservants.* This woman works hard. She doesn't sleep for twelve hours a day; she's up with the sun and providing for others.

- **Shrewdness**: *She considereth a field and buyeth it; with the fruit of her hands she planteth a vineyard.* This woman has the gumption to thoroughly research something, make a major purchase, then turn it into a profitable investment for her family. Although her husband may have been included in the decision, she seems to be the principle player in the transaction.

- **Strength**: *She girdeth her loins with strength, and strengthens her arms.* This woman is no weakling, and she actively works to make herself as strong and hardy as possible. She rightly understands the importance of having a well-maintained temple of the Holy Spirit.

- **Diligence**: *She perceiveth that her merchandise is good, and her candle goeth not out by night. She layeth her hands to the spindle and her hands hold the distaff.* This woman is capable of making merchandise to sell and is willing to stay up late to make the most of her home business.

- **Generosity**: *She stretches out her hand to the poor; yes, she reacheth forth her hands to the needy.* Having provided for her family, she makes a point of generously giving to those beyond her family as well.

- **Preparation**: *She is not afraid of the snow for her household, for all her household are clothed with scarlet.* This woman prepares responsibly for hard times and ensures that her family not only has the means to weather the hardship, but to weather it well.

- *Ambition: She makether herself coverings of tapestry; her clothing is silk and purple.* In the old days, silk and purple were very expensive. This woman has more than good taste; she has the ambition to make things for herself, rather than leaving the job to someone else. As a result of her hard work, she possesses things that are of great value.

- *Respect: Her husband is known in the gates, when he sitteth among the elders of the land.* This woman honors her earthly authority. Instead of sharing stories of his inadequacy, she makes him look good to his colleagues. Because she gives him a place of honor in her heart, he has a place of honor with others as well. This, in turn, reflects well on her as she shares in her husband's good reputation.

- *Quality: She makes fine linen and selleth it; and delivereth girdles unto the merchant.* She is known as an industrious woman and she has her own home business. Her merchandise is not second-rate, but excellent quality, and the buyers know it.

- *Honor: Strength and honour are her clothing, and she shall rejoice in the time to come.* Because of her integrity and virtue, this woman will have nothing of which to be ashamed when she looks back at the course of her life.

- *Wisdom and Kindness: She openeth her mouth with wisdom, and in her tongue is the law of kindness.* This woman does not speak quickly or lash out in frustration. Instead, she makes her tongue just as constructive as the work of her hands. Her family does not fear her words, but instead listens to her wisdom.

- *Selflessness: She looketh well to the ways of her household, and eateth not the bread of idleness.* This woman simply won't let others do what she can do for herself. She puts the needs of others before her own desires and she works hard to be a responsible mentor, helper, and supervisor to those under her care.

To this long list, we can add another virtue: She is trustworthy.

The Bible says that the heart of her husband safely trusts in her.[286] He trusts that she is capable, strong, and resourceful; that she will honor her authority, while at the same time exercising her own authority over others with patience and kindness; that she will use her time wisely; that she will prepare well for hardships; that she will be generous to others; that she will make wise business deals on behalf of the family; and that she will display virtue and trustworthiness both at home and in public.

I believe that this woman did not suddenly learn these virtues as soon as she married, as if marriage were some magic pill for cultivating maturity and excellence. No, she had to practice these virtues first as a single woman. The Bible does not indicate that her excellence lay in the fact that she was a wife, but in the fact that she was a woman who made the most of her time and who served others selflessly. Therefore, whether married or single, a godly woman should strive to earn this praise from those who know her:

Many daughters have done virtuously, but thou excellest them all. Favour is deceitful, and beauty is vain: but a woman that feareth the LORD, she shall be praised. Give her of the fruit of her hands; and let her own works praise her in the gates.[287]

The Fruit of Responsible Singleness

If you have been taking these words to heart, I have both a final encouragement and a warning for you.

The encouragement: A wise and godly young man will be on the look-out for a young woman who loves the Lord with her whole heart and who is willing to let the Lord plan her life. This man will be alert to any signs of ingratitude, selfishness, or discontentment. After all, he knows that this attitude will trickle into her treatment of her husband. If he sees an attitude that is serene and God-glorifying, regardless of the circumstances, and regardless of her stage in life, he will know that this is a woman worth making his wife. Wouldn't you love to know that your husband chose you specifically because he saw that you were glorifying God through your singleness?

---

[286] Proverbs 31:11
[287] Proverbs 31:29-31

246

The warning: This is not to say that we should do God's will because it will make us all the more attractive to a potential suitor. Yes, I know how easy it is to think this way! For example, as I wrote this book, I repeatedly squashed a little voice that whispered, "This book may get in the hands of a lovely Christian young lady who has a godly Christian brother who will find out how virtuous and intelligent I am and think, 'This is the woman I've waited for all my life! How do I get in touch with her?'" Wrong motivation tends to worm its way into our best actions, but God knows the heart!

It will eventually become apparent when a young woman is doing the right thing because she wants to be noticed or because she simply wants to please God! Neither godly young men nor God Himself desires to have anything to do with selfish women or with frauds. Aim to impress a godly man and you'll impress neither the man nor God; aim to impress God and you might impress others as well. Whether you impress others or not, God's approval is worth more than anything else.

The truth: Every habit we form now as singles has the potential to impact not only our future marriage but also eternity. If we think that we can correct wrong behaviors or cultivate right behaviors "sometime in the future," we are fooling ourselves. We must ask ourselves: "Why am I putting this off? What do I hope to gain from procrastination? What could I lose because of procrastination?"

You don't know when you are going to die. You don't know when Jesus is coming back. You might have to give God an account of your entire life tomorrow. When people say, "Live every day as if it will be your last," that's not empty words. That's a wake-up call! Those words are true for somebody in the world today, somebody who *is* living her last day, and you don't know if they will be true for you next. Don't waste your life. Live worthy of the calling of Jesus Christ[288] and He will ensure that you will not be ashamed to give an account of your time on earth.

Watch ye therefore, and pray always, that ye may be accounted worthy to escape all these things that shall come to pass, and to stand before the Son of Man.[289]

---

[288] 2 Thessalonians 1:11-12
[289] Luke 21:36

247

❧ 26 ❧

Real Stories

To illustrate everything that I have said so far, here are two real-life stories. The first story is the story of my younger sister Keren, and how God answered her desires to be married, despite the fact that her journey to engagement broke all societal norms. The second story is my story and how God has not answered my desires to be married—and how singleness is becoming a fantastic adventure for me.

My Sister's Story: God's Yes

In contrast to the modern relationship model, the Biblical relationship model normally involves both families. Every story is different, but I know one couple that broke all the rules of modern relationship development and, as a result, they have a beautiful and unique story.

My father and Jonny's father lived together as bachelors and they kept in touch as their families grew. My sister Keren had a very low opinion of Jonny, the eldest child of his family. His boyish cockiness ignited her prejudice and she endured visits with ill humor. One day, I teased her, "Well, if you hate him so much now, just wait—you'll end up marrying him!" This prediction so infuriated Keren that she never forgot it.

Years passed and Keren began to soften a little toward Jonny. Our families got together from time to time, and Keren and Jonny found that they both shared a love for baking. In order to trade information and recipes more easily, Jonny and Keren began to Skype each other. This was an exception to our family's usual rules about private communication, but it was a risk that my father made prayerfully, in hope of future possibilities for Keren and Jonny's relationship. At first, their communication was very casual, but gradually they began to study the Bible together and to talk in general terms about their hopes and dreams for the future.

Keren began to love and respect the man she saw in Jonny.

"Everything that I had asked God for in a man was in Jonny. He was willing to change and to work hard, he was sober-minded, and he loved God more than anything. I also saw that he valued the wisdom of his parents and he honored them in his life. Furthermore, I saw that he was humble. He didn't talk to me like he was trying to impress me. He talked with me like a friend and as someone else who loved and wanted to follow the Lord."

For his part, Jonny learned that Keren sought God's glory above her own desires. "Some of the things I saw in Keren's life that really stood out to me were her desire to always put the Lord first in her life, her respect of her dad's wisdom and guidance, her character that is so filled with caring for everyone, and the way she always built me up in our conversation."

After several years, Keren had come to value Jonny's friendship so much that she greatly feared losing it, because there was no commitment and therefore no guarantee that he wouldn't find someone else. Keren had spoken to Dad about her desires as the relationship had developed, and my father had prayed for over a year for guidance and wisdom regarding the situation. At last, with much prayer and some fear, Dad asked Jonny where Jonny intended to take the relationship.

Thereafter followed meetings that included both sets of parents, Jonny, and Keren. Including the parents in the process was a step that was not easy for either Jonny or Keren. Looking back, Jonny sees that the step to include both sets of parents taught him a lot about his own motives and desires. "I am really happy that the parents were so involved; they have so much wisdom. However, I admit that at first it was hard for me. I realize now that so much of that had to do with how selfishly I was viewing things. I had preconceived ideas of how a relationship should develop. The way things happened was so against everything that I had pictured."

Keren adds: "I felt that parental involvement was 100% necessary. As much as I loved Jonny and he was my best friend and I didn't want to lose him, I wasn't willing to move forward unless I had the wholehearted blessing from both of our parents. I knew that I would not get God's blessing unless I had our parents' blessing, and without God's blessing, I might as well say goodbye to the whole idea of marriage. It was a matter of taking that step of faith, that whether Dad did the right thing or the wrong thing, the Lord would bless my desire to honor my Dad."

The process had a great number of ups and downs. Sometimes, the direction of the process had to be shifted and plans had to be modified. Jonny, Keren, and the parents had to be very sensitive to the desires of everyone else in the situation. This was by no means an easy or comfortable process, but it was one that was guided by mutual respect and trust. Above all, the parents did not want to allow Jonny and Keren to enter into something about which they were uncertain. Rather, the parents wanted to ensure that any movement toward marriage was accompanied by appropriate desire for each other and by understanding of the serious nature of the commitment.

During the process, Jonny realized that trusting God, not maintaining control, was the ultimate goal. "Finally, I had to lay down my ideas of what a relationship should be, and just give the Lord the control. It was the most difficult thing I have given to the Lord, because I didn't want to lose that control."

Keren realized that she must trust God, even if He denied her the thing she desired most. "I told God that he could have Jonny. He could have all my hopes and my dreams. He could have all my desires for marriage. I could be single for the rest of my life—and I would still love Him. I knew that even if I did get married, if I didn't have God's blessing, it wouldn't amount to a hill of beans. And if I had nothing at all, but I had God's blessing, then it would be more than enough."

Eventually, it became clear that Jonny was interested in making a commitment toward marriage with Keren. A final meeting was needed to ensure that the match was wise. If things went well, Jonny and Keren had the permission and blessing of both parents to commit to marriage.

The week before that final meeting was very difficult. Desire had been kindled, but there was no guarantee that it would be fulfilled, so both Jonny and Keren felt awkward and cautious in allowing themselves to feel strongly attached to each other. When the final meeting occurred, Keren and Jonny found that the way was completely clear for them to make a commitment. With full parental blessing (and much joy within both families), they were engaged immediately.

As they celebrated their commitment, both Jonny and Keren realized that giving God the control of the situation, despite their fears, had resulted in immeasurable peace and joy. Keren, remembering her choice to give up her dreams, reflects, "It wasn't until I gave up everything to the Lord, that He gave everything back to me." Jonny adds, "Now I see that the Lord has blessed our relationship far above anything I could imagine. He has done so much of a better job than I could have done."

Neither Jonny nor Keren regrets including their parents in the decision process. Keren expresses it well: "Now that we are committed to each other and to a lifetime of seeking God together, I love Jonny more than I could have ever imagined loving anyone. And we have two fabulous families included in our romance! This is a much stronger foundation than I would have possessed if I had experienced all of the things that I thought should make up the perfect love story. This is the perfect romance because we are living out an ever-growing romance with our Savior."

My Story: My Yes

Before I tell my story, I must add a caution. I know how easily we can get caught up in thinking about and preparing for an excellent marriage. We want so much to do things right, the first and only time, that we can get distracted from the real goal. We may reach a point in which we focus more on godly living than we focus on Christ Himself. And *that* is where the most subtle and damaging danger lies.

Some people pour their hearts out in ministries of compassion and do many wonderful works in God's name. Some people are incredible Bible scholars and write books about the gospel and bring many to Christ. Yet, for some of them, even though their lives revolve around Christ, they do not have personal contact with Him. They are religious, but they are not in a real, living, growing relationship. These are the people who will someday ask Christ, "Didn't we do this and that in Your name?" And Christ will say, "Depart from me, you workers of iniquity, for I never knew you."[290]

---

[290] Matthew 7:21-23

It is not enough to just do things God's way; we must desire to know God Himself. He does not simply want our sacrifices and obedience; He wants our hearts. He does not simply want servants; He wants sons and daughters. He does not simply want a housekeeper; He wants a Bride.

We must not obsess so much over preparing for a godly marriage that we are distracted from simply loving Jesus Christ. The Enemy would like nothing better than to use our good intentions to separate us from our Savior. That's why I've spent this whole book bringing every lesson back to our relationship with Christ. In the end, it's not about us or about marriage. It's simply about Him. Let everything else go.

If this seems impossible, I pray that my story will inspire you.

I always assumed that, as the oldest, I would be the first to get married. The thought of events happening otherwise was emotionally devastating. When I saw that my sister Keren was drawing closer to Jonny, doubts began to trouble me. "What if she gets married first?" My initial reaction was fury. God couldn't do that to me, not when He knew how much I struggled daily to be content. He said that He wouldn't give me anything that I couldn't bear. Well, if my sister got married first, I wouldn't bear it, and it would be all God's fault! When God asked, "Will you trust Me even if I bless your sister's desires and delay yours?" my reply to God was emphatic: "NO!"

I felt that my surrender, as recounted earlier, had been sufficient. I had not realized that I had put a condition on my surrender. "Yes, I will serve You whether married or single—except if You answer my younger sister's prayers before You answer mine." Now I had to decide between my desires and my God.

I can't point to a day in which the change occurred, but gradually, my "no" weakened and I found myself whispering with tears, "Yes." The day that my sister got engaged, I knew that it had happened. God was asking me for ultimate trust, and anything I did from that point on would either be a confirmation or a denial of that trust.

As I have walked out my "yes," God has rewarded my trust in Him. My disappointment in God's "no" to me did not diminish at all the intensity of my joy in God's "yes" to my sister. I greatly look

252

forward to the joining of our two families. I rejoice to see the beautiful result of godly restraint and wisdom in my sister's relationship. I am inspired by their story to walk out my own story with faithfulness and courage.

One day, as I gave my desires to God for what seemed the thousandth time, I realized that my "yes" to God was no longer a whisper. It was a sky-shattering, fear-defying, earth-cracking, mighty thunder of joy. I no longer feared singleness or loneliness. For the first time in my life, I was completely *free*.

Even though my desire for marriage had not diminished, my singleness had stepped out of childhood into womanhood. I had always thought of singleness like something to be endured or—more accurately—survived. It was a necessary, and hopefully temporary, period of probation. It was something that was my Christian duty to make the best of. I wanted my singleness to be admirable, but did not expect that it could be anything more.

Now, I saw singleness, not as an abandoned woman, but as a queen. And she was *radiant*. Out of all the warriors in God's army, she was one of the most rare and one of the most deadly to the Enemy. She was very strong, very wise, and very beautiful.

Eric Ludy, in one of his books, challenges couples to cultivate a stunning romance in their marriages. He urges them to compete boldly in the competition for "Best Marriage." As I saw my singleness through God's eyes for the first time, I knew that there was another, equally great, competition afoot.

As I had thought of singleness as the lack of a husband, I now knew it to be the fullness of God. As I had thought that commitment was a requirement only for marriage, I now knew that it was a requirement for singlehood too. As I had envied the romance of others, I now determined that I would make my singlehood something to be envied. No more half-hearted singleness. I would serve others with gladness, use my time with wisdom, and learn to know God as a wife learns to know her husband. I would compete for "Best Singlehood Ever."

"You know," I told my sister. "I'm sure that you have no envy for my situation, now that you're happy with Jonny. But I want you to realize that, even as you are experiencing something which is beyond my experience, I am about to step into an incredible world in which you will now never be a part."

It wasn't gloating. It was fact. The woman who is single for only a short time will never possess the unique treasures of a woman who is single for a longer time.

My sister nodded. "You're right. I am not sure I understand it fully, although I wish to. But I know it is true."

Even though Keren will never now fully understand the gift of singleness, someone else might understand. Perhaps God will invite you, as He invited me, to become a single woman as committed to her life of singleness as a woman is committed to her marriage, to become a woman so completely full of the Lord that all the angels of heaven will stand in wonder and awe. I invite you into the company of queens.

If God should one day answer my prayers for a husband, then I shall be very happy. But until that happens—or even if it never happens—I am determined that my "yes" to God will continue to be so loud that all the lies against singleness will turn inside out. I will tell the world how my greatest nightmare has become my greatest dream, through the power of my incredible God.

I did not write this book so that we can prepare for our earthly bridegroom. I wrote this book so that, through our desire for an earthly husband, we can better prepare for our Heavenly Bridegroom. Someday soon, Jesus Christ will return for His bride, and when He does, none of us should be unprepared to meet Him. None of us should be so consumed with our desire for human love that we miss Love Himself when He returns.

If you are single, come on this journey with me. We will prove the power and beauty of singleness. Together, we will prepare to meet our True Bridegroom. When He comes, we will run into His arms and say with all of our hearts, "I have waited my whole life for You!"

[291]*And I heard as it were the voice of a great multitude, and as the voice of many waters, and as the voice of mighty thunderings, saying, Alleluia: for the Lord God omnipotent reigneth. Let us be glad and rejoice, and give honour to him: for the marriage of the Lamb is come **and his wife hath made herself ready.***

---

[291] Revelation 19:6-7